BRANDED NATION

The Marketing
of Megachurch,
College, Inc., and
Museumworld

James B. Twitchell

SIMON & SCHUSTER • NEW YORK   LONDON   TORONTO   SYDNEY

SIMON & SCHUSTER
Rockefeller Center
1230 Avenue of the Americas
New York, NY 10020

For information about special discounts for bulk purchases,
please contact Simon & Schuster Special Sales:
1-800-456-6798 or business@simonandschuster.com

Designed by Dana Sloan

Manufactured in the United States of America

10 9 8 7 6 5 4 3 2 1

Library of Congress Cataloging-in-Publication Data

Twitchell, James B., 1943-
  Branded nation : the marketing of megachurch, college, inc., and museumworld
/ James B. Twitchell.
    p. cm.
  Includes bibliographical references and index.
  1. Brand name products—United States—Marketing. 2. Brand name
products—Social aspects—United States. 3. Church marketing. I. Title.

HD69.B7T7596 2004
658.8'27—dc22   2004052147

ISBN 0-7432-4346-3

To Kate

Contents

1.

Branding 101

There are only two or three great human stories, and they go on repeating themselves as fiercely as if they had never happened before.

—Willa Cather

Why do we need stories? To this may be added two more questions. Why do we need the "same" stories over and over? Why is our need for more stories never satisfied?

—J. Hillis Miller

Branded Nation: If you were looking for two of the most overused title words in the book business, you couldn't do better than this. It seems that every publisher of business books has a ready supply of Brand-this and Brand-that titles: *A New Brand World, Emotional Branding, Brand Warfare, Strategic Brand Management, Be Your Own Brand, Brand Leadership, Brand New, Brand Asset Management, Managing Brand Equity, Building Strong Brands, The 22 Immutable Laws of Branding*, and so on. Most of the three thousand business books published each year are written for people in business who want to make money and who think branding is just the ticket. They may be right, but, as is often the case, the big money is not in doing it but in writing the book about it. So you should know from the get-go that you won't make money from the pages that follow. Turn back; this is not *that* kind of business book.

The other title word is almost as trite. Is there a major publisher who does not have a hand-wringing title using *Nation*? Although *Prozac Nation, Savage Nation,* and *Fast Food Nation* hit the jackpot (with Janet Jackson's *Rhythm Nation* playing in the background), we've recently seen *Adoption Nation, Asphalt Nation, Suburban Nation, Gunfighter Nation, Ritalin Nation, Pharmaceutical Nation, Comic Book Nation,* and even *Corporate Nation* (with an introduction by the ever-anxious national brand Ralph Nader). So maybe it was only a matter of time before *Branded* and *Nation* got hitched in a title and went off together—into *Remaindered Nation*?

I bring these bulldozer words together, however, not to provide business tips or to bemoan the state of American culture, but rather to state the obvious. Much of our shared knowledge about ourselves and our culture comes to us through a commercial process of storytelling called *branding*. The process starts early. A marketing professor estimates that 10 percent of a two-year-old's nouns are brand names. And an English study estimates that one out of every four babies speaks a brand name as a first word. There is no need to recite the dreary litany about how the Marlboro Man is better known than George Washington; how more people recognize the golden arches than recognize the Red Cross; how Mickey Mouse, Coke, or Tom Cruise are part of the With-It! Nation, while the United Nations, elective democracy, or the Peace Corps are part of the Huh? Nation. And no need to mention how American foreign policy and politics have been hijacked by brand meisters. We all know that.

As well, we now appreciate that institutions that were always thought "above" market pressures, such as the law, have been deeply affected. As Richard Sherwin has shown in *When the Law Goes Pop: The Vanishing Line Between Law and Popular Culture,* the goal of modern mega-tele-trials (O.J., the Menendez brothers, Bill, etc.) is to make the case fit a compelling story, branding it as melodrama, mystery, heroic suspense. Gerry Spence, renowned defense attorney, has said as much: winning is just a matter of "finding the right story." He usually starts his summation with the same words, "Now I want to tell you a story." He's not kidding.

But what we may not appreciate is that the most successful recent branding exercise has had to do with how *high* culture is currently being created and shared. Branding in the nineteenth century became the meaning-making motor of consumerism, the key to concentrating the consuming desires of almost every human in the West toward manufactured items. What might not be so obvious is that in the middle of the twentieth century the branding process started to enter the marketplace of cultural values and beliefs. Schools, churches, museums, hospitals, politics (well, we knew about that one), living space, even the judicial system went pop! They—the successful institutions—started *self-consciously* using techniques of branding not just to make their ideological points and generate cultural capital but to distribute their services at the highest possible return. The admen entered the sacred groves, and, rather like the police in your bedroom, once inside, they are difficult to get to leave.

Of course, these distributors of cultural capital would insist that branding was not what they are doing. In fact, abhorring branding as well as all vulgar marketing techniques may be a necessary fiction in the public sphere. It may be important for the minister, professor, judge, diplomat, politician, and curator to regularly excoriate the marketplace while at the same time applying its techniques of fictionalized differentiation. And after we have finished wringing our hands in distress, this may not be so bad. We might find it refreshing, even salutary, to acknowledge the truth. Below all the self-serving voodoo, the marketplace of ideas is a marketplace. Merchants have always been in the temple.

Marketing, a central aspect of the marketplace, has not always been a dirty word. It's an adjunct to sales. And really, isn't all life about marketing, in a sense? You market yourself to your friends, to your employer, your constituents, and they to you. Your children market themselves to their sports team (pick me! pick me!), schools markets themselves (a degree from us is a ticket to success), and even churches market themselves (services at 9 and 11) and their products (forgiveness now, salvation later). Maybe it's just the illusion of *not marketing* that we need to dispense with.

All lasting cultures are based on humans bringing things to market. As the nursery rhyme says, "To market, to market, to buy a fat pig, /

Home again, home again, dancing a jig." We call those things we find at the market "goods," as in goods and services. We do not call them "bads." There are usually two sides to a trade: buyers and sellers. In the modern world there is often little difference between products and services in the same category. The only thing that differs is the story. Branding, in this simple sense, is the application of a story to a product or a service and, as we will see, is utilized whenever there is a surplus of interchangeable goods.

In the modern world almost all consumer goods are marketed via stories. A good marketing plan is the one with a memorable story (Where's the beef?), while an ineffective one is forgotten (remember Herb of Burger King?). Marketing in the economic sense is simply the process of getting this exchange to work efficiently—making money by storytelling. Often what you taste is the story, not the meat patty; the sizzle, not the steak. And that's because it's often the sizzle that carries what we want, namely, the smell, the emotion, the anticipation. One of the best introductions to branding is spending a few hours watching PBS's *Antiques Roadshow* or reading the old J. Peterman catalog. Often the only thing that separates this ratty rug from that priceless tapestry is a story.

J. Peterman knows that the only thing that separates interchangeable objects is a good story. And before he went out of business he told them in his catalog.

4

We have a natural sympathy for consumers. After all, we spend almost all of childhood on the receiving side. Gimme, gimme. Tell me a story. And lots of our adult time, too. But as we grow up, we tend to become more interested in the selling side. In fact, the selling side gets most of the academic attention. The formal study of economics is usually the study of the producer: how he borrows money, how he gauges demand, how he uses machinery, how he tells a story, how he is a *he*. The buying side is usually neglected. Until recently, this was the side of the *she*. He = intellectual, she = emotional is the "Me Tarzan, you Jane" of the traditional take on marketing. Branding is where they meet, and by no means is Jane powerless. In fact, as we will see, David Ogilvy, the advertising impresario of the 1960s, was close to the truth when he said, "The consumer is not a moron, she is your wife."

Storytelling is the core of culture. When the world was made up primarily of needs (food, shelter, sex), there was little sophistication in narrative. We told most of our communal stories about such things as ancestry, nationalism, social class, politics, and the like. But after the Industrial Revolution, when there were massive surpluses, needs were effectively met and wants and desires became central. Stories attached themselves to fast-moving consumer goods (FMCGs) such as soap, thread, patent medicine, canned meats, and a host of other quick consumables.

Branding really exploded after the Second World War as surpluses piled up. Advertising genius Rosser Reeves, who used to run the huge Ted Bates Agency, would stand up before a client, reach into his pocket (his own pocket, although clients sometimes wondered if it was theirs), and pull out some loose change. Finding two quarters, he would announce that his job was to convince the consumer that the quarter in his right hand was worth more than the one in his left. That, he said, was his job. He called it creating a USP (unique selling proposition), but that's branding in a nutshell. Tell a story—that there is a hammer pounding an anvil in your brain as a way to sell Anacin, that Wonder Bread helps build bodies twelve ways, or that M&Ms melt in your mouth, not in your hand—and you have separated your product from other aspirin, bread, and chocolate. Reeves's brother-in-law David Ogilvy, head of the agency that still bears his name, expanded the *proposition* part of USP to tell wondrous stories about Hathaway shirts, Schweppes tonic water, and Puerto Rican resorts.

As you can see, these stories often had nothing to do with the product. Sometimes the story told about a product can change its value, and the story can hinge on the bizarre. Take price, for instance. If bottled water cost 25 cents (which it easily could because it's essentially just tap water) instead of $1, the stories would be entirely different. If tuition at Harvard cost $10,000 instead of $30,000 (which it easily could as the endowment throws off enough cash every other week to cover all undergraduate tuition), the story would be different. If Christie's and Sotheby's were not continually making a market in fine art, chances are that museums would not do as much business as they do. Churches that let everyone into Heaven would soon go out of business. Forgiveness must be paid for; salvation has a price. Tithing has a purpose in generating product value as well as in generating revenue.

Of course we don't think this way. We think that churches, schools, museums, the judiciary, and the like are running on a different track. In no way are they like bottled water! We believe that their cultural value is based not on some transaction between buyers and sellers but on individuals and their yearning for the ineffable *truth*. We seek answers and find The Way. So we yearn for meaning and find religion. We want beauty and find art. We thirst for knowledge and experience education. We go to court to find justice. No logo need apply. Packaging is unnecessary, and competition is unheard of. The public sphere is a brand-free zone.

Maybe it used to be that way when there were few suppliers. But once we had a surplus of pews, university seats, museum galleries, and the like, well, as we will see, things changed. Plenitude leads willynilly to consumerism. Modern culture has been marketized in almost all ways but public perception. The exception is politics. Here we have already come to accept branding as the norm. The transforming event was the packaging of General Dwight D. Eisenhower by none other than Rosser Reeves. The image of Ike was sold to the voters via television commercials called "Eisenhower Answers America." The old general even moaned, "To think an old soldier should come to this." His protégé Richard Nixon was transformed from craggy grouch to buoyant leader, thanks to the handiwork of a master brand craftsman, Roger Ailes. In a few years the process of selling the president was in place. Ailes understood that the presidency is just a political brand and that a politician is the quintessential identification character. All Dick Norris had to do with Bill Clinton was remember how Ailes had done it and stay away from hookers.

By the time of George W. Bush the process had been so completely internalized that the electorate was willing to believe that an old-Episcopal blue blood, Andover/Yale/Harvard, Skull & Bones was really a born-again Christian, Texas good ol' boy oilman. It is simply impossible to imagine that someone like FDR would ever have been able, or have wanted, to be something other than Groton/Hudson River/Harvard/high church. True, he pretended he wasn't confined to a wheelchair, but that was about the extent of the storytelling. Al Gore got stuck in the old brand. Although in reality he was as much the blue blood as Dubya, he was branded out of date, old money, exhausted policies, tired blood. Little wonder onetime Terminator Arnold Schwarzenegger had little trouble being perceived as "Governator." The brand stories fit.

While we have come to accept the narrative of politics (and foreign policy from Operation Just Cause to Operation Iraqi Freedom), we don't like storytelling as an explanation for most other public-sphere interactions. When I was growing up in the 1950s, it never occurred to me that the Episcopal Church was selling something. How repulsive an idea. Selling God! Nor did I ever think, when my family went to Manhattan and dutifully traipsed museum mile, that a great institution like the Metropolitan Museum of Art was selling images of transcendent beauty and that it was battling the Guggenheim up the block. That stuff was self-evidently art. Wasn't it? It lived exempt from time and space. Who dared invoke market pressures? No one cared about the gate. After all, admission was free, wasn't it?

It was only when I became a college professor that I became aware that much of what I was doing was marketing a kind of cultural literacy that was really up for grabs. We in the professorate were doing the grabbing, yes, but when it came to taking it to market we were pretending it had been there all along. Not only that, but we publicly argued that this stuff was really important and that it had always been that way. "Short time's endless monument" Edmund Spenser had called art, but in our hands the curriculum became just another commodity to be sold. The battle for the best entering class was intense, and the criteria were fluid. As our consumers changed, so did our product. Want slave narratives as art? Okay. Want early diaries as feminist literature? Okay. In fact, the better the school, the more fierce the battle and the more malleable the curriculum.

As I grew more interested in how the commercial world was transforming high culture, I realized that the market (aargh, how I hated using that word in this context) for/in postsecondary education was very much like the market for those FMCGs (fast-moving consumer goods). That is to say that the school world is characterized by plenty of things that are interchangeable and offered by many suppliers. My school had become just like many other schools, each with very much the same curriculum, teaching staff, library, and playing fields. On the grocer's aisle that's exactly the condition that invites sellers to start telling stories about their products. In fact, that is exactly the condition

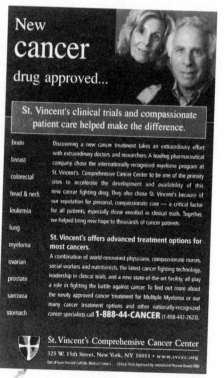

that forces sellers to brand or get squeezed off the shelf. Realizing this made understandable so many developments, such as grade inflation, thoroughly corrupt big-time sports, the outsourcing of most services (including teaching to graduate students), the commercialization of research, and the incredible influence of *U.S. News & World Report*.

And that got me thinking: Had distinction via branding moved from FMCGs to slow-moving cultural institutions (SMCIs), from soap powder and baked beans to political parties, museums, academic institutions, churches, zoos, housing developments, hospitals, and philanthropies for a reason? Is Higher Ed, Inc., in which some magazine establishes the criteria, inevitable? Is there a commercial market for selling salvation, for selling art, for selling knowledge? health care? Even for selling justice? Are the artifacts of high culture becoming just so many stockkeeping units (SKUs) to be moved about and remythographized? And, if so, why should we as belief consumers not want to admit it, and why should those on the selling side be so hesitant to confess their storytelling?

When hospitals all have the same staff and stuff, this is what happens. Branding medical service in the New York City area is a function of interchangeability.

9

The answer is, I think, self-evident. Part of the power of public-sphere branding is that the story is coming from afar—from God, from the Constitution, from perfect forms, from Truth. That contention is the *Über*-brand of Kultur. Perhaps we can better understand branded belief, branded education, and branded art as part of what in the commercial world is called a "themed environment." They even have a special name in marketing: LBEs, or location-based entertainments. That is to say, art, literature, and divinity are created in a site where a certain kind of experience can be exchanged for a certain kind of currency, not just money but, more interestingly, affiliation. To some sociologists influenced by the French, these are the markets of *cultural capital*. The pitch is that the brand of faith, education, or art that comes from one supplier is better than the almost exact same one that comes from another. The competition is intense because the stakes are high. Since the 1980s, a lot of museums, churches, and schools have gone out of business. Many more are living on the edge.

I became interested in the marketing of cultural capital as a result of studying luxury. Modern deluxe does not reside inside the object. It exists in a narrative that is attached by commercial speech—advertising. If I were to ask you to sample various kinds of nonsparkling bottled water as well as water straight from the tap, you probably couldn't tell me *on the basis of taste* which was which. But Evian charges $1.49 for a nine-ounce bottle of the stuff. What you drink is clearly the story, the brand. That's where the taste is. When blindfolded, many people cannot tell the difference between cheap and expensive wines. But more provocative is the fact that many blindfolded drinkers can't tell the difference between red and white wine or the difference between black coffee and café au lait, or not just the difference between Coke and Pepsi but between Coke and Sprite. Without seeing the nameplate, could you tell from the ride alone which car was a Lexus and which a Chevy? Could the same phenomenon be occurring in the nonprofit world? The purpose of this book is to find out.

What Isn't Matter Is What Matters

The meaning of experience has always been communicated in stories. The bard is always a central character in every culture, for without him we would not know what was happening, let alone what has come before or what to expect next. He is the priest of consciousness. While the dominant pre–Information Age stories used to cluster around abstract concepts like nationalism, ancestry, history, and access to divinity, the dominant modern stories cluster around such things as cigarettes, sugar water, beer, and car tires. Think of it: even the simplest things, such as beer, meat patties, coffee, denim, sneakers, gasoline, water, credit cards, television networks, batteries, and airplane seats have deep drum-rolling narratives behind them. The stories are linked into cycles, modern sagas, some lasting for generations, some changing every few months.

From the producer's point of view, installing the story means that he will maximize his profit. Again observe Evian. As I write this, the national average price for a gallon of unleaded gasoline is $1.75. Other prices for a gallon of various fluids:

Lipton Iced Tea: 16 oz. for $1.19 equals $9.52 per gallon
Ocean Spray: 16 oz. for $1.25 equals $10.00 per gallon
Gatorade: 20 oz. for $1.59 equals $10.17 per gallon
Diet Snapple: 16 oz. for $1.29 equals $10.32 per gallon
Milk: 16 oz. for $1.59 equals $12.72 per gallon
Wite-Out: 7 oz. for $1.39 equals $25.42 per gallon
STP brake fluid: 12 oz. for $3.15 equals $33.60 per gallon
Scope: 1.5 oz. for $0.99 equals $84.48 per gallon
Pepto-Bismol: 4 oz. for $3.85 equals $123.20 per gallon
Vicks NyQuil: 6 oz. for $8.35 equals $178.13 per gallon
Evian water: 9 oz. for $1.49 equals $21.19 per gallon

While you might think that consumers would balk and admit that Evian spelled backward is what they don't want to be—namely, naive—no such thing happens. Just the opposite. We *want* the story. The story retails for $1.49; the water is free. The best explanation of

The taste of Evian is not on the palate but in the imagination, and here it is being installed via slightly ludicrous stories.

the consumer's point of view is this conversation from the BBC sitcom *Absolutely Fabulous.* Edwina receives a gift of earrings from her daughter. "Are they Lacroix?" Edwina asks eagerly. "Do you like them?" asks her daughter. "I do if they're Lacroix," replies Edwina.

When you extrapolate the value of these commercial fictions, the numbers become huge; to some observers, obscene. Here's how *Business-Week,* teaming up with Interbrand, a unit of the advertising holding company Omnicom, valued the top ten worldwide brands. As with most such rankings, such as *U.S. News & World Report* rankings of universities, the list changes a little each year so the magazine can be guaranteed future sales. But even if the ranking is based on a number of variable criteria, the basic idea is that strong brands have the power to increase sales and earnings, irrespective of other attributes. Note that these are only publicly held worldwide brands, so some household names such as Gatorade (a subsidiary of PepsiCo) don't count, nor do private companies such as candy maker Mars, Inc. or institutions such as the Roman Catholic Church, the Louvre, or Harvard University.

The World's Ten Most Valuable Brands in 2001

Rank	Brand	Brand Value
1	Cola-Cola	$68.9 billion
2	Microsoft	$65.1 billion
3	IBM	$52.8 billion
4	GE	$42.4 billion
5	Nokia	$35.0 billion
6	Intel	$34.7 billion
7	Disney	$32.6 billion
8	Ford	$30.1 billion
9	McDonald's	$25.3 billion
10	AT&Ts	$22.8 billion

Note that most of these superpowerful brands are in industries with plenty of competition; in fact, they are often selling almost identical products as their cohorts. Coke needs Pepsi. McDonald's needs Burger King. Ford needs GM. If you ever wonder why Microsoft is perpetually tussling with the government, this is part of the reason. From a branding perspective, it might do better with a competitive brand. What the list shows is that whenever you have a surplus of inter-changeable items, the savvy supplier is going to attach a powerful story to his version. "I've never seen a great military, political or corporate leader who was not a great storyteller. Telling stories is a core competency in business, although it's one that we don't pay enough attention to," says Brian Ferren, executive vice president for creative technology and research at Walt Disney Imagineering, number seven on the list. Or, as another master of this process, Roberto Goizueta, late CEO of number one, Coca-Cola, said, "In retail, it's location, lo-cation, location. In business, it's differentiate, differentiate, differen-tiate." He wasn't talking about the product; he was talking about the stories.

This separation into brands via fiction is true not just with obvi-ously interchangeable commercial products such as airline seats, mortgages, credit cards, and long distance service, but with a variety of disparate cultural matters as well. Consider television shows in which branded characters are deeply fixed in roles (think *Seinfeld, Cheers, Hill Street Blues*); television producers (Aaron Spelling and Steven Bochco are brand names); television networks (Discover and PBS have mall stores, as does Disney, and the Fox network has its own brand of news); plot lines (the *Law & Order* story is told on tele-vision in the host show as well as in two extensions, *L&O: Special Vic-tims Unit* and *L&O: Criminal Intent*, a coffee-table book of gritty photographs and another book of trivia, a computer game and a cell phone version, as well as the usual raft of director's cut DVDs); au-thors (Stephen King says he's the "Big Mac and fries" of popular fic-tion); sporting teams (the NBA has been defined by its commissioner as a single brand—the NBA—with-twenty-nine teams); movies (Steven Spielberg and George Lucas are brands, as are the James Bond and Terminator movies); royalty (the Windsors; Prince Rainier and Grace Kelly); talk radio (think how Rush Limbaugh transformed the AM dial); magazines (*Cosmo* opens a clothing store; Oprah is *Oprah*); and even human behavior (ADHD, BPD) and the drugs to treat it (Ritalin, Prozac).

The list of branded goods and services is seemingly endless and in-creasing daily. What it shows is that once we are able to produce

Sell the disease first, then the anxiety, then the cure.

something, almost anything, we will then produce it up until the point of diminishing returns. You name it: meat patties, fictional stories, automobiles, class-action lawsuits, newspapers, or—in terms of this book—pews, classrooms, works of art; if it can be manufactured, assembled, or constructed, the successful versions will ultimately be those with the most compelling narratives. The process is now second nature to us. We even see ourselves in the workforce as being superfluous and just like the guy next to us. What to do? Think of yourself as a . . . brand.

Forbes *magazine has it right: these days kids want to be highly leveraged brands.*

The Modern Brand

Branding, as symbol creation, is, of course, ancient. Start with the word *brand,* and you can follow the entire history of how we name (and control) the meaning of things. Literally, a brand (from Old English *biernan,* "to burn") was something stuck in a fire. As a verb, it describes the process of tempering by high heat. As a noun, a brand is the result of being brazened. A brand is literally a weapon, often a sword, hardened by heating—no symbolism yet, just process and result. You *brandish* a sword or, better yet, brand. Thus a *firebrand* is a hothead, someone who presumably has been too close to the flames and has transformed into something forceful, such as a sword. He is *brazen.*

Exploiting the connection with fire, *brand* became something literally burned into the hide of cows and horses to show ownership. The brand as burned image now starts a curious history because it is joined with *stigma,* which means "blot" or "blemish" and is a signifier of inflicted shame. "Stigma" comes to us from Latin, as the Romans literally branded unruly slaves and criminals. These brands were lightly burnt onto the skin and disappeared within a few years. Many of those branded were Christians. In a provocative bit of cultural jujitsu, early Christianity picked up the symbolic concept and applied it retroactively to the nail wounds of Christ—the stigmata. Here is a rare example of not just a backwards application (metalepsis) but a total reversal of meaning (antagonym). For the wounds received by Christ on the Cross would miraculously appear on the hands of a true penitent: the secondary stigmata, a brand of elevation, not degradation.

In American cultural history, the best-known use of branded stigmas was by the Puritans. Who does not know of Hester Prynne's scarlet letter? What we don't realize is that an entire alphabet was used. So in Maryland, for instance, county justices could brand a criminal with an "H," for hog stealer; an "R," for runaway slave; or a "T," for thief. Colonial America was an ideal culture for such branding. Here was an isolated community with real danger around the edges. Being cast out meant confronting real danger. Being branded increased your danger. Your story traveled with you—literally.

During the nineteenth century, the concept of *brand* also consolidated an older, less ambiguous, definition. The brand became a return address or a trademark burned on such products as liquor and wine casks, timber, metals, and the like. This is still a common usage. Very often a brand shows how ownership can literally attach to a moving product. We all know the branding of, say, the flying A on the flank of a steer as a mark denoting ownership. Soon it becomes the nameplate of a car, the flying B of Bentley. The brand becomes a social construction of possession, no longer of transgression, and not yet of inclusion. This meaning was consecrated when, in 1905, Congress passed trademark legislation. The brand legally became "a name, term, or design—or a combination of these elements that is intended to clearly identify and differentiate a seller's products from a competitor's products," which is still how it is formally defined.

In the modern world we have, again true to the stigma history, reversed the magnetic poles with self-inflicted tattooing. Not just adolescents but grown-ups wait patiently to have themselves branded with various witticisms on various parts of the anatomy. We also proudly wear the initials of affiliation, branding ourselves with what are often designer names. So Donna Karan's DKNY, Chanel's Cs, Tommy Hilfiger's Tommy, Gucci's Gs, or Ralph Lauren's RL are displayed on our bodies as signs of inclusion, not exclusion. We occasionally recognize such branding as a kind of bondage. We talk of style slaves and fashion victims. But even though many of us are deeply susceptible to the manufactured allure that inveigles us into making "buying decisions," we are not necessarily that keen to admit it. The branding process, however, works the same way: in or out, on the skin or over it. We want to be part of *this* story, not *that* one.

So, in a way, brand has moved from noun to verb and back to noun. I think it's best understood as a storytelling *process*. Observe Levi's. A century ago the Levi's brand was a way to display what are called in marketing the "features and benefits" of a machine-made fabric: denim. The brand was literally stamped on both the packing boxes and the pants. The brand denoted and connoted: it said, "this is *from* Levi Strauss & Co., it *is* Levi's denim, and it *means* that Levi's is rugged." Later the brand appeared as that big label for all the world to see, right there on your hip, a symbol. By extension, the brand became more than a promise of experience; it became the experience it-

See that beauty mark? Mercedes-Benz has the temerity to brand a brand, literally.

Which brand do you want to slide into today?

19

self: You are rugged. Levi's was not just *on* your hip, it *became* hip, just as you do when you wear Levi's. Then, rather mysteriously in the 1970s, just as it seemed indomitable, the Levi's brand lost its cachet and became something to avoid.

Perhaps more appropriate than a narrative process, the brand has become a kind of theater in which various dramas are performed. Some years ago John Stuart, then chairman of the Quaker Oats Company, said in an often quoted comment, "If the business were split up, I would take the brands, trademarks, and goodwill, and you could have all the bricks and mortar—and I would do better than you." But holding the experience, as it were, is not without risks. For while a brand can take years to evolve, it can evaporate in just months if it loses its interpretive audience. Or if it gets the wrong audience. The tipping point tips both ways.

Modern commercial brands are tippy because, unlike most other stories, they are not written down in an *ur*-text. They appear in advertising, in packaging, in logos, in slogans, and in the minds of consumers. They are just "out there" in the cultural ether, social constructions without the telltale provenance that holds them in place. We know them, yes, but we're not sure how. In this sense, the modern brand is like a smell. Although humans are sensitive to scents, we are unaware of the impact of odor until we reach the extremes. Then it's all reflex. Whiff, and we gag. Whew, and we swoon. Yuck, we say when we are too close to carrion. Yummy, we say when we are not close enough to perfume. Smells, like the other sensations, carry stories to the brain, but they do it almost at the speed of sound and our response is often visceral and violent. And that's what a great brand ultimately is, a sensation, again the infamous sizzle, not the steak. That's why brands are so hard to control.

Here's another way to think about brands: they are commercialized *gossip*. Not gossip in the tabloid sense of who is sleeping with whom but gossip in the much more profound sense of secret meaning to be shared by insiders. "Psssst, here, listen to this." Gossip moves in whispers because they're far more important than shouts. *Buzz* is such a good onomatopoeic descriptor because it gives the sense of bees in a hive. You pay attention to gossip; it's important. That's why you lean over and cup your ear, alert your sniffer—prepare for the good stuff, the real dirt, the gravy, the perfume. It even has a temperature; it's *cool,* or it's *hot.*

Gossip may seem trivial to dictionary writers and newspaper readers but ask anyone in marketing how important gossip is. The reason *buzz* is the coinage *du jour* on Madison Avenue and in Hollywood and Washington, D.C., is because what they sell is fresh brands for old products. Back in the post-Prohibition days, liquor companies found that the best way to move a new product was to hire bar drinkers to whisper that a certain branded drink was really powerful. After all it was just bourbon, rye, or scotch that was often coming out of the same vats, but the power of "Pssst, try this stuff, it's better than moonshine" was potent. Humans cannot resist the intimacy of secret knowledge. In advertising, commercial gossip is no longer called *whisper copy;* it's *viral marketing.* Universities, art galleries, churches, philanthropies, and other sites of cultural capital are no exception. They have realized not just the power of "getting the word out" but the power of "getting the right word out to the 'right people.'"

Brand Community: The New World Order

We know the words. Brands are the new lingua franca. What marks the modern world is that certain brand stories have become ligatures that hold experience together. We speak of *brand families* of objects on the shelf, never really appreciating that such families may well extend into the human sphere. We use the term *brand loyalty* without really appreciating the power of affiliation. We all know the way certain automobile owners wave at each other solely on the basis of the brand of car they drive (Saab, for instance), how certain computer users form chat groups that extend friendship beyond simple discussions of shared equipment or operating systems (Apple, for instance, or Linux), how the alumni of certain schools seem to bond even if they were not in the same class (Dartmouth), even how dog owners will cross busy streets to chat with someone with the same breed of dog. Humans yearn to become sociable, to tell stories and share feelings. Brands facilitate this process.

The most famous brand community and one that has been studied to within an inch of its acoustic exhaust pipes (often at some risk to the ethnologist) is Harley-Davidson. Here is a bit of pig iron, chrome, and leather that is 20 percent more expensive than its German and Japanese counterparts and probably 30 percent less well made. But it has the almost total reverential devotion of thousands. Clustered like pilgrims around an icon of worshipful concentration is a community of aggressive outsiders linked with a brand so deep in pretend lore that in the Harley Owners Group both machine and owner share the same name: "Hog."

What makes Harley so interesting a story is that thirty years ago it was almost bled of meaning. The company was driven into the ground by AMF, the maker of bowling equipment, as they cheapened the product and shifted the audience to suburban kids. But thanks to the Hells Angels, some misunderstood movie sequences with Marlon Brando (he's actually riding an English Triumph), great product names (Knucklehead, Panhead, Shovelhead, Hardtail, Super Glide, Hydro Glide, Electra-Glide, Dyna Glide, Chopper), a symphonic exhaust system that produced a recognized sound (*potato-potato-potato*), and an elaborate chrome presentation allowing for customization, this object has become a talisman. The brand has become sensational—literally and figuratively.

As has often been pointed out, any brand that encourages its acolytes to literally transfer its logo onto their body as a tattoo, any brand that has believers using the owner's manual as a Bible for marriage ceremonies, any brand that has pilgrimage celebrations such as Bike Weeks, any brand that has a special version of the Ford pickup truck fitted out with a cargo bed specially designed to coddle the bike, well, whatever that brand is, it's getting almost religious.

You can see the same cult-community status (albeit not so tight) woven around such magical objects as the Mazda Miata, Krispy Kreme donuts, Zippo lighters, Jeeps, Tupperware, various cigars, and wines, to say nothing of the entire communities created by designer-label clothing such as Dior, Gucci, Armani, and Ralph Lauren. Often even a simple product can attain such status solely on the basis of seeming exclusivity. This is gossip struggling for the condition of the Word. Remember how Coors beer used to be the magical brand in the 1970s, even starring in a movie in which Burt Reynolds risked life and limb to transport it to Atlanta? Or what Nike running shoes used to be like? Or the Prada baguette purse? Often ownership is self-consciously fetishized, as when Land Rover holds special rallies and training programs to show how rugged the car is, and by extension how outdoorsy is the owner, who, in truth, rarely leaves the condo. That 95 percent of these vehicles never leave the blacktop is missing the point of brand. As with the SUV, the story is about power and the freedom to get away. Forget the product.

The search for community explains why the concept of *cool* occurs in the mid–twentieth century, as producers of interchangeable objects struggle to cross the tipping point and create a sense of unity based on shared use. What is cool if not the certification of membership in a branded community? Sometimes the endeavor is a little obvious, as with this famous Tareyton campaign developed just as advertisers were realizing how important a thoroughly concocted community could be.

Brands do more than tell stories, they create community.

Brands Are Made to Be Consumed and Witnessed

Susan Fournier, of the Harvard Business School, has tried to account for the compelling nature of certain brands. She records the day-to-day interaction of ordinary people with common FMCG (fast-moving consumer goods), articles such as the soap, shampoo, and cleaning materials that cluster in the closet. In other words, just as there are communities of brand users, there are communities of brands. Things fit into patterns, constellations, jigsaw puzzles. Brands rhyme. They are loyal to one another. She reports in a journal article, "Consumers and Their Brands: Developing Relationship Theory in Consumer Research," that brand stories act like religion not just by holding people together but also by holding individual experiences together. Like parables, the stories behind how you use a certain brand of, say, toothpaste, how your parents used it, how it has appeared in your life, what makes you believe in it and want to associate with it—all these point to an absolutely natural extension of human relationships not just to other humans but to . . . of all things . . . *things.* She concludes:

> *Whether one adopts a psychological or sociohistorical interpretation of the data, the conclusion suggested in the analysis is the same: brand relationships are valid at the level of consumers' lived experiences. The consumers in this study are not just buying brands because they like them or because they work well. They are involved in relationships with a collectivity of brands so as to benefit from the meanings they add into their lives. Some of these meanings are functional and utilitarian; others are more psychosocial and emotional. All, however, are purposive and ego centered and therefore of great significance to the persons engaging them. The processes of meaning provision, manipulation, incorporation, and pronouncement authenticate the relationship notion in the consumer-brand domain.*

In other words, brands are the passwords in the new tribalism, the basis not just of interactions but of interior actions. They are becoming the new Esperanto, the currency of exchange, the meaning of *habitus,* the intersection of self and other. We cluster around them as we used to cluster around sacred relics; we are loyal to them the way we are loyal to symbols such as the flag; we live through, around, and against them. Brands have become members of the new and improved family of man.

The Diderot Effect

Although Professor Fournier has given brand affiliation a deep meaning, the realization that commercial things come in patterns is generations old. The entire process of creating a coherent commercialized self by assembling brands has a name to ethnographers. It is called the *Diderot effect*. The insight into how commercial objects dovetail was first noted by the late-seventeenth-century essayist Denis Diderot. In his "Regrets on Parting with My Old Dressing Gown," the French philosopher explored what would become a modern condition. As we will see, it explains much of the power of the collections of Museumworld, the curriculum of Higher Ed, Inc., and the denominational coherence of Christianity. It may also explain why we choose the educational, religious, and artistic experiences and sensations we do.

Here is Diderot's argument on how things fit together, how things predict and complement one another. As he looks up from his desk and glances around his study, Diderot notices that it has been transformed by mysterious forces. It was once crowded, humble, chaotic, and happy. Now it is elegant, organized, and a little grim. What happened? Diderot suspects that the cause of the transformation is right before his eyes. It is his new dressing gown. A week after he began to wear the gown, it occurred to him that his shabby desk was not quite up to the standard of his robe. So he got a shiny new one. Then the tapestry on the wall seemed a little threadbare and new curtains had to be found. Gradually, the entire contents of the study were replaced. Why? Not because he wanted a new study but because he needed a sense of coherence, a sense that nothing was out of place, a sense of a center, what today would be known as *brand coherence.* He wanted the stories to fit.

In modern marketing this is called creating a "consumption constellation," entering a brandscape, conforming to a fashion, making an ensemble. No matter what it is called, the pleasure and the pain remain the same. Achieving that sense of completeness is, in that linguistic barbarism unique to our times, creating a *lifestyle*. A lifestyle is an emblematic display of coherent brands, a demonstrated understanding of stories.

Thanks to the Machine, Most of Our Stories Are Commercials

Cultural critics may cringe to admit it, but most of our shared stories are about manufactured stuff. This was predictable. The Industrial Revolution applied steam power to machinery. Machines make similar objects. When too many objects are produced, their manufacturer is confronted with a serious problem. He has a *surplus*. Surplus is the curse of mass production. Logically, he should cut the price and "work the inventory off" by thus increasing sales. But he may find it more expeditious (not to say profitable) to distinguish his product by telling a story about it. Here, he says, my product makes you more popular, live longer, be happier, seem sexier; it is better made, lasts longer . . . anything that pretends distinction for what the consumer logically knows is fictitious. The producer spreads commercial gossip, spritzes his product with some fumes, tries to make his story not deep but shallow, not profound but compelling—cool. The story's purpose is not to inform you about the product but to inch you closer to the buyhole.

If you look at the stories we share, I mean *really* share—so much so that we cannot even remember how we learned about them—you will see something rather startling. These stories about manufactured products have roots in mythology. Take the cartoon characters or identification characters of commercial products, for instance. The Jolly Green Giant seems a mimic of the giant of lore, the Pillsbury Doughboy seems the perpetual infant, Tony the Tiger is the affable lion, characters in advertisements for light beer seem to be jesters of various kinds, while performers in sneaker ads are like Olympian heroes, Harley-Davidson users are portrayed as eternal outlaws, blue jeans wearers are often going where none have gone before, the Marlboro man invokes the independent outsider, Betty Crocker the archetypical good mother, and so forth. Commercial stories, while shallow, are usually drawn from the preliterate or prerational world. All right, they may not be the hero with a thousand faces, but they are from the same town.

Places you've always wanted to go. Things you've always meant to do. It's never too late to make it right. The new Boxster. An elegantly re-sculpted exterior. A meatier 225 hp boxer engine. A more adventurous existence starts at $42,600. Contact us at 1-800-PORSCHE or porsche.com.

What's the story of your life, starting now?

The new Boxster

PORSCHE

A car is more than pig iron and plastic; it's a story. Advertising tells it.

As Margaret Mark and Carol Pearson have recently argued in *The Hero and the Outlaw: Building Extraordinary Brands Through the Power of Archetypes,* the myth behind these images, the reason we have this shared pantheon of lowercase gods, seems to be the necessity for certain kinds of quick-fire story exchanges. The stories come in a flash because we've consumed them before in other texts. They are nothing if not efficient and redundant. You get the story in a logo, a slogan, a package, a tune. There is nothing more here than the smell, so to speak, just flyby gossip. That is what makes them so powerful and so wide-ranging.

Brands can go into almost any culture precisely because they can overlay indigenous myth so efficiently. They are *syncretic.* Take, for instance, Halloween, which started as a Druid ceremony expressing the concerns of dying light and the onset of winter, was co-opted by Christianity and reformatted as All Hallows' Eve, which was, in turn, taken over by the candy companies to become Halloween, a night of harvesting sweets. Although UNICEF tried for a while to make trick-or-treating an act of feel-good generosity, it was not successful. However, even as you read this, Halloween is being commandeered by the brewers, who ardently wish that this night would belong to Michelob, Coors, and the other usual suspects. Halloween is now turning into Oktoberfest. As with much of our calendar, brands set the clock.

The secret to great brands is that they are often nonsensical. Coke is the real thing, all right, but we have no idea what that means. Apple thinks different, to be sure, but we have no idea what that entails. A diamond is forever. Duh? So what? Just do it! Just do *what?* Texaco is a star, McDonald's is a golden M, IBM is blue: the very superficiality is part of why these stories move so far so fast. They *can't* be read deeply, but they can't not be read.

The Logic of Things and the Seeming Illogic of Consumers

If we were logical and we had to buy something, anything!, wouldn't we all go down to the library and check out *Consumer Reports,* find the best version, and then all buy it? And you would know if this had happened because when you went to your local grocery store, you'd see only a few aisles of products. You'd see maybe two or three types of toothpaste, not twenty. In fact, if you were to reduce product redundancy from your average Safeway, you'd end up with a store about the size of a 7-Eleven. And, if we were logical, generic labels would ultimately rule the shelves.

But this doesn't happen. In fact, if you look at the irruption of floor space, you see just the opposite. The average grocery store has been expanding. It's now about 44,000 square feet. The average number of items (stockkeeping units—SKUs) carried in a typical supermarket is 30,580. This is more than double the space and objects that existed in the 1950s. Why?

This explosion is not because there are more different products but because there are more nearly redundant products. There are more than thirty versions of Crest toothpaste. Check out the soap aisle and

How far can an Oreo go? Brand extension at work.

remember that there are only about three major producers, all glutting the shelf with nondifferent cleaners. The big-box stores clustered over by the interstate highway are mute testament to the fact that we are looking not for intrinsic differences but for narrative ones. What separates us as a modern culture from much of the rest of the world is not that we are able to hold an array of different versions of the same object but that we are able to hold an incredible number of different versions of the same stories. This phenomenon is now happening in an increasing variety of noncommercial venues. In a word, it is the result of branding.

The explosion of seemingly unnecessary choice is a characteristic of a free market, yes, but what we have developed is an explosion of almost perfectly interchangeable choices in which attached narratives are the *only* variable. Before the Industrial Revolution, soap was soap, malt liquor was malt liquor, the church was The Church, and storytelling was communal and fixed and finite. It was said that until Coleridge's time one man could know most of a culture's stories. And that Coleridge did. But once the machine was introduced into the Garden, all hell broke loose. Soap became Ivory, malt liquor became Glenturret single-malt scotch whiskey, the church became Southern Methodist, art became idiosyncratic and the signature became primary. No longer was this painting a still life, it was a Monet. This transformation was wrought by continuous-production machinery, yes, but it is also the result of a profound shift in the imagination called *Romanticism*.

The Poeticizing of the Material World: Romanticism

To understand how stories became attached to manufactured things—branding—we need to appreciate two seemingly unrelated transformations that occurred during the nineteenth century. These crucial shifts in perception are the common acceptance of the *pathetic fallacy* and the rise of *Impressionism*. Together they opened the way for commercial branding and in so doing eventually transformed the suppliers of cultural capital as well.

One of the radical assertions of Romanticism was not that it made feeling into an epistemology (you know it's right because it feels right) but the startling contention that inanimate things and nonhuman life share feeling. Admittedly, this was often proffered as a way to shock, but it soon became a way to inform and expand consciousness. Here's just a bit of the feeling phenomenon as expressed by William Wordsworth in "Lines Written in Early Spring." Unlikely as it may be, the process he limns at the end of the eighteenth century is at the heart of commercial branding.

> *I heard a thousand blended notes,*
> *While in a grove I sate reclined,*
> *In that sweet mood when pleasant thoughts*
> *Bring sad thoughts to the mind.*
>
> *To her fair works did Nature link*
> *The human soul that through me ran;*
> *And much it grieved my heart to think*
> *What man has made of man.*
>
> *Through primrose tufts, in that green bower,*
> *The periwinkle trailed its wreaths;*
> *And 'tis my faith that every flower*
> *Enjoys the air it breathes.*
>
> *The birds around me hopped and played,*
> *Their thoughts I cannot measure:—*
> *But the least motion which they made*
> *It seemed a thrill of pleasure.*
>
> *The budding twigs spread out their fan,*
> *To catch the breezy air;*
> *And I must think, do all I can,*
> *That there was pleasure there.*
>
> *If this belief from heaven be sent,*
> *If such be Nature's holy plan,*
> *Have I not reason to lament*
> *What man has made of man?*

When Wordsworth states that he believes that flowers *enjoy* the air, that the birds have *thoughts,* that the budding twigs *sense* pleasure, he is willingly and almost belligerently threatening the concept of knowing. This unarticulated paradigm—what was called the Great Chain of Being in Elizabethan times—essentially orders the values of life for a culture. With the exception of the burst of Romanticism about the time of the French Revolution, it usually excludes sentience from the natural world. Birds don't have joy, twigs can't sense pleasure, and birds most certainly don't think.

The high Victorian John Ruskin coined the term *pathetic fallacy* to describe this misattribution of human characteristics to nature. For Ruskin it is the mediocre intellect that can perceive the forms of nature in terms of its own projected emotions. It is sensationalism turned maudlin. But it is exactly this emotional projection that lies at the center of commercial storytelling.

Wordsworth was no feeble intellect. He was a painstaking poet and, in an ironic sense, an innovator in modern commercial storytelling. He made projected sensation the subject matter of art. What was his infamous definition of poetry? "The spontaneous overflow of powerful feelings recollected in tranquility." And who is a poet? Just "a man speaking to men." In other words, the sensations of an individual are the stuff of knowledge and, by extension, of culture. Wordsworth made it safe to have feelings about the modern world. In fact, he insisted on it.

But he did not go far enough. Other artists did. And in so doing they ushered in one of the truly radical shifts in temper, *Impressionism.* While this shift is best seen in oil painting later in the century, we can glimpse it first in poetry. What makes it important is that it demands collusion on the part of the viewer, a willingness to, as Coleridge said, "suspend disbelief" and accept on what he calls "poetic faith" information that is on its face irrational. Think of van Gogh's *Starry Night.* How can you look at such an image and not see that it is a response to nature, not a portrayal of it? In the well-worn trope, the Romantic artist is holding a lamp up to nature, not a mirror. You have to respond.

Remember Keats's "Ode on a Grecian Urn" from your high school days? In the poem the speaker is looking at an ancient urn, and he starts asking questions of it. First, he wants to know what story is being told on the urn. Young lovers are caught in frozen pursuit on the urn, and he wonders who they are and how they feel. Next, he walks around the urn and sees another scene. This time the scene is of a priest leading a heifer to some kind of sacrifice. He wonders what religious ceremony is being enacted.

> *Who are these coming to the sacrifice?*
> *To what green altar, O mysterious priest,*
> *Lead'st thou that heifer lowing at the skies,*
> *And all her silken flanks with garlands drest?*
> *What little town by river or sea-shore,*
> *Or mountain-built with peaceful citadel,*
> *Is emptied of its folk, this pious morn?*
> *And, little town, thy streets for evermore*
> *Will silent be; and not a soul, to tell*
> *Why thou art desolate, can e'er return.*

As you can see, Keats is asking for information that is *not* on the urn. If the little town were on the urn, he would know if it were up in the hills or down by the seashore. What is happening is that he is starting to animate the urn and give it human characteristics, rather as Wordsworth did with nature when he attributed feeling to birds and flowers. Keats is essentially treating the object like something/someone which/who can respond to his questioning—a thing that can tell a story. He is treating it, in other words, in a singularly modern way—like a brand.

In the final stanza, all the pins are removed and Keats out-Wordsworths Wordsworth. Here are the lines:

> *O Attic shape! fair attitude! with brede*
> *Of marble men and maidens overwrought,*
> *With forest branches and the trodden weed;*
> *Thou, silent form! dost tease us out of thought*
> *As doth eternity: Cold Pastoral!*
> *When old age shall this generation waste,*
> *Thou shalt remain, in midst of other woe*
> *Than ours, a friend to man, to whom thou say'st,*
> *"Beauty is truth, truth beauty,—that is all*
> *Ye know on earth, and all ye need to know."*

Any schoolboy appreciates what is going on, or at least what seems to be going on. Keats seems to be hearing what the urn is saying. In other words, it talks! And, far more important, it seems to be saying something rather profound, although it's not clear what exactly. But who cares? It's the shock of reciprocity that is startling.

You say, so what? Well, normally I wouldn't care so much, but look at this ad for the Neon. What the hell is that car doing talking to us? This is not a god, like Poseidon speaking of the sea, or a crow in Aesop's *Fables* commenting on human greed. This is a manufactured object with something to say to us! Rather like the famous October 23, 1929, issue of *Variety* that announced, "GARBO TALKS OK," it may not really matter much what the car or the urn or the silent movie star has to say. The point is that silence rarely speaks and that, while objects may be storied, they are not storytellers. But of course in the modern world they are. They are because we have anthropomorphized them, thanks to Romanticism.

Branding gives things a social life; even a Neon can be your friend.

The Pathetic Fallacy Is the Truth of Branding

Not only are we not shocked by the Neon ad, we drawn closer to the car. By the same token, we are friendly with such outlandish creatures as the Pillsbury Doughboy, Mr. Clean, Aunt Jemima, Ronald McDonald, Tony the Tiger, and the Ti-D-Bowl man who lives in the toilet. Clearly something has happened between Keats and modern advertising. Mr. and Ms. Product and their kin are not from Utopia but from Adopia, a parallel universe, a kind of commercialized version of Romantic nature, inhabitants of Brandville. We all know many of them, often better than we know some of our own family. And we know them because of (1) the storytelling necessity of separating fungible products, (2) the predictable humanizing of the manufactured world to generate those stories, and (3) our learned and practiced willingness to move back and forth between the real world and Adopia, suspending judgment in the hope of building some kind of magical relationship that will generate meaning for what is really just beer, chocolates, sugar water, or a meat patty.

Colin Campbell, an English sociologist, argues in *The Romantic Ethic and the Spirit of Modern Consumerism* that indeed something tectonic happened to the Western imagination to make such application of stories to machine-made objects possible. He contends that at the end of the Age of Reason we lost interest in rationalizing and started dreaming. That's what Romanticism was all about, not just the application of engines to production but the application of the imagination to consumption. The object of our dreams became commercialized, the stuff of getting and spending. That's what the Industrial Revolution was all about. Maybe we have always been this way. Until the nineteenth century, only kings and princes could yearn for the meaning of things, but with continuous-production machinery, the rest of us could have a go at it. To supercharge the process, we had to be willing to suspend disbelief, to essentially become consumer poets. We had to be willing to become emotionally involved with not just animate nature but inanimate commerce.

The Industrial Revolution didn't suddenly make us want things and the stories that went along with them. The Industrial Revolution was the result of our materialism, not the cause of it. But we don't always know what we want. If we knew what things meant, we could choose among them on the basis of some inner need. But we don't know. So in a sense we are not materialistic enough. That's why stories can get in between us and the objects. We desperately want meaning; things can't supply it, so we install it via narrative, via branding.

When a culture has few objects, it tends to spiritualize the objects of the next world. Heaven is richly imagined in poor cultures. African and Latin American Christians have rich inventories of Heaven. When we have a surfeit of stuff, we tend to spiritualize parts of it in the here and now, forgetting the luxury Beyond. That's why few people in the West today even have a sense of what's in Heaven. If we can trust what we see in medieval art, they certainly used to. Wordsworth shows that this secular spiritualizing happens as we observe in the natural world; Keats shows it operating in the world of man-made objects.

Hence branding (storifying things) is not so much the result of production as it is the result of consumption. It's the stories we're after as well as the material goods. The coupling of concocted stories with machine-made objects, plus the willingness to "suspend disbelief" and accept that such stories could be true, if only for a moment, allowed the phenomenon of branding to take hold. Essentially, we made dreaming a central part of consuming: look, desire, dream, buy.

It's an irony, Campbell admits, that Romanticism, the putative enemy of material consumption, should have paved the way for the marketing of excess stuff by foregrounding the life of sensation, privileging the process of daydreaming, and encouraging the attribution of spiritual yearning to the nonreligious world. In splitting the personality into active and contemplative and praising the latter, in foregrounding fiction and reneging on reason, in making impulse and emotion acceptable, in valuing loitering and drifting, in encouraging solipsism and the rise of the individual response, the enemies of Getting and Spending made the Industrial Revolution of Getting and Spending possible. Technology may have provided the machines, but the poets loaded the software.

We have still not fully understood the ramifications of moving from needs to wants, from mandates of biology to choices of experience. We do know this: discretionary spending—be it for entertainment or art, travel or education, gourmet food or religious experience—

represents an increasing portion of our endeavors. For many of us, especially when young, gathering unnecessary objects has become a site of creative choice and pleasurable sensation. As Herbert Muschamp, design critic of *The New York Times,* has recently observed, "In the last 50 years, the economic base has shifted from production to consumption. It has gravitated from the sphere of rationality to the realm of desire: from the objective to the subjective, to the realm of psychology." It may be that modern artists, the priests of taste, will again show us the way to the next step of consuming sensation. In fact, two English pop artists, Neil Cummings and Marysia Lewandowska, have given it a go:

> *Modern exchange is not materialistic. It is not objects that people really desire, but their lush coating of images and dreams that mesh with a wider promotional culture fueled by advertising and the broadcast media. Exchange helps to animate objects with value and in so doing it weaves a dense social web of aspiration characterized by a cycle of desire, use and disillusionment. Disillusionment inevitably follows exchange; it is never the object which is consumed—instead, it is the relationship between us and the object of desire.*

It's ironic that the counterculture that started with the Romantic privileging of the avant-garde should have provided the heart of consumer culture. The poets provided not the machinery of production but the machinery of consumption. The Puritans may have said, "Work, work, work," but the Romantics said, "Spend, spend, spend." They made shifting consciousness into a goal and the natural world the means of achieving it. They democratized deluxe, sacramentalized the mundane, and made the physical world transcendent. Marketers, or "attention engineers" as they were known in the Victorian times, did the rest.

Brand Poetry

Could it be that successful brands make it through the sieve of clutter the same way that certain works become recognized as literature?

They change how we *feel.* Visually, brands are achieving the condition of art. Since the 1990–91 exhibition at New York's Museum of Modern Art called cautiously *High & Low: Modern Art and Popular Culture,* no one has doubted that the imagery of advertising was edging over into the high-cult world of art. The case has been consolidated by such recent books as *The Fine Art of Advertising,* by Barry Hoffman (creative director of Young & Rubicam), *Advertising in America: The First Two Hundred Years,* by Charles A. Goodrum and Helen Dalrymple (both of the Smithsonian Institution and both published by the art house Harry N. Abrams), and the German art publisher Taschen's massive collections of American ads, which are essentially presented as reverential picture books. Not entirely by happenstance is the person responsible for designing the illustration for the advertising agency called the *art director.*

But if you really want to see the acceptance of advertising as art, go into any college dorm and look at what is posted on bedroom walls. Adolescents decorate their walls with the aspirational images of their future. A decade or so ago, you could walk into the campus bookstore and buy poster-size reproductions of the works of great masters to thumbtack to your dormitory wall. There is now a company called Beyond the Wall that sells students ads from Nike, Citizen Watch, Bain de Soleil, Valvoline, Sony, and the rest, blown up to poster size at $10 a copy. What American college students decorate their space with is much like what is on the walls of Third World housing. Such poster images are the mezzotints of modern life, the art of materialism.

Beyond the Wall may call its jumbo ads "Poster Art," but the crossover is deeper and more profound than this image migration suggests. A brand narrative itself becomes poetic as it starts to act like a trope, a figure of speech. A brand becomes not just *what* we think about an object, but *how* we think about it. Lest this sound too ethereal, realize that this is precisely the nature of metaphor. It states something in the place of something else. Language, both visual and verbal, brands experience, makes consciousness possible by creating a code of understanding. It captures and delivers sensation. That's why most definitions, like that of the American Marketing Association, focus on *differentiation:* "A brand is a name, term, sign, symbol or design, or a combination of them, intended to define the goods or services of one

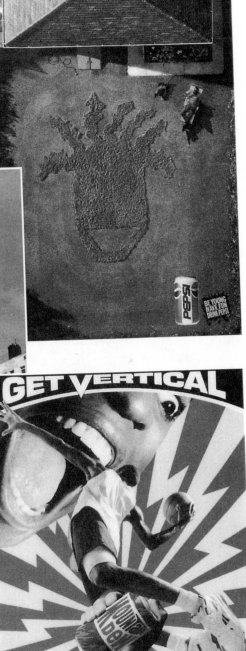

Take down your van Gogh.
Put up your Pepsi poster.

seller or group of sellers and to differentiate them from those of competitors." When that differentiation works, the brand generates *frisson*, it provides sensation, a shift (albeit minuscule) of consciousness.

Here is Joseph Conrad taking a purely literary approach to this process: "The meaning of an episode was not inside like a kernel but outside in the unseen, enveloping the tale which could only bring it out as a glow brings out a haze" (*Heart of Darkness*, Chapter 1). Brands operate the same way. They draw their meaning not from their "kernel," the actual product, but from what surrounds them. They create an aura of differentiation around a product that distinguishes it from all others. Rather like the nimbus or halo that was represented in gold leaf in Renaissance paintings, the brand does not just tell the product's story or the holder's place, it determines the viewer's response.

Just as a brand casts an expanding aura around a product, it also focuses concentration on an emotional core. One of the traits of a good story is that it can easily be concentrated into just a sentence or two—the gist of a kernel. One of the reasons that study guides such as Monarch and Cliffs Notes are the staple of every schoolboy is that powerful stories often have easily expressed kernels, highly concentrated plots, called *'cepts* in academese, for *concepts*. What of these: A young man unwittingly slays his father and marries his mother. A Moorish prince is tormented by suspicions of his white bride's infidelity. A curmudgeonly old skinflint is humanized by a trio of apparitions on Christmas Eve. A staid gentleman-scientist performs an experiment on himself that lets a libidinous monster come out of Hyding. An ordinary man wakes up one morning to discover that he has been transformed into a cockroach. A savvy lad rafts down a river with a black slave. An obsessed man chases a whale while his crew suffers.

In academic lingo, a story expressed in a single nucleus is called a *holophrasm*. It reduces chapters to a paragraph, complex ideas to a nubbin. Oddly enough, great art tends to be intensely concentrated. So too with great brands. The brand gathers its centripetal power because it generates what is called in adspeak *ownership*. Below are the holophrastic kernels of some well-known brands:

Nordstrom = service

Palmolive = smoothness

BMW = experience

BIC = disposablility

Maytag = dependability

Mercedes = prestige

Nike = coolness

Apple = liberty regained

Pepsi = youthfulness

Oil of Olay = timeless beauty

Saturn = Americana

Kodak = memories

Porsche = speed

Lauren = anglophilia

De Beers = forever

Gerber = baby

Gucci = glitz

Disney = magic

Marlboro = cowboy freedom

Gillette = sharpness

FedEx = overnight

Volvo = safety

Often this condensation can occur visually. As with a Picasso line, a Gauguin color, or a quirky van Gogh shape, we immediately recognize and respond to the golden arches, Texaco star, Lucky Strike bull's-eye, Shell's shell, Holiday Inn sign, Playboy bunny, Nike swoosh, CBS eye, red cross, or Rolls-Royce flying lady. Sometimes we find the kernel inside a tune, as with the percolating sound of Maxwell House coffee, Coke's "I'd like to teach the world to sing," McDonald's "You deserve a break today," the CNN war music, the Teabury shuffle, or a cat food's "Meow, meow, meow" song. Sometimes color triggers the brand sensation. Not only do we know the difference between Pepsi blue and Coke red, we know that Pepsi blue is not Tiffany blue or Kleenex blue or IBM blue and Coke red is not Marlboro red, which is not Heinz red or Budweiser red. We know the difference between Hertz yellow, Kodak yellow, Sunoco yellow, and Caterpillar yellow, between Heineken green and John Deere green.

Brand kernels also reside in what are called identification characters, or *ID characters*. Here we can really appreciate how close brand narratives are to folktales and how deep they are in human history. Our affiliation to a brand mimics a human relationship. Consider these provenances:

- From our human world, such as the Philip Morris bellhop, the Morton Salt girl, the Marlboro man, Aunt Jemima, Betty Crocker, Mrs. Olsen, Uncle Sam, Mr. Whipple, Little Miss Coppertone, Little Debbie, Uncle Ben, Madge the Manicurist, Josephine the Plumber, Ben & Jerry;

- From folklore, such as the Keebler elves living in the Hollow Tree, the Snap, Crackle, and Pop residing in Rice Krispies, or the Jolly Green Giant inhabiting Happy Valley;

- From cartoon town, such as Elsie the Cow, Mr. Bubble, Bibendum (or "Old Bib," the Michelin tire man), Poppin' Fresh (the Pillsbury Doughboy), E.B. (the Energizer Bunny), Tony the Tiger, Cracker Jack, the Underwood devil;

- From crossover land, characters from the world of half-human/half cartoon, such as Mr. Peanut, Ronald McDonald, Johnnie Walker, the Quaker Oats' Quaker, the Smith Brothers (Trade and Mark), Mr. Clean;

- From Greek mythology, such as Hermes carrying flowers for FTD, Ajax the white knight with his magical lance, the Merrill Lynch bull, or Pegasus at the Mobil station;

- From our world who have gone into the otherworld and returned, such as Robert Young, who became Marcus Welby, M.D., to return as "I am not a doctor" Dr. Robert Young, and some who never come back, such as Colonel Harlan Sanders, the Hathaway shirt man, Schweppes' Commander Whitehead, Duncan Hines;

- From animals made human, such as Charlie the Tuna, Spuds Mackenzie (the party animal), Morris the Cat, the Playboy bunny, Smokey Bear;

- From cartoon characters who have been pressed into commercial service, such as Bugs Bunny going to work for Nike, Yogi Bear as spokesman for Arby's, Bart Simpson hawking Butterfingers, Rocky and Bullwinkle peddling tacos for Taco Bell;

- From the natural world, such as Nipper the dog, the White Owl, the John Deere leaping deer, the Exxon tiger.

The reader/consumer can interpret the grain, the kernel, the aura, the tune, the color, the named product, and the identification character in any number of ways, and these ways will change as the consumer changes and as the consumption community varies. In the words of legendary industrial designer and branding guru Walter Landor, "Products are made in the factory, but brands are made in the mind." The brand is software that runs the product, but there is considerable variety of interpretation. In this sense the brand is really an element of product design. The consumer is active in formatting that design, which is why over time the brand story moves first to the personal, then to the human, and finally to the emotional.

That's why we find advertising loaded with the rhetoric of inter-personal relations: "Thank you, PaineWebber." "Thank you, Tastykakes." "I love what you do for me, Toyota." "Thanks, Delco." "Thanks, Crest." Conversely, the sense of self-worth is also apparent: "I'm worth it." "Master the moment." "Be all that you can be." "I found it!" "Looking good makes us feel good." "You deserve a break today." "You, you're the one." "You've come a long way, baby." In their brand narratives, companies are solicitous in their concern for us: "Ford wants to be your car company." "You asked for it, you got it—Toyota." "Have it your way." "Something to believe in." "We bring good things to life." "It's the right thing." With the product, you have a constant friend: "You're in good hands." It's "me and my R.C.," "me and my Arrow." Branding does not create these relationships; they have al-ready been established long before we start consuming their com-mercial narratives. Branding exploits them.

From the simple insight that humans can bond with manufactured objects via stories has come the most important development of mod-ern life: the endless tying of fictions to the fabricated stuff of every-day life. Listen to marketers talk, and you appreciate the depth of seriousness that this process has achieved. How else to explain brand cycle, power brands, brand extension, megabrand, umbrella brand, brand equity, brand essence, brand harmonization, brand identity, branded environment, cobranding, corporate brand, subbrand, brand buoyancy, brand audit, brand architecture, brand building, brand pro-filing, brand DNA, brand fingerprint, brand hierarchy, brand map-ping, brand probe, brand values, brand creation, challenger brands, and hundreds more? Just as Eskimos have many words for snow, brand managers have an entire vocabulary for commercial fiction.

The Academics of Branding

The academic world has only recently paid attention to the power and complexity of branding. Academics may even be able to provide insights to marketers. Linking brand stories with other narratives may prove productive in understanding how these microfictions work. Most obvious: just as a brand is a storied experience, it also can't be two stories at once. Somehow the concept of *genre*, the idea that a work fits into a pre-established format and that if it violates the expectations it will confuse the reader, relates to branding. So we may be stymied that Yamaha is both pianos and motorcycles; or understand that *Playboy*, which tells the story of imaginary sex, cannot make a go of real-life resorts; that Hooters, a restaurant known for ogling and chicken parts, may not be able also to run an airline; that the World Wrestling Federation, which "owns" violent fantasy, cannot also "own" real violence such as football; or even that Campbell's is soup and not sauce and so had to name its sauce line Prego. Again, the ancients knew this. They developed a concept of the Unities, which essentially held, among other things, that you couldn't mix story types. A tragedy is not a comedy is not a pastoral is not an elegy. But you can extend a story, which is why a romance can move from a short story to a novella to a novel.

This emotional coherence may explain one of the perplexities of branding, to wit: why some brands can be extended and others can't. If you think always of the root story—the kernel—it may make sense why Pierre Cardin cannot sell dishware and BIC couldn't market panty hose but Jell-O can sell yogurt and ice pops. Caterpillar uses its brand to sell tractors, shoes, and clothing because its emotional story is simple: We're tough. But the company couldn't sell high-tech harvesting equipment.

Story coherence is a key to understanding much of modern pop culture. Take celebrity, for instance. Coherent narrative is why Mary Tyler Moore can move from story to story, always staying inside the same character (from Laura Petrie to Mary Richards), or Kelsey Grammer can play Frasier Crane on *Cheers* as well as on *Frasier*. But note that the characters on *Seinfeld* were flops in other stories because they moved out of the roles of George, Kramer, and Elaine.

Jerry, however, has been savvy enough to stay . . . brand Jerry. Meanwhile, Larry David, who was real-life George, can become real-life pretend Larry David. In the commercial world, this narrative coherence is why Richard Branson can lurk behind the Virgin brand and extend the concept of wily good bargain from record label to retail chain to media production company to cola to air travel to cell phones and even to a line of condoms. Story changes; character is stable. Typecasting is the tribute entertainment pays to branding. If you don't believe it ask Donald Trump, Oprah Winfrey, P. Diddy, and, alas, Martha Stewart.

How to expand brand narratives has proven as difficult as it is expensive. The temptation is always there, if only because a new commercial brand might cost $100 million or more to introduce but a third of that for extension. Understanding the process in the commercial sphere may allow us to predict whether such public-sphere innovations as university branch campuses (as opposed to separate schools), stand-alone churches (as opposed to denominational affiliations), and museum outposts (such as gallery spaces in various buildings or even different cities) will succeed.

Once we understand where branding comes from (surplus production of fungibles, be they hard goods or services), how it works (affiliation via fiction), and what it moves toward (emotional attachment), we may be better able to appreciate what has been happening in the noncommercial world. Instead of imitating Chicken Little, we may regard the current upheavals in the culture industries as predictable and even refreshing. Critics may howl, but having nonprofits behave like for-profits may not be detrimental. In fact, it may be invigorating and profoundly democratic, even meritorious. I don't mean to overlook the problems of what is often dismissed as "the world for sale" or "every business is show business," but, as we see every day, there are worse systems than the marketplace, be it for pig iron, tap water, and politics or for pews, classrooms, and works of art. Furthermore, as commercial brands seem to be entering a period of exhaustion, the culture industries are entering a fascinating time of renaissance. Churches, museums, and universities have rarely changed as much as they have during the last few years. Many of them have gone under. Whether or not the "new and improved" versions can survive (let alone *should* survive) in the New Brand World remains to be seen. But this much is certain. The branding of non-profits, like globalization, is not *going* to happen. It *is* happening right now.

2.

One Market Under God

THE CHURCHING OF BRANDS

> *A good ad should be like a good sermon: it must
> not only comfort the afflicted—it also must afflict
> the comfortable.*
>
> —Bernice Fitz-Gibbon, *Macy's, Gimbels, and Me: How to
> Earn $90,000 a Year in Retail Advertising*

> *Whether God exists or not, the concept is very real
> indeed among atheists and believers alike. So if we
> accept that God is a concept and that organized
> religion is the official marketing body, is God
> delivering on the brand promise? Or do we need a
> repositioning strategy for the new millennium?*
>
> —Debate on Brandchannel.com Forum, September 2001

What does religion look like from a marketing point of view? Mind
you, I'm not talking about God. That's a belief, not a brand. A brand is
a story that travels with a product or service or, in this case, a concept.
In the beginning of Christianity was the Word, and, as I'm sure you've
already guessed, the Word was the Brand. Although the history of religion is in a sense the history of marketing, the development of branding as a competitive device is quite recent. And remarkably Christian.
In fact, selling God, the activity known as proselytizing, is a uniquely

Christian/capitalist concept. Let me explain as a brand manager might.

At the macro level, all religions offer the same transaction. They exchange the meaning of life for some investment by the believer. A story in exchange for attention is the quid pro quo. Sometimes this exchange requires only attention, but more often it involves money and work. Pay up now, be saved later. There are lots of suppliers of this promised product. The *World Christian Encyclopedia: A Comparative Survey of Churches and Religions in the Modern World,* published every other year by Oxford University Press, counts them up. It takes two volumes and runs to eight hundred pages. Why? Because there are almost ten thousand distinct religions in the world. Each day about two more are added.

The product of most religions is usually safe passage to the next world, and, until recently in the West at least, it was very alluring and remunerative. I say "until recently" because when there was no surplus of objects in this world to load with sublime meaning, most of the world's religions, the large suppliers, created a parallel universe filled with magnificent material. Afterlife of some kind is the promise of most religious brands. Understandably, access to this life usually occurs after death, although *epiphany* is the sensation the penitent achieves in this world. Epiphany is a hint of what's to come, a whiff of the next life.

In each religion there is a sacred text that carries the brand and allows the belief system to be codified and passed along. So in Hinduism, the earliest of the major religions, God appears in this world in different guises, such as Krishna, and promises elevation via reincarnation until you achieve full consciousness. The sacred storyboards, so to speak, are the Vedas, the Upanishads, and especially the Bhagavad Gita. Buddhism is uniquely nontheistic but promises the achievement of higher consciousness through the chanting of mantras. A Buddhist may achieve "the death of the enlightened" and experience complete liberation, Nirvana. Judaism, another ancient religion, posits a creator, Yahweh, whose sacred text, the Hebrew Bible, promises no palpable destiny other than that righteousness will be rewarded. While Orthodox Judaism is practiced in most parts of the world, in pluralistic America there are Conservative and Reform choices, a testament to how modern markets not just accommodate choice but generate it. Christianity, the next of the major religions to evolve, has a well-defined but complex God (the tripartite Father, Son, and Holy Spirit), an addition to the Hebrew Bible of the New Testament, a well-defined afterlife, and a judgment day. Before the Reformation there were about eight major mendicant orders competing for market share (Dominicans, Benedictines, Franciscans . . .) of the Church of Rome, and now there are about eight major denominations (Episcopal, Methodist, Baptist . . .) of the Protestant Reformation. The newest of the world's major religions is Islam, founded more than a half century after Christianity, with Allah as the one God, the Koran as the sacred text, and a paradise entered after death by those who submit their will to Allah.

What is remarkable is that these systems rarely compete head-to-head with one another for market share. With the exceptions of Christianity and Islam, they seldom convert fresh believers. Crusades and jihads are historically rare. More common is that the suppliers of Heavenly Access compete fiercely inside themselves for brand exchangers. You are born into them, and you squabble among yourselves for who gets the biggest piece of the pie.

From a marketing point of view, world religions resemble huge umbrella brands such as the Japanese Mitsubishi, Matsushita, or Mitsui. The organization is almost organic: hundreds of disparate cells competing inside a mother organism. And it's here in the Christian denominational system that the history of marketing really begins as the disparate cells compete against each other. Sometimes they really slug it out. In fact, as Toby Lester reported in a recent article in *The Atlantic,* everyone who has studied new religious movements around the world agrees that the most factious cells are being generated in Christianity, especially in Asia, Africa, and Latin America. Fundamentalist Islam is the next most factious.

Epiphany Is the Immediate Product, Heaven the Ultimate Promise

As we know from commercial branding, an enduring story always has to deliver an *affect.* The story has to move the listener, to exchange a feeling for attention. The feeling that all religions attempt to brand is the feeling of salvation. That sense of "Whew! now I can rest." That sensation goes by a number of names in English: enlightenment, rebirth, Paulist conversion, sublimity, out-of-body experience, and transcendence, among others. The sensation usually happens in a group at a particular time following certain rituals. What makes this a comparable experience is that it is an *upward* thrusting through turbulence toward a still point. As such, it shares with many other experiences the sensation of rebirth, of starting over, of a second chance.

In Christianity that sensation is even laid out in a central story. The story is of the birth of Christ and deals with how the three wise men felt when they beheld the Christ child. They were "wise men" for a reason: they were skeptics. But viewing the divinity of God in the body of a mortal filled them with a peace that passeth all understanding. The formal term is *epiphany.* They beheld God as man.

Transcendence via redemption is deep in the yearnings of human life; it is the dawning of a new day, morning again in human life, a reason for being here. As Aldous Huxley pointed out in the startling *The Doors of Perception,* the religious version is sometimes experienced pharmacologically. Ingesting LSD or peyote may give you a sensation of out of body, but it is usually not done in human clusters. It's called a *trip* for a reason.

This generation's LSD is a drug called Ecstasy, and its promise is in its name. What this drug holds out is a high eerily close to that of its ritualized cousins in religious settings. In fact, it promises a "sense sublime," which is indeed part of the up-and-out-of-body sensation of the born again. Entering culture as part of "rave" entertainment produces sensations of immediate detachment and lightness, loss of drives such as hunger and sleep, and especially a sense of renewed confidence and optimism. That this sense of renewal should be tied to music and communal excitement is no happenstance. The ecstatic religious sensation is vertical, yes, but it is also horizontal. It goes *up* in individuation, but it also goes *out* in community.

Ecstasy à la Franklin Graham

As with all sensations, epiphany can be marketed. A couple of years ago I went to a Franklin Graham crusade on the campus of the

University of Florida, where I teach. Franklin is the son of Billy, and his shows are direct descendants of the tent revivals of yesteryear. These were, in turn, adaptations of Methodism and the American excitement of the Great Awakenings. The three-day revival was called Festival 2002. *Revival* currently has a bad name, as does *crusade,* but if you observe the interactions in slow motion, you can see humans yearning for sensation and the marketing machinery that supplies it.

The Graham Festival has been repeated so often that it runs like clockwork. A month before the event, the advertising starts. A week before, banners go up. Then in come the buses. Local churches band together to promote the event. Essentially, they help isolate and excite the crowd. The bigger the crowd, the better, but the crowd needs to be self-selected. This out-of-body sensation depends on the bandwagon effect and as such depends on keeping dissension at a minimum. There are gatekeepers at the door. At the event I attended, they spent most of their time turning back rowdy university students. To get the experience working, you must see your seatmates moving forward toward the experience and you must not see any turning back. And although it doesn't hurt to have pickets outside to generate the sense of "them against us," inside it's all "us against them."

We start with much music and witnessing. It goes on and on. Although the event lasts about three hours, the actual sermon is over in a finger snap. Thanks to television and a rock concert, everything is blown up to gargantuan size with sound amplifiers and massive video screens. After almost two hours of music, Franklin Graham appears. He looks just like his dad. He is wearing an extraordinary outfit. On his head is a baseball cap with a red Ralph Lauren polo pony logo. His shirt is blue denim, and over his heart is another bright red Ralph Lauren polo pony. Nowhere else in the auditorium was there any imagery of affiliation; no crosses, no robes, no bells, no soaring imagery. In fact, the revival took place in the University of Florida basketball arena, complete with the commercial logos of Gatorade and Nike hanging down from the ceiling.

Mr. Graham was not shy about commenting on his choice of sartorial affiliation. Yes, he proudly said, that's Ralph Lauren. And tomorrow, he promised, he'd be wearing the logos of the Fighting Gators. From time to time the television camera focused on his baseball hat and his shirt as if to say that there was something valuable, observable there. I have thought long about why Mr. Graham foregrounded the polo pony. Why both the hat and the shirt? His audience of mostly lower-middle-class country folk (about twice as many white as black) were not consumers of such upper-tier brands. They were Wal-Mart, Sears, J. C. Penney, not Hilfiger, Gucci, Lauren. In fact, the audience was a hodgepodge of low-church Protestant denominations that had banded together to support the revival. They didn't know one another, and they didn't share the same churches. During the week they competed for followers, but not then. The only thing they had in common is football at the University of Florida and shopping at the mall. But they did share the same yearnings. They had come to this revival to experience something, to be reborn, to sense community, and then to go home refreshed. They knew the sensation they wanted, and they knew Mr. Graham would provide it. They were wired.

While I could not recognize the various denominations of Christianity around me and while Mr. Graham made it clear that God would not recognize various religions ("Mohammed didn't die for your sins," he said to enthusiastic applause. "Buddha didn't die for your sins. Only one died for your sins, and that's the Lord Jesus Christ, son of the Living God"), the audience did recognize the commercial badge of arrival: the polo pony brand. They had seen this logo at the mall just as surely as they had seen the Nike swoosh on the football team's uniforms and the coaches' visors. Affiliation, once announced, becomes interchangeable. Want to know what salvation feels like? Well, it feels like being able to afford this, which is what Mr. Graham was saying.

I don't mean to have those little ponies drag too much weight, but in the modern world of marketing there is considerable syncretism, the layering of similar experiences, cobranding. So, for instance, one can see how the Catholic religion layered its All Hallows' Eve over an ancient Druid ceremony to celebrate the dying of light in the autumn. And we can see how first the candy companies and then the beer brewers have layered their sales campaigns over Halloween to make it commercial. Overlapping is second nature in Branded Nation because the brands are what we have as common language. To sell Ronald Reagan's second campaign, his handlers used the quasi-religious

"Morning in America" montage of daybreak imagery. To market hotels and cars, Sheraton hotels, and General Motors, invoke "redemption." Xerox implies miracles. Mercedes shows the gods on your side if you drive its SUV. And it works both ways. What is a popular fashion accessory? The cross. The religion of stuff is the stuff of religion.

Brand affiliation is as much a part of belief communities as secular ones; in fact, perhaps even more pronounced. That's because religion is a *collectively produced commodity* and, as such, depends on continually iterating the reward of joining as well as the price of deaffiliating. The use of shunning and excommunication are uniquely part of the religious experience, as is the quick division between the saved (us) and the condemned (them). Material consumption is less restrictive but no less articulate. You are either with the brand or against it.

The jeweled cross is iconic, branding the wearer as believer.

Redemption co-opted to become a brand characteristic of a car or a hotel room.

"Morning in America" montage of daybreak imagery. To market hotels and cars, Sheraton hotels, and General Motors, invoke "redemption." Xerox implies miracles. Mercedes shows the gods on your side if you drive its SUV. And it works both ways. What is a popular fashion accessory? The cross. The religion of stuff is the stuff of religion.

Brand affiliation is as much a part of belief communities as secular ones; in fact, perhaps even more pronounced. That's because religion is a *collectively produced commodity* and, as such, depends on continually iterating the reward of joining as well as the price of deaffiliating. The use of shunning and excommunication are uniquely part of the religious experience, as is the quick division between the saved (us) and the condemned (them). Material consumption is less restrictive but no less articulate. You are either with the brand or against it.

The jeweled cross is iconic, branding the wearer as believer.

Redemption co-opted to become a brand characteristic of a car or a hotel room.

True Redemption.

Put your game to the ultimate test across 4,536 holes of championship golf.
Redeem your Starpoints™... no ifs, ands, or blackouts.

Become a Starwood Preferred Guest at spg.com.

THE LONGEST ROAD IN THE WORLD IS THE ROAD TO REDEMPTION.

THIRTY YEARS AGO, GM QUALITY WAS THE BEST IN THE WORLD. TWENTY YEARS AGO, IT WASN'T. THE STORY OF OUR LONG JOURNEY BACK.

GM presents an overnight success story, a decade in the making.

Ten years ago, we had a choice. We could keep looking in the rearview mirror, or out at the road ahead. It was the easiest decision we ever made.

The hard part meant breaking out of our own bureaucratic gridlock. Learning some humbling lessons from our competitors. And instilling a true culture of quality in every division, in every department, in every corner of the company.

Today, with quality at the core of our values, we're building the best cars and trucks in our history. GM is now challenging the automotive world in fuel efficiency, advanced emissions controls, styling and design, and manufacturing productivity.

It didn't start yesterday. And it doesn't happen overnight. But last year we launched over twenty new models on the way to posting our second straight year of market share gains. And a vehicle lot of you rediscovered that an American car can be a great car.

The road to redemption has no finish line. But it does have a corner.

And it's fair to say we've turned it.

HOW SIX CYLINDERS DELIVER THE POWER OF A V8

The 4.2-liter GM Vortec 4200 ... and punch with 4 valves per inline 6, found in every 200_ cylinder, dual overhead mid-size SUV, delivers the cams and variable valve horsepower of a V6 with timing – features rarely only six cylinders. We used an found in competitive V6s. all-aluminum composition And with a 10:1 compression and simplified design to reduce ratio, its cylinders fire with the weight. We packed both power efficiency of a racecar.

The latest news, reviews and a glimpse of the road ahead. See it all at www.gm.com/story.

The road back began at dawn.

GM's culture of quality started with a literal wake-up call. In a series of mandatory six a.m. meetings, the gospel was spread throughout the company. Ten very painful but very productive years later, GM is now delivering:

• Industry leading emissions controls, using the least amount of precious metals.
• More return customers than any other car manufacturer in the world.
• The top two automotive assembly plants in North/South America in the J.D. Power and Associates Initial Quality Study.
• 149 automotive awards in 2002.

Coming this summer: The rule-breaking, game-changing Chevy SSR.

Coming this summer: Elegance and muscle re-mingle in the exhilarating Cadillac XLR.

Coming this fall: The legendary Pontiac GTO roars back with a 5.7-liter V8.

CHEVROLET   PONTIAC   OLDSMOBILE   BUICK   CADILLAC   GMC   SATURN   HUMMER   SAAB

In Branded Nation no religious image is too sacred not to be exploited.

Branded Religion Is Big Business

By his connection with Ralph Lauren, Mr. Graham is demonstrating that he is somehow saved, that he has arrived. The allure of salvation is big business. There are more clergy in America than Ford and Chrysler together have workers. And if religion were a company, it would be number five on the Fortune 500, its $50 billion of revenues putting it behind IBM and just ahead of GE. Church land and buildings are worth uncounted billions. And the figures don't include volunteer work, worth an impressive $75 billion a year.

In America, the religion business has always been in turmoil. It is a marketing free-for-all. The reason is clear: we have no state-sponsored religion. The First Amendment, ironically, has encouraged a proliferation of sects, all of which have been forced to compete. With no national sponsorship, the battle for converts became positively Darwinian. For many churches this never-ending competition added the perpetual pressure to stay solvent. That, in turn, always argued for attracting the widest audience, paying attention to the take-away value, and focusing always on the end user while all the time pretending to a higher calling. Marketing became a necessity. Necessity is the mother of invention. And so, predictably, most of the innovation in branding came from the selling of salvation.

Though some Protestant ministers did preach against greed, wealth, and untrammeled competition, just as many found an alliance between spiritual affairs and a market-driven economy to their advantage. At least the successful ones did. From Monday to Friday you could pretend that you had your eye on Heaven, but over the weekend you had better be packing them in. Or you'd be sent packing.

If you want to succeed in the American market, you'd better make church compelling. And compelling it was, and still is. The tent revivals of the 1800s sold cider and musical entertainment along with salvation. At Methodist camps in the 1850s, young people roller-skated to a waltz version of "Nearer, My God, to Thee." In the 1980s two televangelists, Jim and Tammy Faye Bakker, hawked a gospel of materialistic goods and an eternal life in the hot tub. If some service gathered a crowd and newspaper coverage, some church at the edge of the market was going to be using it. Mainline churches might cock an eyebrow, but if the Pentecostals found an audience with the hootenanny, some downtown church currently losing parishioners would soon give it a try. As Lawrence Moore, the historian most in touch with the history of competitive church marketing, says slightly tongue in cheek in *Selling God: American Religion in the Marketplace of Culture,* American churches have invented lots of fun—serious, competitive fun.

With no state protection, suppliers have to behave almost like athletic teams, continually playing against one another, racking up runs or believers. Such competition makes them concentrate on innovative marketing, something European religions have never attended to— hence their relatively low turnout today. American religion has had to generate excitement, frisson, some kind of emotional payoff, even though sometimes the sensation is hidden beneath a stern exterior. When the Pew Research Center for the People and the Press studied forty-four nations, it found an inverse relationship between per capita GNP and the importance of religion to its citizens—with one outstanding exception. When it comes to religion, the United States behaves like a Third World nation, but with a twist. The very quality that fosters self-reliance also fosters the intense competition of belief systems. In this culture you don't whisper, you shout.

The result is a thriving evangelical subculture, complete with its own music, magazines, movies, and other forms of entertainment, including Christian rock concerts, theme parks, and cruises. The high church is no different. Even Anglican-Episcopalians generate enjoyment, albeit often in the more subtle form of hauteur. Or at least they did before their brand unraveled in the 1970s.

As Moore mentions at the beginning of his insightful *Selling God,* this drive for audience excitement makes the academic observer almost like a sports fan. As he says, "I follow religion with much the same exuberant spirit that many of my friends follow baseball. Readers offended by the suggestion that religion exerts an appeal analogous to that of a form of commercial entertainment might as well stop here. Much more of the same will follow." I say the same thing. This is not a flippant observation but a self-evident one: yes, we are an exceptionally pious and religiously diverse culture. But what we really are is an intensely competitive one. And that's because our brands are intensely competitive. Oddly enough, that is no oxymoron but a truth of marketing: low variation of product produces high affinity and cut-throat competition. Coke versus Pepsi.

When a business this big is in turmoil—and this one *always* is—the situation is full of market surges and collapses. Consider the roller-coaster history of the Methodists, the Baptists, the black churches, the Mormons, and the current explosion of the Pentecostals. The fastest growth is occurring in the low-Protestant Pentecostal ranks. These churches, which demand high commitment, are clearly gathering adherents from the middle ranges, from denominations such as the Presbyterians and Congregationalists. If you think this is a stable market, just remember: the Methodists were nowhere in 1776; they were everywhere in 1876; and they were receding in 1976.

Witness the current marketing plight of the Catholic Church. Here is a $7 billion brand in distress. It's a brand without an active manager, struggling with a shrinking market share due to a perceived lack of differentiation, a failure to maintain relevance, and an aging consumer base. The priestly malfeasance is continually played off not just a background of a church that cannot condone divorce, premarital sex, or birth control but a commercial culture that has witnessed the swooning brands of WorldCom, Enron, and Martha Stewart. To be sure, the Catholic Church still has a strong customer base and there is tremendous brand equity, but the marketplace of alternative religions will rearrange affiliations. The question is not just where future parishioners will come from but where the future priests are.

What's extraordinary about the market in supplying epiphany is that regardless of individual upheavals in specific denominations, each week 40 percent of U.S. adults attend a church or synagogue, a percentage unchanged since the 1970s. However, churches have made only slight gains in pursuit of the charitable dollar, getting just over half of individual giving and bequests. We are finding the epiphany experience elsewhere in obvious places such as New Age rituals, as well as in more subtle places such as luxury shopping. Dramatic gains elsewhere in Protestantism, mostly in freestanding, inter-denominational churches, have equaled the mainstream's losses. Meanwhile, Judaism hasn't budged. The Conservative and Reform branches, however, are a tribute to Christian denominational choices and exist primarily in the United States.

So although the market for religion hasn't shrunk, market share is changing all the time. It's just like the soap aisle down at the supermarket. Both growing and declining churches face unprecedented marketing challenges. Hence, words familiar from boardrooms— market research, customer satisfaction, takeaway value, positioning, asset management, brand equity—resound in pastoral and diocesan offices. "Pay attention to your brand or lose your business" has replaced "Tend your flock." Often the most insight comes from brands that are being pushed off the shelves by inattention instead of those pulled off by consumer desire. Let's have a look at one such supplier that shows the penalties inflicted by poor brand management.

Brand in Distress: The Episcopal Example

Observe the current state of the once-dominant Episcopal Church. Episcopalians committed an unforgivable marketing sin: they forgot their brand because they lost the story. Or, perhaps more accurately, it was taken away from them. Here's my interpretation from a marketing point of view.

A generation or two ago the Episcopal Church was at the top of Protestantism. It was the luxury brand. Go to the top of commercial banking, law, politics, education, and Episcopalians would be there, all decked out in Mayflower finery. In 1950, *Fortune* magazine reported that about a third of CEOs were staunch Episcopalians. And the Church as institution reflected the business model. It was organized from the top down, a vestige of the old Anglican system, which in turn was a mimic of the Catholic, one based on the church/state unity featured in the concept of the divine right of kings. The head of the Anglican Church is the king or queen, although the archbishop of Canterbury is the CEO. So too in this country, the bishops of the various geographical entities, under a presiding bishop, were responsible for the brand. They ran the show and, to a considerable extent, the country as well. More presidents of the United States in the twentieth century were Episcopalians than any other denomination.

The allure of Episcopalianism was not in the creeds or the stone buildings or the stained glass or the twinkling clerics. Its promise was social affiliation. In fact, in a twist peculiar to our commercial culture, the Episcopal cultural dominance is at the heart of Ralph Lauren's Anglophilia represented on the hat and chest of young Franklin Graham. In the tradition of American retail, Franklin is borrowing Ralph's expropriation of what the Episcopal Church used to, in marketing terms, *own*—namely, the power of ancestry. That polo pony is drawn from the sport of kings and implies the value of blue-blood heritage.

The best exploration of the Episcopal brand during its heyday is a book written in the late 1970s by a husband-and-wife team, Kit and Frederica Konolige. *Power of Their Glory: America's Ruling Class, The Episcopalians* made the case that the brand story was decidedly secular. The book's thesis was not popular when it was first published. The Konoliges argued that the Church's promise was linked to the "St. Grottelsex" prep schools, urban clubs, the Ivy League, squash courts, museum trustees, top business echelons, and politics—anything but faith. Yes, here was an all-encompassing brand that sited you on Sunday, but it was especially helpful during the week. Episcopalian society was formal, graceful, Junior League, English, white, intellectual, rational, New England, *Social Register*, and sensible shoes. Not by happenstance is the Episcopal Cathedral in Washington, D.C., called the *National* Cathedral.

In its own self-satisfied way, the Episcopal Church was fun. It oozed confidence. You could see that wry good humor and bonhomie in the love of self-deflation. A typical joke told about them by them: A newcomer to heaven asks Saint Peter why the first few rooms are so raucous—reeking of alcohol, laughter, and dancing. "Why, those are the Methodists, Baptists, and Presbyterians," explains Saint Peter. "But why is it so quiet in the last room?" asks the newcomer. "Oh, those are the Episcopalians. They drank, laughed, and danced on earth. They don't need to do it here." Wink-wink. Most churches don't go in for nicknames, too jovial. But in palmier days Episcopal churches were relabeled with clever sobriquets—a sign, perhaps, of overweening confidence. So, for instance, Saint Michael and All Angels in Dallas became Saint Mink and All Cadillacs. Ask any Episcopalian if his church has a nickname, and you'll be amazed. George W. Bush comes from this tradition. He nicknames everyone. It's a perk of power.

In the middle of the twentieth century, the Episcopal brand suddenly lost it. Although it's tempting to say that this is because of internecine squabbles over too much liberalism, the problem was in the brand story. What the Church promised, it could no longer deliver. Marketplace meritocracy ruined it. Just one example: Up until the 1960s, the Church controlled the elaborate system of social positioning via education, the promise of access to the upper echelons of political, legal, and educational as well as corporate life. The clergy were the gatekeepers at such places as St. Paul's, Groton, and Middlesex. Why did they lose the gate?

As Nicholas Lehmann argues in *The Big Test: The Secret History of the American Meritocracy,* the SAT did blue bloods in. The minute getting into elite universities depended on doing well on two hours of test taking, not on having two hundred proper ancestors, the game changed. And as we will see in the next chapter, the upper-tier schools, especially Harvard, now run the cultural show. In 1950, get into Exeter, and your chances of going to school in Cambridge, Massachusetts, were excellent. Want to get into Harvard today? Don't go to Exeter. Stay home and be a star.

Although the Church's formal membership has always been small—from a peak of 3,647,000 in the late 1960s, down to about 2 million today—the Episcopalians' strength was never in numbers but in power. Like the Jews, with whom they share many similarities (small numbers, old traditions, and social codes of behavior), they could protect the brand best by concentrating it. But it worked only if they delivered not safe access to the next world but predictable access to this one.

Having spent a handful of Sundays in 1999 visiting the Episcopal churches in my small university town, I can testify that things are in disarray. Many individual churches are at sea. They have come loose from the parent denomination. Savvy congregations are retaining more of the shrinking money in their collection plates, forcing denominational officials to cut the national budget. Since 1991, the mother Church, for example, has had to reduce its national staff by about one third.

Some branches are even affiliating with rogue countries in faraway places . . . such as Africa, for goodness' sake! The fact that a renegade bishop in Africa is providing breakaway congregations a sense of schismatic tradition is unsettling to WASP blue bloods. And the fact that he is sending missionaries *to* the United States from Rwanda is simply too much. But then another part of the church is affiliating with the (gasp!) Lutherans. In every church I attended, I heard squabbles about who could get into the priesthood, the incessant bickering about changes made to the Book of Common Prayer, and the general melancholy of a church whose future money flow was slowly moving to the cemetery.

The Episcopal Church is indeed a church of gray hairs. The Cadillac division of General Motors can tell you what that means to a brand. Ironically, many of these internecine disputes are ending up in the American courts or on the front page simply because this Church owns so much inventory. The muscular Christianity of the Old School is going the way of Palmolive soap, Prell shampoo, and the Fleetwood Brougham.

One sees this melancholy transformation in the edifices themselves. Go into any major downtown area and look at the wonderful old Episcopal church. Go there on Sunday. You'll see the problem. Go to Manhattan and look at the splendid asymmetric Gothic church designed by the famed architect Richard Upjohn at the corner of Sixth Avenue and Twentieth Street. In its heyday parishioners included John Jacob Astor, Jay Gould, and Cornelius Vanderbilt. In the early 1970s, the building was sold to a drug rehab center and from there became the famous/infamous Limelight, a dance club *cum* drug warehouse. The experience was so traumatic that the Episcopal diocese promised that no more church sales would be done out of "financial necessity." So how did Saint Bartholomew's Church, at Park Avenue at Fifty-first Street, solve its problems? Café St. Bart's, a nifty sixty-four-table bistro with signature desserts, famous for its Caesar salads, salmon ravioli, and good wine selection.

The Church Ad Project

In this context, the repositioning of Episcopalianism is instructive. Part of the Church actually started to join the commercial fray. Have a look at the following ads.

Turnabout is fair play. Selling church affiliation à la Madison Avenue.

These ads come from what used to be called the Episcopal Ad Project and is now called the Church Ad Project. It was started in the 1990s by George Martin, a minister and adman in Minneapolis who realized that an entire generation was bypassing his church. The ads are visually clever and linguistically sophisticated. But what they really are is ironic. They capture the wink-wink tone of the old Church, that wry self-satisfied sense of belonging, but without offering anything new or distinctive.

In other ads, we see pictures of Santa and Jesus with the question "Whose birthday is it, anyway?"; a picture of the Bible under the line "The Original Power Book"; a snowboarder flying next to the line "You're self-confident and self-reliant. But it never hurts to have a back-up"; a picture of a chalice under the line "Over 10 Trillion Served"; an external shot of an Episcopal-looking church: "The leading place to invest in futures"; under a picture of crucified Christ, "Body piercing is nothing new to us"; a picture of the prayer book under "Weekly prophet sharing"; the Energizer Bunny against the headline "Has the true meaning of Easter gotten a little fuzzy?"; and the Ten Commandments tables in front of "For fast, fast, fast relief, take two tablets."

Where Church Marketing Comes From

In many marketing respects, what we see here is the selling of bottled water. There is little if any product differentiation because Protestantism has become a commodity. The suppliers are redundant, and church space is oversupplied. That's why denominations need separation via branding. When you have an interchangeable product, the story becomes the necessary fiction. How you tell it becomes crucial. And the telling of it is progressively coming from the marketplace, from the supermarket, from the shelves of machine-made goods. Turnabout is fair play. For generations the influence went the other direction, from Church to marketplace.

Certainly the paradox of how contemporary America can be both the world's most religiously diverse nation and one of the most religiously intense is analogous to how we can be one of the most materialistically profligate as well as one of the most environmentally active. On one hand, we struggle to separate religion from life; on the other, we enthusiastically admit it. If you wonder how "brands have become the new religion," as a recent Young & Rubicam study asserted, it's because religion is the old brand. We know it. We know what it promises. So from a historical point of view, it's no happenstance that modern branding started in the early twentieth century as men who had studied for the ministry turned their talents to selling machine-made products. And it's no happenstance that the Church should be using precisely the same fabular machinery to refind its flock.

Once we realize that magical thinking is at the heart of both religion and branding, it will become clear why they can momentarily merge. Branding fetishizes objects in exactly the same manner that religion does: it "charms" objects, giving them an aura of added value. An archbishop of Canterbury supposedly said, "I do not read advertisements—I would spend all my time wanting things," quite forgetting that indeed he does "read" advertisements and that he does spend much time "wanting things" as well as exchanging them. His ads just appear in different texts.

It is no happenstance that the advertising men, or "attention engineers," who helped bring about the rise of Consumer Culture were steeped in the Protestant tradition. They understood both the nature of yearning and how to franchise it. They knew the language of sincerity. They knew the power of promise—large promise. They knew how to make a sale and close the deal. Marketing was a white upper-middle-class *Christian* endeavor, in part because most of the educated population was Protestant and in part because the procedure for selling manufactured resolution to life's present problems was so similar to what religion had developed to sell future redemption. Above all, they knew the power of story.

Look at the early apostles of advertising. Among the most important ministers of commerce with deep evangelical roots were Artemas Ward, son of an Episcopal minister, whose slogans for Sapolio soap were almost as well known as the Song of Solomon; John Wanamaker, a staunch Presbyterian who considered entering the ministry and whose marketing genius helped make both the modern department store and the holidays such as Mother's Day that give us time to use it; Claude C. Hopkins, who came from a long line of impoverished preachers, started preaching at seventeen, and translated his talent into copywriting for beer, carpet sweepers, lard, and canned meats; James Webb Young, who sold Bibles door to door as a true believer until he went to work at J. Walter Thompson, where he did much the same job; Helen Lansdowne, the daughter of a Presbyterian minister, who studied three years at Princeton Theological Seminary before applying her talents to selling all manner of products to women; Theodore MacManus, one of the few devout Catholics in early advertising, who held honorary degrees from three Catholic colleges and was the master of the "soft sell" until he quit, disgusted with advertising, especially its huckstering of cigarettes as health foods; Rosser Reeves, son of a Methodist minister, who mastered the "hard sell" and left as his legacy the Anacin ads with all the hammers pounding their anvils; Marion Harper, Jr., the president of his Methodist Sunday school class, who went on to manage McCann-Erickson; and F. W. Ayer, a devout Baptist and

Sunday school superintendent, who gave his own agency his father's name, N. W. Ayer & Son, because it sounded more established and then coined the motto "Keeping everlastingly at it" to make sure the point was made.

Most interesting was Bruce Barton, son of a Baptist minister, who went on to found BBDO as well as write one of the most interesting books connecting religion and marketing, *The Man Nobody Knows* (1925). In this book he analogizes Jesus to an account manager who is eternally busy at "my father's business," selling redemption by the newly named but ancient devices of branding. Jesus and his little band of twelve entrepreneurs are shown carrying the Word to the modern world. He is no "lamb of God" but a full-fledged salesman out on the hustings. The omniscient narrator, the voice of advertising, often glosses the text with up-to-date information, but essentially the chapters represent a Christological musing on American business. Here's a bit of how it reads:

> *I am not a doctor, or a lawyer or critic but an advertising man. As a profession advertising is young; as a force it is as old as the world. The first four words ever uttered, "Let there be light," constitute its charter. All Nature is vibrant with its impulse. The brilliant plumage of the bird is color advertising addressed to the emotions of its mate. Plants deck themselves with blossoms, not for beauty only, but to attract the patronage of the bee and so by spreading pollen on its wings, to insure the perpetuation of their kind.*

> *It has been remarked that "no astronomer can be an atheist," which is only another way of saying that no man can look up at the first and greatest electric sign—the evening stars—and refuse to believe its message: "There is a Cause: A God." I propose to speak of the advertisements of Jesus which have survived for twenty centuries and are still the most potent influence in the world.*

> *Let us begin by asking why he was so successful in mastering public attention and why, in contrast, his churches are less so? The answer is twofold. In the first place he recognized the basic princi-*

*ple that all good advertising is news. He was never trite or com-
monplace; he had no routine. [In the second place] he was advertised by his service, not by his sermons. Nowhere in the Gospels do
you find it announced that:*

> *Jesus of Nazareth Will Denounce
> The Scribes and Pharisees in the
> Central Synagogue
> To-Night at Eight O'Clock
> Special*

*If he were to live again, in these modern days he would find a
way to make his works known—to be advertised by his service, not
merely by his sermons. One thing is certain: he would not neglect
the market-place. Few of his sermons were delivered in syna-
gogues. For the most part he was in the crowded places, the Temple Court, the city squares, the centers where goods were bought
and sold. . . . Where will you find such a market-place in these
modern days? A corner of Fifth Avenue? A block on Broadway?
Only a tiny fraction of the city's people pass any given point in the
down-town district on any given day. No; the present day marketplace is the newspaper and the magazine. Printed columns are the
modern thoroughfares; published advertisements are the cross-
roads where the sellers and the buyers meet. Any issue of a national magazine is a world's fair, a bazaar filled with the products
of the world's work. . . . Jesus would be a national advertiser today.
I am sure, as he was the great advertiser of his own day.*

To Barton, Jesus was a businessman; advertising is a business.
Jesus spoke in parables; advertising speaks in parables. Christianity is
a branded product; advertising sells branded products. Jesus performed miracles; advertising works magic. The similarities are too
powerful to overlook. As Barton once said at a meeting of advertising
agencies, "If advertising speaks to a thousand in order to influence
one, well, so does the Church." However much Barton's Babbitry in
the cause of faith may seem Philistine, it cannot be denied that he
made the connection between the two merchandising systems.

The powerful allure of religion and branding is the same: we will be rescued. This act of rescue, be it effected by the Man from Glad or the Man from Galilee, transports us to the promised land of resolution. We will find the peace that passeth understanding. We will find the garbage bag certified by the American Association of Sanitary Engineers. The stigmata will be removed. Ring around the collar will disappear. Ditto halitosis. Sin, guilt, redemption: problem, anxiety, resolution—the process of transformation is clear. The more powerful the redemption/resolution, the more otherworldly becomes the final site of salvation.

If you wish to see the similarities between religious and advertising pitches, recall the television commercials of the 1950s. The old-time television commercial was an almost perfect mimic of a religious parable. It was a microtext of drama, an epitome of ecclesiastical exemplum, a morality play. We sat meditatively in front of the electronic altar, absorbing sermons from corporations on how to get "the most out of" our detergent, our floor wax, our family, our love life. In the television commercials we all knew by heart, someone—a young female if the sponsor was a household product, a middle-aged male if it was for a cold remedy—was in distress. This Everyperson was middle-class and white. S/he needs rescue and consults some other figure, who promises relief. This other person testifies, gives witness; the product somehow appears, is tried, and voilà! resolution. From on high, the disembodied voice of the male announcer then made the parable unambiguous by reiterating the curative powers of the product. Our Everyperson was well on the way to Valhalla.

Along the way to this Happy Valley ran a parallel universe peopled with emissaries from the eternal Beyond. In the Christian scheme this is the heavenly world, filled with all the sainted worthies. In the world imagined by advertising, in what Richard Simon has called "adtopia," this world is populated by a new breed of beneficent spirits. These spirits magically reside not in nature, holy books, magical signs, or chants but in objects as mundane as automobile tires, rolled-up tobacco leaves, meat patties, green beans, and sugar water. The Man with a Thousand Faces simply has a few more, and he spends most of his time inside containers on shelves down at the A&P.

It is as simplistic to say, "Here are the nasty advertisers capturing our imaginations and manipulating them for their own profit" as it is to say, "Here are the nasty churchmen capturing our imaginations and manipulating them for their own aggrandizement." These transformations are not imposed on us any more than Zeus really terrorized the ancients. We need the gods more than the gods need us. That our gods are now in the hands of commercial manipulators, that folklore has become fakelore and folklure, that holy grails have become spot removers, and that the magic of the Eucharist has been stolen by liquor campaigns is possible only because of the yearnings of humans and the power of institutions to direct those yearnings. However much we may feel comforted by thinking "They are doing this to us," in truth we are doing it to ourselves. Like it or not, Brands "R" Us.

The Domination of Denominations

The center of gravity is now shifting as the successful denominations are becoming aware of the process. The advertising impulse, the movement to branding, occurs whenever there is a plenitude of similar suppliers with interchangeable products. When you can't distinguish between products on the basis of their intrinsic value, you depend on fictions. The suppliers of religious experience since the Protestant Reformation have been called *denominations*. The interdenominational competition has been intense. So intense, in fact, that a new formation called the *megachurch*, which is seemingly nondenominational, is churning the lower Protestant levels.

Here's what has happened. From the time of the Civil War the little stone church on the corner or the white clapboard nestled on the town green or the heavyset brick building on red clay was an outpost of a huge marketing organization. Although it looked as if each franchise was directed by independent pastors, in truth the order of the denomination came from headquarters in Manhattan or Nashville. From these headquarters came not just hymnals, Sunday school lessons, building plans, and choir robes but the actual services, complete with the time-tested routines of delivering a specific experience. This culture produced commercial advertising, and it would in turn be profoundly influenced by commercial advertising.

Whatever that paradigm was in its many variations, one thing is certain: starting in the 1950s, the sensation of *new beginning* and *starting over* was competing with other religious suppliers, as well as with a new entity: electronic media. That is not to say that the communal sensation of historical religion fell out of favor. Quite the opposite. It's still central in most of our lives. Witness how the twelve-step treatment has migrated from the church, where it formed the basis of conversion, to such places as drug addiction, shopping excitement, sex appetites, and even eating chocolate. There is no contradiction that Americans in large numbers say they believe in God, while most mainline denominations have experienced declining membership for decades. Recent surveys show that 70 to 90 percent of Americans have some faith in God, yet only about 40 percent attend church or temple on a regular basis. So clearly something is happening in the center of this market.

Go to any mainline church, and you'll see what's happened. The center is literally empty. The fringe remains. In 1995, the nation's six biggest mainline Protestant denominations had 21.3 million members, down 25 percent from 1965. The traditional denominations such as Methodists, Presbyterians, Episcopalians, and the United Church of Christ have been hit the hardest. They have lost more than a quarter of their consumers in the past two decades. Growth has slowed even for the Southern Baptists, probably the chief beneficiaries of America's move to the Sun Belt and fundamentalism. The Pentecostals have clearly consolidated some of this restlessness.

More interesting from a marketing point of view is that in recent years the only traditional mainline denomination to gain adherents has been the more liberal Unitarian-Universalist churches—the emotional opposite of the more rigid Pentecostals. Partly, this is due to an increase in families attracted to the Unitarian tradition of local control and nondoctrinaire services. But partly, the growth is due to Unitarians' willingness to include a growing wing in the Church that is unabashedly New Age. Unitarians would blanch to hear this, but they have been doing an excellent job of niche marketing. They have also been able to tag along with the diversity and feminist political movements.

These *newly churched* are the Bobos of religion. They are the bourgeois bohemians David Brooks isolated in his delightful book with the quasi-religious title *Bobos in Paradise: The New Upper Class and How They Got There.* What Bobos have to choose between is the old denominational delivery system of the Protestant tradition and the new entertainment mode of getting in touch with your feelings. The Unitarians have been able to welcome such touchy-feely developments as holistic healing centers, Robert Bly's "Iron John," Bill Moyers and Joseph Campbell, James Redfield's *The Celestine Prophecy,* the appearance of angels as totems and crystals as inspiration, weekend spas, Buddhism, Transcendental Meditation, and Deepak Chopra, as well as Chicken Soup for this and that. Ralph Waldo Emerson would have been pleased—well, okay, amused.

In a market filled with choices, the low-cost supplier will usually be both featured and boycotted at the same time. The criticism lasts until the next low-cost supplier appears. Once doing church becomes like doing shopping or doing lunch (or even doing drugs), the inevitable contradiction appears. The consumer is allowed to become passive while the retailer is active, and the hard sell, the guilt-and-shame sell, becomes the soft sell, the feel-good sell. Brands and brand stories replace content-based material. Sooner or later, feeling is foregrounded.

In the delivery of the religious sensation the process goes like this: first the marketer as minister, then the minister as marketer. Sooner or later, with interchangeable products, product-driven marketing ("This is what we have to sell. Take it or leave it.") becomes consumer-driven ("What have you got for me?"). "Consumers listen to us" becomes "We listen to consumers." Shoppers become customers become clients become friends. Forget the hellfire and brimstone; pass the remote control.

The Multiple-Provider System and Branding

What Martin Luther and the Reformation did to religious suppliers, and what Henry VIII and the Anglican schism supercharged, was the abrupt decentralization of production. Instead of having mendicant orders compete with one another in delivering a uniform service, the Protestant system formalizes separation and distinction. But if what religion "sells" is the sensation of epiphany, the promise of forgiveness and salvation, the inkling of order in the universe, the promise of a life beyond this one, then the great transformation of early modern life was the furious repackaging of the product. It becomes personalized. By the eighteenth century, the Arminian controversy was hardly controversial. In fact, it became the norm. The views of Jacobus Arminius, who asserted the importance of individual will, were taken up by John Wesley, who essentially argued that the individual needed no translator between himself and God. And after Wesley there was a free-for-all. The consumer was king.

The Wesleyan movement transformed into Methodism, which had a startling impact on the democratization of religion. It was as if the single-supplier marketplace had been tipped over to become a slew of local markets. In this explosion of diversity we see one of the most fascinating aspects of branding. In the Roman Catholic centralized system, the competing orders had to explode upward in order to segment the audience and provide a story via such media as architecture, painting, or the decorative arts. The Benedictines, the Franciscans, the Jesuits, and the other orders could not change the service—which was mandated by Rome—so all they could do was change the wrapper. The evolution of the cathedral, complete with ever-changing internal decoration (what is now called *art*), is how they competed. The cathedral grew higher and higher, the decoration more intense.

But the democratization (aka denominalization) of Christianity allowed the service to change *outward*, and hence the brand story resides inside the local unit. Packaging ceased to become important. Ditto interior decoration. What became important was the interpretation of the text, the various rituals and regulations, the creative endeavors of the congregation inside the denomination. The religious experience became, like so much of the consumerist society, intimate and local.

In a sense, the umbrella brand of the Holy Roman Catholic Church became the brand family of Protestantism.

And what are the major Protestant denominations? The Church of England, the American Episcopal Church, the Presbyterians, the Religious Society of Friends (aka Quakers), the various Baptist Conventions, the Unitarian Universalist Society, the Lutherans, the United Church of Christ, and the United Methodist Church. How are they organized? From the bottom up. Believers affiliate with a local church. It usually includes those who have professed their belief in Christ, have been baptized, and have taken the vows of membership. The local church is the context in which to hear the Word of God and receive the Sacraments. Groups of local churches work together as a district and are supervised by a clergy superintendent. These districts are part of an annual conference, the basic unit of the denomination. Central Conferences are the regional units outside the United States. Conferences in the United States are usually grouped into geographic jurisdictions. Checks and balances are built into all aspects of church life. Not by happenstance does a denomination's organization resemble that of the U.S. government.

The Religious Economies Theory

Where I sit in my office at the University of Florida, I am surrounded by churches. Of course a university campus is a magnet to denominations, just as it is to all kinds of marketers. Across the street, all bunched together, are a University Lutheran Church, St. Augustine Catholic Church, Baptist Collegiate Ministry, the Presbyterian Church (or Disciples of Christ, as they also call themselves down here), Episcopal Campus Ministry, the University United Methodist Church, and the Emmanuel Mennonite Church. The Hillel Foundation is constructing a large building for Jewish students right next to what is becoming the focal point of branding this university: the University of Florida Foundation building (which I'll discuss in the next chapter). A block or two away are the United Church of Christ, a synagogue, a Quaker meetinghouse. In between these churches are the golden arches and neon burgers of fast-food franchises. On the campus each Wednesday there is a migrating version of the International Society for Krishna Consciousness, which feeds students a free vegetarian lunch.

This tight bunching of religion providers occurs because of what is on my side of the street. To many, the university is Gomorrah. But the same nesting occurs downtown, with many of the same outfits doing the same business, albeit in larger quarters, with columns out front, steeples with crosses on the roofs, and parking in the back.

Now, from a marketing point of view, does the clustering of

churches have anything to do with the clustering of other objects? To some sociologists, the reason there are so many kinds of houses of worship is no different from the reason there are so many brands of detergent or toothpaste at the supermarket or the bunching of car dealerships at the edge of town: competitive economics. The law of supply and demand shapes the earthly delivery systems of epiphany, forgiveness, and salvation. The consumers in pews are fickle, ready to bolt to a competing brand if the current one seems stale or uninspired.

This economic approach, called the *religious economies* explanation, has led some scholars to conclude that competition, rather than the undermining of belief, actually spurs it. Not only does it make clergymen work harder, they say, it also means there is a greater likelihood that any one person will find a brand that suits his or her spiritual tendencies, be they New Age or biblical literalist. The more different brands you have, the more consumption increases and the more the brands deepen. Having five different suppliers of bottled water expands the market for what at one level is just tap water and at the same time builds affiliation. Religious pluralism is precisely why the American market is so vibrant while in most of the rest of the world dominant religions constrict the flow of competing narratives and enervate the brands.

In *Acts of Faith: Explaining the Human Side of Religion*, two sociologists, Rodney Stark and Roger Finke, use this market explanation to understand the U.S. paradox: Why is religion here both pluralistic and devout? Using data from an unusually thorough survey of religious behavior in 1906 conducted by the U.S. Census Bureau, they explore the link between religious diversity and commitment. (Alas, such information is no longer gathered by the government—a sign of our tender ecumenical times.) Then the sociologists used the same statistical formula that the Federal Trade Commission uses to measure the amount of competition in consumer markets (such as those for toothpaste and soap) to look at pluralism even more closely. They found that in towns of similar size, church attendance was highest when there was the greatest choice of worship. In short, brand commitment varies directly with choice: the more variations, the deeper the affiliation.

Marketers have always known this. Competition often increases consumption. In countries where only Coke is sold, there is less consumption of soft drinks than when Coke and Pepsi battle it out. McDonald's sells well when clustered along with Wendy's and Burger King. Cars sell best when dealerships are bunched together. You'll sell more hardware if your competition is right next door. That's why Home Depot goes in right next to Lowe's, Staples next to Office Depot. Even if your prices are exactly the same, you'll pump more gas if there's a station across the street.

Religious economies theory would predict that Europe could wake up religiously if its churches started acting like their American counterparts. Monopoly churches are headed for dullsville. But watch out! Sometimes plenitude and pluralism are too exciting. You can have too many gas stations. Having too many sects of Islam may increase the possibility that brand affiliation will become violent, but having some will make you more Christian. And vice versa.

Congregations as Consumption Communities

If the rational-choice theory is correct, one might ask, What's next for American Protestantism? If the social benefit of prestige is removed (good-bye Episcopalians), and if all denominations essentially offer the same product as well as the same sense of affiliation, what can a producer do to create a new brand, tell a new story, deliver the old sensation, and still stay in the purview of religion? Clearly, the emotional product—the therapeutic sensation of redemption, of epiphany, the promise of a new start, of forgiveness—must remain in place. After all, the essence of otherworld systems is that they deliver exactly this promise.

Perhaps the way to start predicting the future is by observing what has been happening in the retailing of hard goods. We are now buying brands as a way of generating intense and specific community. The study of these consumption communities goes by any number of names—psychographics, ethnographics, macrosegmentation, to name a few—but they are all based on the ineluctable principle that birds of a feather flock together. As one might imagine, the keenest knowledge about these groups comes from those who have the most to gain by understanding and selling such information, namely, marketing specialists. Tell a savvy marketing analyst your most recent purchase, and he will tell you with amazing detail what you'll buy next.

Take zip codes. Marketing firms have separated neighborhoods into some forty or so designations called PRIZM (Potential Rating Index for Zip Markets) clusters. Each of the clusters is defined by detailed demographic, lifestyle, and consumption information, often including brand-level data. For example, the Shotguns & Pickups cluster is partly defined by a high usage of chain saws, snuff, canning jars, frozen potato products, and whipped toppings. Members of this cluster are exceptionally unlikely to use car rental services, belong to country clubs, read *Gourmet* magazine, or drink Irish whiskey. By contrast, in the Furs and Station Wagons cluster members are much more likely than the typical consumer to have a second mortgage, buy wine by the case, read *Architectural Digest*, drive BMW 5-series cars, eat natural cold cereal and pumpernickel bread, and watch *The Tonight Show*. Members of this cluster are unlikely to chew tobacco, hunt, drive a Chevette, use nondairy creamers, eat canned stews, or watch *Wheel of Fortune*.

Outfits such as the Percept Group, a consulting firm in California, work almost exclusively with churches, using this kind of data. Here's how it describes its service:

> *Zip codes are another simple and easy way to define your study area. Most of us are already familiar with our local zip code areas as they tend to follow natural community boundaries. You may specify a single zip code or a group of zip codes as your study area. If you wish to define your study area with multiple zip codes, they do not necessarily have to all be next to one another. . . . Normally Percept only uses the top zip codes which represent 80% of the respondents. This eliminates zip codes that represent unusual situations like visitors from out of state who happen to complete a survey on the Sunday that you administered it. If you wish to use this option, you may also choose some cutoff value other than 80% (although we do not recommend choosing values below 70% or more than 90%).*

What they don't say, and perhaps what really doesn't have to be said, is that they use PRIZM data to fill in the blanks about the consumption habits and by extrapolation the pastoral needs of congregations. Hence Percept can draw a seemingly detailed picture not just of the prospective congregation but of its pressing concerns. It sells its services to individual churches as well as entire denominations. In certain parts of the country, the Presbyterian Church, for instance, is a client.

The Consumer Is King

No need to feel embarrassed about this kind of targeting if you are of the Bruce Barton school. Christ knew his audience and positioned his Word to fit the audience. It's not that some customers are better than others, it's just that some need different pastoral care. To be sure, from the return-on-investment point of view, it rewards the pastor who can find congregants with the necessary disposable income and time to maximize the power of the brand. They are *repeat* consumers, whose affiliation increases both the coffers and the dependability of the service.

You have doubtless seen the nice young men in the white shirts who come knocking on your door to talk to you about your life. Sometimes they are on bicycles, but always they are so neat and tidy. Ever wonder how they ended up in your neighborhood? Ever wonder why they always ask you about you? They seem to know you. The Mormons—or The Church of Jesus Christ of Latter-Day Saints or just LDS, as it now prefers to be branded—make intensive use of demographic data to locate new opportunities. The church conducts regular surveys worldwide, and each local unit, or ward, also reports member data to world headquarters in Salt Lake City, Utah. It is especially interested in what demographers call "marriage markets." Find a neighborhood in which diaper sales are increasing, and soon you'll find these young gentlemen on their bikes.

The consumer of the religious sensation most in demand is called by various names: the seeker, the unchurched, the as yet uncommitted. Here's why. There is no future in trying to sell your brand to an already converted user of a product. What you want to do is to sell to someone who has not bought the story, made the choice, converted. You don't advertise hair coloring to people whose hair has turned gray. You don't sell beer to beer drinkers. You don't sell cigarettes to smokers. You say you do. You say you are only trying to get brand switch-

ers. But in truth, if you want to succeed in marketing, you will have to sell your product to those who have not even started to buy seriously.

Pick up any teen magazine, and you will see the truth of this proposition. Check the age of women in hair-coloring ads. The models are usually nowhere near the event. That's because the wily marketer sells to the audience that precedes use, not the one that is already using. Its members are the ones who pay attention to the brand story. Remember when the tobacco execs were testifying before Congress and they all said they never targeted kiddies? Everyone in marketing howled in disbelief. The first rule of Marketing 101: Target the audience just on the entry edge of consumption. Find them before they buy, before they listen to competing brands, and you will get them for life. A little expense up front, and they will consume far longer than some middle-aged wanderer who will haphazardly take or leave your brand. If you ever wonder why American advertising is targeted at adolescents, it's because it would take about $350 of marketing to get a fifty-year-old male to change his beer choice, but you can get an eighteen-year-old to try your brand for about $50.

Plus, once you get the entering wedge of young consumers—*early adopters,* as they are called in the jargon—you'll soon find a tsunami of fellow believers cresting behind. I observed the wedge parabola of consumers as the Reverend Graham invited the initiated down to the space in front of him. First there was a trickle of young people. Were they in cahoots with the revivalist? Perhaps. Then a slow surge of "Count me in." Finally the stragglers. At five-minute intervals of singing songs of joyful induction, Mr. Graham stepped to the microphone and offered the comforting words "We can wait for you. The buses will not leave without you. Your friends will understand."

A marketer cannot overestimate the sensation of watching others demonstrate desire in determining your own eagerness to consume. Desire often resides not internally but in the panic of others. Paul Ormerod points out in *Butterfly Economics: A New General Theory of Social and Economic Behavior* that such communicable panic may even be hardwired. In the mid-1980s, entomologists did a series of experiments with ants. Two food sources were placed equidistant from and on opposite sides of a nest. The food piles were kept equal in size no matter how much the ants took from each. There was no reason for the ants to prefer one brand, so to speak, to the other. Logical economists would predict that the ants would divide the piles evenly waiting in equidistant lines. But no. Instead, because ants can signal one another as to where food lies, the distribution fluctuated wildly, even swinging from an 80:20 ratio to a 20:80 one. Follow the leader is no simple childhood game but a deeply installed herd behavior.

The Megachurch: Brand Central of the Next New Thing

Piling on is not an isolated phenomenon of human behavior. As Malcolm Gladwell, staff writer for *The New Yorker,* demonstrated in *The Tipping Point: How Little Things Can Make a Big Difference,* herd mentality is at the heart of such enterprises as fashion, suicide rates, teenage smoking, war, best-selling books, and numerous other endeavors that spread like the flu. In fact, Gladwell coins three rules of epidemics (The Law of the Few, The Stickiness Factor, and The Power of Context) to explain geometric explosions in what is essentially human taste.

Take a look at any medium-sized city today. You can see what happens once this tipping point is reached in church affiliation. In almost every city of more than 200,000 population there is a church growing like Topsy, doubling every few years. These new churches are the result of a strange confluence of marketing, population shift, consumer demand, consumption communities, the entertainment economy, and the good old-fashioned yearning for a feeling of epiphany and the bandwagon effects that generate it. These churches even have a new name: they are called *megachurches.*

You can recognize them easily. They are on the outskirts of town. They look like junior college campuses, surrounded by vast parking lots, with their own buses and signboards out front. They have a new congregation, disproportionately young and energetic. Although most of these churches are white, the African-American ones are also exploding. Made up of black, upwardly mobile professionals ("buppies"), these churches in places such as Houston, Philadelphia, and Washington, D.C., are furiously subverting what it means to be denominational. As opposed to old-line denominations, they are efficient at using a web of specialty group labor. Listen to them talk, and you will hear a refrain of growth—"We're growing"—as if that were a sign of redemptive success. And they deliver the emotional product: the promise of the conversion experience inside an affiliated group, complete with video screens and music. These new freestanding institutions may revolutionize what in the patois of marketing is called *doing church.*

You might have predicted this brand consolidation from the demographics alone: half of all churchgoing Americans are attending only 12 percent of the nation's four hundred thousand churches. To look at it another way: half of American Protestant churches have fewer than seventy-five congregants. See all those little churches on the sides of country roads? See all those big downtown churches? Ever wonder who fills them up on Sunday? No one. The mainline denominations are drying up. Their churches have more pew than flock, and unless they change, they'll have more history than future. Small congregations of fewer than a hundred at worship, in rural communities and inner cities, are shutting their doors at the rate of fifty a week. They are going the way of small, underendowed private schools and museums.

So where are the believers going? Protestantism is experiencing the same brand shifts that occur when Sam's Club or Costco comes to town. Consumers move in trickles, then droves. The one thing these warehouse churches have in common is what they also share with Franklin Graham's revival: they usually belong to no traditional denomination. This new delivery system is electronic, local, and efficient. Scholars may call them "postdenominational church" or parts of the "new apostolic reformation," but the layperson knows better. Megachurches are often called "purpose-driven" or "seeker-sensitive" churches, "full-service," "seven-day-a-week" churches. Detractors call them "shopping mall" churches. Those still less impressed call them McChurches or Wal-Mart churches.

You can see this purposeful identity ambiguity in the names the churches call themselves: Wooddale Church, Over the Mountain Community Church, Mountain Valley Community Church, In the Pines Community Church, Saddleback Valley Community Church, Willow Creek Community Church, Fellowship of Las Colinas, Mariners Church, Calvary Chapel, Church of the Open Door, Community of Joy,

House of Hope, Gateway Cathedral, New Life Fellowship, Seneca Creek Community Church, Cedar Run Community Church, Sea Breeze Community Church. As opposed to their brethren, which proudly proclaimed their presence by posting small signs on the outskirts of town notifying all passers-by that a Methodist or Episcopal or Presbyterian church was nearby, these places have something in common: they whisper no word of denomination. But note the reiteration of "community" in their names.

Have no doubt about it: along with community, a central selling point of such religion is growth. You sense it the minute you pull into the parking lot. By the time you are inside you are aware that while there is no interest in soaring space, no arched apse, there is an obsession with horizontal space and filling up seats. Instead of balconies there is often stadium-style seating, just as at a Cineplex, complete with sound and video systems.

Although the megachurches have borrowed heavily from the electronic media, they have little in common with the Elmer Gantrys of 1970s and '80s televangelism. There are no sweating, heavy breathing, and threatening damnation unless the phones ring. In fact, Jay Leno and David Letterman, not Jimmy Swaggart and Jim Bakker, are the templates of the genial minister-as-host. True, the ultimate goal is to convert the passive observer into an active contributor, but the goal is not to line the pockets of the preacher but to increase the size of the church. Bigger is better.

While growth and large size used to be viewed with some suspicion in the traditional denomination and resolved by building newer and smaller churches, the megachurch does not depend on intimacy. Just the opposite; it thrives on anonymity. It's a bandwagon, climb aboard! Piling on is even legitimated by a new organization called the American Society for Church Growth, which takes an increase in congregation as a valid goal and shares demographic data from census tracts as a way of acknowledging its purpose.

From a doctrinal point of view, increasing size is not just a natural by-product of righteousness, it is a harbinger of the Apocalypse. If it weren't a good product, would people be buying it? Hence, using commercial marketing terms such as "market segment," "niche," "satisfied customer," even "ROI" (return on investment) raises no eye-brows. In fact, such phrases trip easily off these pastoral tongues.

The reward of growth is not just to deliver the sensation of affiliation and redemption but to deliver economies of scale to the endeavor. Such size and stand-alone independence make for the efficiencies of mass production while subtracting the inefficiencies of having to support denominational overhead. Now everything goes back into the pot. Big congregations, far from being a deterrent, are a marketing asset. They provide the anonymity that allows newcomers, shoppers, the curious (*seekers,* in the parlance), to feel comfortable comparison shopping the church. Just as in the mall, window shopping and shopping around are central and important parts of the experience. Drive to the mall. Go inside. Look, dream, go inside an individual store, and buy a branded item. Such large size also generates huge pools of excited and committed volunteer labor. Face it, a church really needs only a minister and a flock. Everything else is day labor. So they can concentrate on what makes a brand powerful: maintaining growth. What you sell is the perception that *whatever* it is you are selling certainly is in demand.

In the nineteenth century, retailers happened onto the central truth of selling. Victorian retailers would often pile goods near the front door and stand looking on amazed at what happened. As Emile Zola wrote in his novel *Ladies' Paradise* (1883), a common street sight in Paris was the milling of shoppers at the store entrance. "It should seem to people in the street as if a riot were taking place . . . that the shop was bursting with people, when often it was only half-full." Once inside, women were trapped in a glittering Aladdin's cave where everything was easy to touch and proximity to the ineffable was disconcerting. Before they became in-house police, the primary job of floorwalkers was to escort ladies safely through the emporium so they would not be disturbed by the transcendental excitement of goods and the virus of consumption. The early department stores were called Lands of Enchantment for a reason; they were magical, alive with contagious desire.

Growing churches and congregations, like growing businesses, have learned the importance of generating "church at the door." Shoppers equate crowding with value. Is there any feeling as eerie as being alone in a mall? So a megachurch often behaves like a successful mall, consolidating other frayed institutions such as school, family, government, neighborhood, and even employment. In a sense, a megachurch mimics the Norman Rockwell town center, complete with the town square—the *commons.* Having people milling around is crucial. By taking on roles as various as those of the Welcome Wagon, the USO, the Rotary, the quilting bee, the book club, the coffee shop, and the country club mixer—and, of course, the traditional family and school—these "next churches" have become the traditional villages that many Americans think they grew up in and now can find only on television.

Megachurch Community

In this context, the mall and megachurch look alike for a reason: they are institutionalized communities, growing outward, not upward. They are forever adding new wings, just like the local hospital. On one hand, they distribute the goods—deliver the care; on the other, they willingly, even eagerly, experiment with marketplace transactions. New product lines can open up in a wink. Stores are forever changing places. New machinery is wheeled in. The modern customer is as accustomed to eclecticism as he is to comparison shopping. The Next New Thing is just around the corner. After all, this is the embodiment of choice, the heart of competitive branding. The megachurch thrives on innovation as the denominational church affirms tradition. I can't tell you the number of times I've heard "Well, *this* is certainly not the church you are used to" coming from the pulpit as an accolade. Whatever "this" is, it's the essence of the brand that separates one church from all the interchangeable others.

So the mall and megachurch offer a panoply of choices under one roof—from worship styles to boutique ministries, plus plenty of parking, background music, clean bathrooms, and the likelihood that you'll find something you want and come back. In mall marketing there is a phenomenon called the *Gruen transfer,* named after the architect of the first self-contained mall, who realized that bunching up similar stores increased, not decreased, consumption. A *micro*-Gruen transfer is what happens when a shopper goes looking for a particular object and then just drifts into becoming a shopper, a person with a diffuse impulse to buy, to spend. Sociologists quickly noted this wandering-from-store-to-store phenomenon about mall shoppers, and it is one of the raisons d'être of the enclosed mall. Wander all you want, but stay inside. But there is also a *macro*–Gruen transfer. Put Lowe's next to Home Depot, and chances are you'll increase the sales of both. As we consume in clusters, so too do we worship.

That's why at the really successful megachurches you see all manner of entertainment and sensationalism that you would think the church might hold at arm's length. Here there are aerobics classes, fast-food franchises, bowling alleys, counseling centers, and multimedia Bible classes where the *son et lumière* rivals that of MTV. The megachurches can make these quicksilver shifts because they are freestanding; they have no tradition or denomination to represent. They have *mass,* in both senses of the term.

The megachurch also shifts media easily because it self-consciously mimics the kind of excitement generated elsewhere. In anthropology this is called *syncretism,* the ability of an institution to layer itself over other sequences. So here are four examples of the megachurch co-opting other delivery systems.

Music

Perhaps the most startling aspect of the megachurch is that it is in the middle of the Entertainment Economy. To be sure, music has always soothed the savage breast, and music is at the heart of almost every religion because it can also do exactly the opposite. Of all the senses, music plays to the emotions with the least interference. It is not tied to emotional life; it *is* emotional life. Epiphany to follow. The sound of the megachurch is, however, not the music of the pipe organ, the hymnal, and the robed choir. It is the sound of the FM radio, contemporary, changeable, tuneful, and, best of all, simple, sing-alongable. And there is a lot of it. Almost half of a typical service is music.

Almost without exception, the music of the megachurch is generated onstage by a band. That's right, a real live band. All the instruments once abhorred by latter-day Puritans as sensual—the saxophone, drums, electronic guitar, and keyboard—provide not just the enter-

and-sit-down music but the stand-up-and-follow-the-bouncing-ball tunes. Old-time denominational music was often adapted from eighteenth-century poetry, but contemporary church soft rock is composed by the same people who provide shopping mall music. Go to Crate and Barrel, the Pottery Barn, or the Gap. Admire the music, and you can purchase the CD at the register. Go to the megachurch, and you'll find the same situation. The music is supplied out of several services, which also send arrangements on disc or via satellite. You can often buy the tapes and/or CDs at the door—all copyrighted. In *Billboard* magazine, which charts the various kinds of music, this genre is called *Contemporary Christian* and is one of the fastest-growing areas of the music industry.

Spectacular screens

Whereas you once had to squint at a hymnal to find the tiny words of the endlessly repetitive and dull hymns, the new system uses a follow-the-bouncing-ball video. Overhead projectors show you the words (as well as the perpetual copyright notice). This is karaoke Christianity. Jumbotron salvation. You can sing along flawlessly.

These high-resolution screens also allow you the comfort of your favorite pastime, watching television. The same screens are a central part of Franklin Graham's ceremony as well. In the megachurch, however, there are often two or more screens giving you various points of view. That you can't control what you are seeing doesn't seem to be an audience concern. Even better, it's just like watching football or hockey.

In addition, the screens allow the pastor a video chalkboard to illustrate his message, flash a cartoon, or show a filmstrip. In a sense these screens are the descendants of the stained-glass window, another nonverbal storytelling device. But stained glass is static and hard to view up close. These overhead screens force you to view what is being programmed. In fact, you can't keep your eyes off it. The resolution is just so good. So if there is a personal testimonial, or a two- or three-person dramatic sketch, or even a biblical gloss, you can be sure you'll see it perfectly no matter where you sit. And that you'll see it as the organizers prefer, up close and personal.

The screen becomes the electronic altar, literally. And while these screens may seem a luxury, they are cheaper than buying two thousand hymnals and two thousand prayer books. Also smarter. For one thing, projecting words and lyrics on a screen means no mass page flipping by parishioners. You are never lost during the service. The singing I heard in these churches was uniformly booming and enthusiastic, partly because of the simplicity and almost childish repetitiveness of the music, but also because the people had their chins up and their hands free. Thus the spontaneous clapping and swaying of hips and, occasionally, the single hand outstretched to God were epiphany simplified and democratized.

Parking

Parking is crucial. Twenty to thirty years ago the average Methodist's car brought four people to church. Now it brings less than half that, 1.68 to be exact. Megachurches makes a fetish out of parking for a reason. They usually have huge lots, shuttle buses, and cute little signs, just like at the airport or Disneyland, to remind you where you parked your car. Again, the insistence on being in a crowd but not being crowded is central. Most impressive, to me at least, were the men—volunteers—outfitted in headsets just like air traffic controllers, directing cars. Having the entry rituals start in the parking lot is crucial. You sense the surge of highway traffic—the ideal bandwagon, you often pass by the local police, who earn overtime but provide something even more important: the sense that something really important is going on. It's hard not to be caught up. You are en route to Somewhere Important.

Child care

The history of church and child care makes an interesting commentary on competitive church branding. In the nineteenth century, children were taken to church. They sat in the family pew. It was unthinkable to change congregations, let alone pews. The children behaved and were quiet. Church was a test, a chore. Then, with the Sunday School Movement in the early twentieth century, children were separated for some of the service. By midcentury they were separated for all the service. They disappeared—and with them the family pew and all that it meant about the abstract qualities of heritage.

In the modern megachurch the children have returned with a vengeance, not in the service but in the church. From a marketing point of view, this makes sense. You don't sell to users. You sell to the unaffiliated. The youth programming is almost as prominent as that for adults, if not more so. There is no assigned seating. The megachurch often becomes the after-school place of choice. And woe to any church that does not have a state-of-the-art communication system so that Mom and Dad can be informed either via pager or ticker of the whereabouts of Junior. During the services I saw that there was often a subscript ticker on the supersized screen announcing that "The parents of child #267 need to come to the Sunday school" just like the news crawl on CNN or the market report on CNBC. Not only does this address the safety concerns of the modern parent in a crowded mall, but it gives the illusion that anxious parents will never really have to be separated from their children. They are just visiting different stores, connected by pagers.

Criticism of the Megachurch

Such congregational poaching has not come without criticism from the displaced denominations. In the world of fungible products, you don't capture market share without having to contend with the howls of those you displace. With the arrival of Wal-Mart come the cries of unfair, unfair. From whom? From Sears and J. C. Penney. And who howled when Sears and J. C. Penney (and especially their catalogs) came to town? The downtown merchants. (In fact, the use of brown wrapping paper as a way to package goods to send them through the mail was a result of the embarrassment of buying from a catalog. "It comes to you in a brown paper wrapper" is now used for pornography, but it was first used by Sears and then picked up as branding by United Parcel Service.) And who shouted "unfair" when the downtown merchants came? The corner store. And whom did the corner store displace? The door-to-door salesman, the drummer. In a strange sense, things have come full circle as the independent megachurch pastor shares many similarities (independent, local boy responsible for his own territory) with the Victorian drummer. The drummer earned his nickname because that was his task: to drum up business.

So what are the cries of displaced suppliers of the conversion experience as marketed in the Church Growth Movement? Predictably they are from the old-line denominations. The charges are congregation stealing, cheapening the experience, superficiality, providing flyby sensations instead of real theological substance. The megachurch is the dumbing down of American religion, epiphany lite, minister as personality, service as TV with musical interludes, cherry-picking of smug baby boomers, obsession on the "front door" never minding the flood leaving the "back door," fair-weather churches feeding easy-to-digest junk food to the already overweight.

Conveniently forgotten is that this is exactly the pattern not just of religion but of marketing in general. Someone develops a new wrapper or a new delivery system for an interchangeable product and overnight the market has to adjust. Brand-new brand. Megachurch ministers retort that their approach to secular culture has respectable precedents throughout modern Christian history. Think only of such stalwarts as the Methodists and Disciples of Christ, for example, who were the upstarts during the first half of the nineteenth century. Recall the "excitements" of Methodist camp meetings or the Chautauqua movements. In the twentieth century, the Assemblies of God grew from 50,000 in the 1920s to 1.7 million today by promising a new kind of participatory experience. The megachurches are just doing the job more efficiently.

And hasn't this always been the trajectory of religious branding—the movement from Upper Sublimia to Lower Vulgaria? Martin Luther translated the Scriptures into German vernacular, and the Lutheran Church adapted then-contemporary folk music, including drinking songs. What were they met with? Howls of "Violation!" The Methodists under the Wesley brothers "agreed to become more vile" to reach the common people, even preaching in fields and town squares. They coached their adherents to speak "in the most obvious, easy, common words, wherein our meaning can be conveyed." For this they were reviled. The democratizing of the conversion experience has always let loose a predictable fusillade of criticism. As General

William Booth, the founder of the Salvation Army, memorably said, "Why should the Devil have all the best tunes?"

If you want to see this secularization happening, just observe the changing visage of Christ. In fact, one of the best books on branding centers on the changing image of Jesus. Art historian Leo Steinberg makes the point in *The Sexuality of Christ in the Renaissance and in Modern Oblivion* that the image of Jesus has been a long-contested marketing device of competing orders. We forget that only a few generations ago the image of Jesus was transformed from Semitic and distant into Caucasian and neighborly. This shift was effected by an art student in Chicago named Warner Sallman. The Sallman image appeared in almost every Christian church, was the frontispiece of presentation Bibles, was tacked on bulletin boards and featured on calendars, and, until the Supreme Court took it down, was hung in almost every American school, often right beside Gilbert Stuart's George Washington.

The Warner Sallman image of Christ became an identification character to brand objects, literally.

SUNDAY SCHOOL
INTERMEDIATE TEACHER
JANUARY FEBRUARY MARCH 1942

Willow Creek: Mega-Megachurch

Of all the megachurches, the most interesting from a marketing point of view is one just southwest of Chicago called Willow Creek Community Church. As opposed to the other bucolic names that megachurches often have, the Willow Creek name came, appropriately enough, from the fact that the congregation once met in the husk of the Willow Creek movie theater. Rather like malls that take their name from what they destroy, so this church takes the name of the entertainment it now competes with. Ask anyone in the Church Growth Movement, and he or she will know its name. Willow Creek is to American religion what Home Depot is to fix-it-up, McDonald's to meat patties. It's the Next Thing in Protestantism—the low-cost discounter of epiphanic community.

First the obvious: this is not a church in any traditional visual or architectural sense. It resembles a nifty little junior college or a small

What do you get when you cross a church with a community college?
Willow Creek Community Church.

business concern that manufactures something clean, like drugs or computer parts. Remember how banks and colleges used to look like Gothic churches? Think Yale, University of Chicago, or Princeton. Now churches look like branch banks—the revenge of marketing. Bill Hybels, the entrepreneurial pastor of Willow Creek, stated that what he wanted his parishioner to say as he came to Willow Creek was "I was just at corporate headquarters for IBM in Atlanta Wednesday, and now I come to a church here and it's basically the same." Hybels got his wish.

On one side of the *campus*—and that's what it's called in the church literature—is a greensward, on another side is a five-acre reflecting pond, and in between are the black slabs of endless parking. And I mean endless—3,100 spaces. Rule number one of modern retailing: you are only as big as your parking lot. As I write this, the lot is currently being ripped up to accommodate still larger additions to the main building. Getting parishioners off the Interstate and into the parking lot costs the church more than $100,000 a year for local police in their official cars. And it's worth every penny. Here is rock concert affiliation. This brand is so popular that the police can barely control the consumers!

To help you get parked, there is a swarm of men wearing reflective vests talking to one another on headsets like the ones burger flippers and options traders wear. They are also talking to a controller perched atop the church building. Once parked, you can take a shuttle bus to the various doors of the church, just as you do at Disney World. The parking lot has the cute cartoon signs necessary for mall shoppers or airport trippers so that the car can be located. Needless to say, the lot is spotless, as is the rest of the campus. In fact, it's almost antiseptic.

Willow Creek is set up to be a gathering place. There is no one portal done up like a passage into another world with a huge arch and fonts. Nothing that says, "Main Entrance: Abandon Hope All Who Do Not Enter Here." Instead, here is the easy entrance to the modern business—lots of doors. These are not the electric sliding doors of your local grocery store, but close enough. Go inside and you will find not an ounce of old-time religiosity. There are no icons, no crucified Christs, no little telltale signs of stained glass or covered dishes or polished silver or gold that one associates with Don't Touch! Be Careful! Be Quiet! Act Devout! He May Be Watching!

Straight ahead of you is a 4,540-seat auditorium. The seats are just like those down at the Cineplex 16. No drink holders, however. And no prayer pads or slats for kneeling. You pray sitting or standing, not on your knees. A key to understanding Willow is this observation from Reverend Lee Strobel, a onetime close aide of Mr. Hybels and now out on his own: "When I was in London I went to St. Paul's and it wasn't very user-friendly. The lighting was bad, the seats were uncomfortable, and you couldn't hear what the guys at the front were saying. . . . You can't convince the unchurched that they have to sit on a hard seat in a draught for an hour every Sunday morning because that's what people did 500 years ago."

In the carpeted foyer, overhead video screens announce details of the day's activities. This could be a hotel lobby or an airport. On the video monitor is a digital clock counting down the time before the service begins. There are a brightly lit information booth, wide corridors, and clear signposting; but again no icons, no font, no vestry. And there are never any "out of order" signs. The church makes a fetish of having everything working. Just like the mall.

When you enter the gunmetal gray auditorium, the automatic curtains are lowered so there is a calm half-light. Down front is a flood-lit center stage complete with all kinds of drop-down screens and scrims. When the pastor (although that term is never used—first names suffice) delivers the sermon (and that word is never used—*message* is the term), you can see him from different points of view on the various screens, just as you can with the new DVD technology that allows you to shift angles of vision.

But the video technology is not what initially impressed me. I was blown away, almost literally, by the sound system. I could hear Mr. Hybels breathing even though I was halfway up the tiered auditorium. Not pant-blowing like Elmer Gantry but just quietly drawing in a breath. And so when the music starts—and you know when it starts because the place shakes—the reverberance is literal. And when it's quiet, you can actually hear breathing. I haven't been to many rock concerts but my kids tell me the sound systems make isolation impossible. You don't listen to the sounds, you feel them.

To enable the congregation to join in song, overhead screens display the lyrics. A ten-piece band heats up a rhythm as latecomers are hurried to their seats. A slow crescendo then sets the tone. When the band on the stage stops playing, the crowd of four thousand–plus erupts in a loud football cheer. The minister takes the stage to explain, "The applause that took place just now was not for any particular performer. It was for God." Everyone agrees. "And so," says Mr. Hybels, "let's thank the performers." Clap-clap.

After a little skit illustrating the upcoming sermonette (it lasts for less than the length of a few commercials), Bill Hybels takes the stage. Well scrubbed and dressed in a casual sort of way (yes, from time to time he wears the polo pony on his shirt), he takes as his topic for the day the necessity for "virtue development" or "life at the boiling point" or some such easy-to-recognize general theme. As he eases into a fast, savvy line of patter, it is easy to imagine him as a motivational guru firing up a bunch of lackluster corporate execs or flipping burgers at a neighborhood cookout. By rapid turns, he's intense, relaxed, controlled, and loose. The services themselves are not impressive. No threats, no intimidation, no doctrine. With the exception I'll mention below, I was never ruffled.

Over the weekend there are four exactly interchangeable services.

These are the boomer "seeker services," the loss-leader entertainment. The church calls them, with deflective candor, Christianity 101 or Christianity Lite. Then midweek there are two "believer services." That's the grad school, the place for transcendence . . . and tithing.

The weekend seeker services are not worship services, to speak of. They are edutainment. They are aimed at a population that generally is skeptical. Hence the take-it-or-leave-it aspect. It's pure soft sell, like a Super Bowl television commercial. It's Sunday-supplement religion, comforting to believers and informative to the curious. Hybels's focus on the "felt needs" of his baby boomers means that these weekend messages reflect a nurturing, forgiving God who will help with family life, day care, job stress, recreation, and the drive home.

Willow Creek's staff makes sermonizing decisions on the seeming whims of the marketplace. In doing so, doctrine is not handed down from Above, either from Heaven or from any bishop. The subject *du jour* approach is quicksilver fast and nothing if not relevant. Religious programmers simply analyze what the consumer needs and likes. For instance, Hybels asks his staff to copy the styles of secular entertainment, and at the beginning of the week they check the incoming e-mail and often spin a service around the concerns expressed in it. It's lite, sure. But it's compelling. Just like *60 Minutes* or the *Today* show.

The sermons are almost embarrassingly personal. Hybels is forever referencing his own family, neighborhood, history, and experience. Gregory Pritchard, at the time a theology Ph.D. student who went on to write *Willow Creek Seeker Services: Evaluating a New Way to Do Church,* found that over a year's time (1989–1990) the word "I" was used more than 6,000 times to create intimacy while specific Scripture was cited only 169 times. This man feels your pain, but he's not going to inflict Jesus on you to solve it. At least not on the weekend. When William Jefferson Clinton entered his season of enforced humility in August 2000, he came to Willow Creek to discuss the problems of "moral failure." Not by happenstance was Mr. Hybels one of the president's trusted religious advisers. And when Mel Gibson was concerned about how to market his controversial *The Passion of the Christ,* he too came to Willow Creek in January 2004 for a sympathetic audience.

From president to parishioner, this is a church in the business of

WILLOW CREEK SURVEY 2002

Thank you for completing this survey! This information will be used to understand our church and to closely evaluate ministry opportunities. This is anonymous, so please give us your honest and thoughtful responses to the questions. If you have already filled out this survey at a previous service, do not fill out another one now. Use a pencil or pen; an usher can provide one for you. At the end of the service, please place your survey in one of the baskets located in the lobbies. Thanks again!

SECTION ONE

Please tell us about your church involvement

1. **How long have you been attending Willow Creek (including Axis and Willow Creek Wheaton)?**
   - O_1 I'm visiting for the first or second time
   - O_2 One year or less
   - O_3 2–3 years
   - O_4 4–5 years
   - O_5 6–10 years
   - O_6 11 years or more

2. **What *most* influenced you to attend a service at Willow Creek for the first time (including Axis and Willow Creek Wheaton services)?** *check one option*
   - O_1 A friend or relative brought me to a service or an event
   - O_2 I heard about Willow Creek from a friend or relative
   - O_3 I drove by the church and decided to visit
   - O_4 I moved to Chicago and someone recommended Willow Creek
   - O_5 Media coverage caught my attention
   - O_6 I was attracted to a particular program or ministry here
   - O_7 I heard about a special event or service
   - O_8 I learned about Willow Creek through the web site
   - O_9 Other: _____

3. **How would you describe your church involvement before attending Willow Creek?**
   - O_1 I did not attend church
   - O_2 I attended church primarily on holidays/special occasions
   - O_3 I attended church regularly
   - O_4 I attended church regularly and was involved in serving and/or a small group

The first of more than thirty questions on a Willow Creek survey of church involvement, spiritual life, and depth of affiliation.

coping. Willow Creek deals with getting on with it first in this life; then with getting on to Heaven. In looking over the sermons for the last decade (they are listed on the Church's Web site), you can see an almost chicken-soup-for-the-soul inventory of subject matter. Adjustment is key: adjusting to your children, to your spouse having an affair, to apathy, to abortion, to debt, to divorce, to drugs, to competition, to being lonely, to not measuring up, to repetition, to sloppiness, to lust, to anger, to being passed by, to racism, to growing older, and well, to just about everything that men especially would prefer not to speak about in public.

The minute the service is over, you can pick up your own personal audio tape or CD of *exactly* the service you just witnessed so that you can revisit the coping lessons in your car or at home. State-of-the-art duplicating machines in the basement crank out three thousand copies, which are stacked in the lobby by the time the service ends. For two bucks you get everything but the copyrighted music.

The marketing insight of Willow Creek is that it is able to equili-brate the vertical with the horizontal. It is the horizontal Christianity that is represented in the physical plant. People are all over the place—dehydrated community. Just appear, and you are One of Us. On one side of the entrance to the auditorium, the building expands into a food court (and that's exactly what it's called) looking like what you might see in any modern airport—a number of cafeteria lines and small tables. There is seating for 750, and the congregants can eat Chinese noodles or hamburgers. From the prices charged, the food court is a moneymaker. Off the food court, there are more rooms—gyms with three basketball courts, numerous rooms for teen and child activities, as well as the performance auditoriums for the irrepressible earsplitting music of a baby-buster group called AXIS.

When I first attended there was a Starbucks kiosk complete with advertising. But a year later when I returned, it had been replaced by Seattle's Finest. When I asked why the shift, I was told, "better deal." Too bad, because I had always thought the genius of Starbucks was the same as Willow Creek's. The famous coffee shop ad that went "Not home, not work but the third place" belonged in this church. After all, the *third place* is exactly what Willow Creek is attempting to be. Not home, not work, definitely not your father's church, but something including all three.

Up in a mezzanine over the food court is a remarkably good book-store. Naturally it's biased toward megachurch issues, but it's also quite ecumenical. It offers more than seventy-five thousand spiritu-ally oriented titles from four hundred publishers, plus tchotchkes for Granny and video games for Junior. There is also a selection of reli-gious CDs that you can sample just as you do in the mall. Mixed in with the books are racks of greeting cards, all with appropriately non-ironical, sincere messages about helping others cope. The bookstore is also a moneymaker. There's no discounted pricing of the type you see at Barnes & Noble.

As with so much of the modern marketing, the emphasis on adolescence cannot be missed. Just as marketers never attempt to convert users of a product if they can concentrate on those who have yet to make a choice, so too with Willow Creek. There is great emphasis on what the young people are doing. How are they *feeling?* From the vibrating sounds of their music, I'd say they were feeling just fine. Willow Creek does the nifty trick of reversing the adage that children should be seen and not heard. I've never been in a noisier church, and from time to time, we in the main auditorium were provided video feeds of what the teens were doing. Alas, they came with audio.

On the other side of the complex are the hushed executive offices for the more than 260 full-time and 220 part-time employees and the extensive kiddie care industry complete with guards to make sure Junior is really safe. Over in this wing is a chapel totally void of iconography (I peeked behind the curtain, hoping to see just a glimpse of sacred imagery), counseling suites, and the usual seminar, study, and "breakout" rooms of the various self-help subgroups. Everything is neatly labeled in Helvetica, the floors have the telltale color-coded lines for how to get from here to there, the walls are greenish, the stairs all have no-slip strips, and the whole aura says Mayo Clinic. In fact, this side of Willow Creek looks like a hospital because, as I reflected, that's exactly what it is. There is even rubberized flooring in the stairwells just like the hospital. This is a cultural safe place. I almost expected to see one of those signs with a small child being hugged announcing a Safe Zone.

When the Harvard Business school sent a little cadre of MBAs out to have a look at the operation in 1991, they saw another side of Willow—the financial statements. The MBAs reveled in the numbers: yearly revenues topped $12 million (today it's more than double that), of which barely more than half went to staffing and operations, about 30 percent to operating costs and salaries, 12 percent to debt reduction for the $34 million building, and 2 percent to miscellaneous.

No funds go out of Willow Creek to administrators upstairs. Just the opposite. Funds come to it. While Willow is independent of any top-down denomination, it has expanded sideways into its own Willow Creek Association. The association is a network of more than two thousand churches, each contributing about $200 annually to receive a newsletter, discounts for Willow Creek's list of religious publications, and invitations to pastors' conferences. Clearly its marketing advice is in demand. The average Willow Creek–style church has four hundred worshipers (about four times the national average), but more important it is concerned with growing. Better yet, the affiliates' names are entered into a finders atlas, which shows newcomers which churches will be sympathetic to Willow-esque branding. If this sounds suspiciously like a denomination, so be it. What it really represents is a franchising of the formatted service.

How do the numbers look? In 1995, Willow Creek had $22 million in revenues: $13 million from member contributions; the rest from food sales, the church store, and fees from the Willow Creek Association. The salary for Bill Hybels, the CEO, is comparative chicken feed: about $85,000 and a housing allowance. I'm not a businessman, but these figures are, to business types, otherworldly. Not just what comes in—about $15 a week per person (which is not out of line for churches)—but that so much of what goes out—the labor—is done by volunteers (which is extraordinary). That means a lot of people giving a little money but doing a lot of work for the brand. And there is a steady trickle of new members. What compares with it? The Salvation Army, the Girl Scouts, and various paramilitary organizations of dubious distinction. All in all, concluded the Harvard study, Willow Creek was a tribute to reading the Rosetta stone of the consumers, the "knowing your customers and meeting their needs," being there with the story when the audience was ready to hear it.

How the Brand Works

How does the story get told? Willow Creek works rather like the old Communist Party; the entire enterprise is based on a network of interlinking cells. These cells are the central part of that horizontal organization, how community comes to be. There are the *support groups,* yes, but they are also the narrative nodes. In an analogy worthy of the old party, Lee Strobel, a Willow Creek leader who wrote one of the best-selling books in megachurch literature, *Inside the Mind of Unchurched Harry and Mary,* illustrated the concept by referring to an ad for the Continental Bank of Chicago (now BankAmerica). In the ad we see a huge, impersonal bank with the little boutique bank nestled inside. Continental, the campaign said, was "the big bank with the little bank inside." Willow Creek is a monolith with a lot of miniliths inside. Maybe a better analogy would be the modern department store.

About two thirds of the more than 25,000 worshipers at Willow Creek belong to these small in-house boutiques—more than a hundred of them, some for singles, some for couples, some by sex and age, many by location. The real organizational marketing goes on here, below stairs, as it were. In 12-step fashion, there are support groups galore. There's a group to help *you*. Preabortion. Postabortion. Philanderer or philanderee. Drug recovery. Divorce recovery. Oversexed. Undersexed. Postpartum depression. Prepartum depression. Obsessive-compulsive disorder. Single parent. Single parent with children at home. In addition, there are groups that help you with your finances, your career, your hair, your wedding, you name it.

Presiding over all these cells is the genial paterfamilias, Bill Hybels. Religious explosions like Willow Creek Community Church always depend on a charismatic character who connects the dots missed by other suppliers. What makes Hybels extraordinary is not that he's a compelling speaker (he is) or that he's a tireless organizer (ditto) or that he's amazingly intuitive (ditto), but that he's a branding genius. Stories are not second nature to the brand. They are first. And he knows it. He is absolutely sincere when he says, as he has been saying over and over, "We don't think our success is about marketing. You can't market Jesus." Which, of course, is precisely what he has done. *That's* the story.

Here's how Hybels did it. In 1975, as a twenty-three-year-old, he wondered why so many people claimed belief yet so few went to church. So for eight hours a day, six days a week, for six weeks, he and some members of his youth fellowship went door to door asking questions worthy of George Gallup. The questions flowed into one another so he knew how to follow the concerns of his respondent upstream to the spring of concern. Here's the conundrum he was trying to solve: If so many are self-called Christians, why do so few go to church? Do so many sports fans stay away from the game? Do so many shoppers avoid the mall? Why the disconnect between claim and attendance?

The answer was surprising. The impediment to family faith was, in a word, *men*. They balked. Here's how he discovered this. He started his questions with "Do you actively attend a local church?" If the answer was yes, he politely went on to the next house. Why waste time? If the answer was no, however, he asked, "Why not?" and charted the responses. Here were the common refrains: "Churches are always asking for money." "Church services are boring, predictable, routine, and irrelevant." "All you do is stand up and sit down." "I don't like being shamed." When he could speak just to men, he really found out the secret: men don't like being religious in public. It's not that they are not eager for the epiphanic experience; it's that they prefer it not to be displayed. Promise Keepers, the fundamentalist Christian group that fills football stadiums with men, has been hectored for its sexist policy, but it has understood male reticence. In the company of women, men don't want to be told to sing, to say stuff, or to give anything. They don't like losing control. They like the sense of voluntary activity, of doing something, of questing, exploring the edge on their own.

If there is one marketing secret Hybels learned, it is this: Men are the crucial *adopters* in religion. If they go over the tipping point, women follow, children in tow. The male ants in the food line determine the crowd behavior. But men are exquisitely sensitive to the very thing women seem to like in church—namely, authority. When they have to cede too much independence, they won't budge. And Hybels knew exactly how to comfort them. He gave them a new name. His parishioners were known as *seekers*. And he gave the service a new subject, *felt needs*. "Now let us pray" is not as efficacious as "Join me in prayer," which is not as successful as what I heard at Willow: "I'm going to pray, and you may want to join in."

Hybels took the niche marketing approach a stage further. He even renamed his target. He called his seeker "Unchurched Harry." As the owners of professional sports franchises have learned, if you can hold the men together, keep them feeling that they are important, allowing them to bond with one another while maintaining the sense that everything is voluntary and unforced, they will form a nucleus of furious energy. They commit. Just look at the season ticket prices charged by the major ball clubs, and you can see that this is the inelastic demand of commitment.

Iron John is not an unconsidered term, for men in groups will go through blistering fires to be forged together. These are the guys who charge a hill to blow up a pillbox or drill down a well to rescue someone who is trapped. Men in groups are super potent (and super dangerous). The special men's sections of Willow Creek are called *Iron on Iron*. All right, all right, the forge of Iron on Iron is in reality a group of portly men who get together to talk over breakfast, but it shows how difficult it is to get men to congregate. When women want to talk, they pick up the phone and go out to lunch. When men want to talk, they make a production out of it.

What Hybels understood is that while men may read in private, in public they seem to crave the company of other men. They like it when it's organized for them. So the church has seminars on subjects such as "How a Man Grows in Christ" and "Building Purity"—always without women. Usually the groups meet in clusters of six to eight men, but there are occasional meetings of upward of a thousand. This move from squad to battalion is the key to male affiliation. As the brochure says, Willow Creek is "committed to turning irreligious men into fully devoted followers of Christ" because, as any political leader can tell you, the conversion experience is far more potent for males than for females.

If you want to appreciate Hybels's talent with men, just observe this note sent to the listserve of those lightly affiliated with the church.

From "Bill Hybels" <weekends@willowcreek.org>
To <enews@arrow.willowcreek.org>
Subject Boiling Point—
Date Wed, 2 Oct 2002 143040 -0500

Dear Enews Friends,
Sorry for breaking into your day but I just had an idea that I thought you might be able to help me with. This weekend I will be continuing with my series "Life at the Boiling Point." I will describe how serving people in the name of Christ adds heat to our spiritual lives, and gets us closer to the "boiling point." I

would like to end the message with some true life stories from people who have experienced significant spiritual growth as a result of putting on a serving towel and volunteering in the name of Christ.

Would you be willing to write a brief paragraph describing the spiritual benefits that have come your way since you decided to put on a serving uniform and get into the game? Your story has the potential to inspire many thousands of people. I will protect your anonymity, as well as be sure to give God all the glory in the deal. How about it?

Thanks!
Bill

P.S. Our enews communiqués have had to be one-way up to this point (so that I can do my day job!). But this time I would really appreciate hearing from you, so please just click on reply and let it rip!

There is such a sense of muscular and manly Christianity to this query. The male recipient is being asked to help a fellow in distress, the subtle shift from "putting on the serving towel" to the more manly "serving uniform," the allusion to "getting into the game" and the invoking *teamwork,* as well as the final "let it rip" speaks, to me at least, of guys helping guys. It's hard to resist.

The care of men is one of the most interesting positionings of the megachurch. Young men are, let's face it, a bit endangered in the old-line denominations. It has not always been this way. In the late nineteenth and early twentieth centuries, the average young man used to spend upward of twenty hours a week in the single-sex company of other men. That's what such clubs as the Elks, the Masons, and the Moose, as well as the Grange, were all about. Many of these organizations were church-related. Plus, men would spend almost 10 percent of their disposable income on such things as uniforms, clubhouses, and trips.

These male-only organizations have dried up. That's why such voluntary assemblies of men as deer camps and cigar bars are so interesting to ethnographers. Often men go to such places not to hunt or smoke but because they know they will be in the company of other men. Often the strip club is more a testament to the desire of men to separate from women than to watch women undress. It's why barbecuing is so popular and why golf clubs have been so slow to admit women. Carpooling works for women, not men. If you could promise that *only* men would be in a carpool, perhaps it might be successful. While it may be too simple to say this is a reaction to the women's movement, the male yearning is undeniable. Men hunt in packs. For many men the locker room, the steam room, the hunting shack, and the SUV become places of retreat and relaxation. Sociologists have a term for such male-only places: *loafing sheds*.

When you look at Willow Creek men's groups, you find that along with divorce, self-help, couples counseling, singles groups, ministerial and evangelical clubs, there are places for men to be just with men, loafing sheds. Here are some. Accounting Groups do the books; Campus Operations includes setting up, parking, cleaning, and tending the grounds; a section called CARS takes care of maintaining, detailing, and repairing cars; Faithful and True for Men offers "support and encouragement to men seeking to maintain sexual purity and integrity in a sexually charged world"; Pastor of the Day offers "a listening ear and spiritual direction to those who call or come to church with spiritual questions or concerns." There are also the more predictable Sports Ministry (basketball, volleyball, football, golf, and 5K runs); Men's Ministry (talk about life); Front Door Team (tours and greeting); as well as the essential Production & Programming (sound system, staging, camera, lights). There is also a Cross-Roads group that meets to ride motorcycles.

The sensitivity of Willow Creek to male concerns is at the heart of the brand. Most churches can deliver the redemptive feeling, forgiveness, and salvation. Most penitents are already prepared, as Franklin Graham aptly displayed. Play music and they'll come forward. But few can provide lasting community for men. A poster hangs outside Bill Hybels's office. It says, "What is our business? Who is our customer? What does the customer consider value?" These questions are lifted not from St. Peter but from Peter Drucker, the patron saint of management, and they affirm the reversal of the usual gatekeeper/epiphany-dispenser mentality in favor of a consumer-sensitive response, with a special concern for men.

Conclusion

A brand is a commercial story, a folk tale on the take. Because it's a story, it promises an emotion. As such, it is evanescent, always in the process of being told and retold. It can be easily hijacked, subverted, destroyed, rewritten. As Walt Whitman once said, before there are good stories, before there are poetic tellers, there must be "great audiences." That's because a storyteller is really always dependent on his audience for direction. Like telling children bedtime stories, the teller/bard/pastor/curator/schoolteacher needs to know not just which version they want but which version they are ready for. If he'll listen, they'll tell him. "Tell me about Little Red Riding Hood and this time really describe the wolf," says the maturing child. "Tell me about redemption, except this time forget the fires of Hell," says the modern seeker.

What separates the Willow Creek brand from most of the other megachurches is that its redemption story is so benign and its sense of community is so strong. From a personal point of view, I must say that while I did not exactly come to mock and stay to pray, I did come to observe and stayed to wonder. Can this be done? Can you have a religious brand that does not exclude? After all, the history of great religions is never that they promise to deliver a feeling; they also promise to withhold a feeling. Excommunication of one sort or another is always lurking even in the most benign brand. The other side of Franklin Graham's salvation crusade is the abiding promise (which he makes a number of times) that others are going straight to Hell. The fastest-growing denominations in the United States are the Mormons and the Pentecostal Baptists. Both of them promise hellfire for deserters.

On my last visit to Willow Creek I may have glimpsed the edge. I spent the fall of 2002 at the University of Illinois teaching in the Advertising Department. I was asked to give a talk to the faculty on what I was interested in. So I talked about Willow Creek and what interesting niche marketing it had done. I was met with many arched eyebrows, typical of academics confronting competing institutions. That Sunday (October 13) I returned to Willow Creek, where I had not been for a year. The massive expansion of the church facilities called "Chapter 2" was well under way.

Seeing construction going on is crucial for certain brands, especially when you are focused on growth. Las Vegas, for instance, rebuilds itself every decade—it's a sign of brand affirmation. Build it, and they will come. Just seeing building cranes and derricks along the skyline gives the onlooker a sense of vitality and enthusiasm. But I had a sense at Willow Creek that the recession had occurred at the same time as this rebuilding. I sensed panic. For the only time at Willow Creek that weekend, I heard a plea for money. Here's how it happened.

Entering the church, I saw a large wooden cross on the stage. I had never seen iconography before. The message was titled "Live at the Boiling Point: Heat Through Giving." This series of sermons had begun a month earlier, and had addressed the promise of elevated consciousness as faith becomes more a part of your life. But the earlier sermons had not necessitated this huge wooden cross. Something had happened.

The service began with some members of the band climbing up on a stool and then falling back into the arms of colleagues. That was called "taking the plunge." Then two props were wheeled out onto the stage: a prison cell made of metal tubes and a huge hundred-dollar bill. Here's the argument: Our Lord wants you to be a giving person. That's why he's given you so much. So you should give back. Take the plunge. You can give back by visiting the poor (enter the jail cell). And you can give to the church (go to the huge hundred-dollar bill and fold back just a tenth). But remember what He gave to you (cue the cross). You are not tithing a church; no, you are *repaying* God. Take the plunge. I was not the only one who was shocked. I looked around and saw that others were equally upset. I had never heard this side of Willow Creek before, the upper-television-tier Jimmy Swaggart side. I had assumed that this occurred on Wednesday night. Did Chapter 2 have anything to do with it? Was Bill Hybels checking the P&L statement?

To return to the audience side of the transaction, it was clear that they were shuddering a bit. Maybe the true believers were tired of carrying the freeloaders like myself. As I've just mentioned, part of joining a lower Protestant church is that others will be punished. The congregation may prefer to believe it is coming from On High, but since *it* has to make the sacrifice, there should be a payoff. Somebody should be shamed. No one is shunned at Willow Creek. But this came close.

And it made me think: Can a brand offer a mimic of village life, provide small groups and family clones, have a nice food court and basketball court, let the teens play with the sound system, and have lots of support groups without ever being a stern disciplinarian? Or, to change the analogy slightly: We depend on the law to organize certain human transactions. We consider that law comes from some mythic source. With us, that's the Constitution. The myth of the *ur*-text holding everything together is central to the American brand of jurisprudence. It's not good to believe that it's every judge for himself or, worse, that there is a high degree of uncertainty built into the story. This also true with religion. If we ever countenanced the possibility that man makes his gods in his own image, would we ever give ourselves over to the priest?

Franklin Graham represents the tough-guy approach. Follow me or burn in Hell. Bill Hybels represents the other side. Follow me and find surcease. Can that soft side succeed? Can the benefits of social ties, socialization, good feeling, and compassion carry the day? Is there enough take-away value? Or does he have to invoke the Plunge from time to time? From a historical point of view, the focus on death, moral superiority, and the economies of the closed mind (my way or Hell for you) has carried the power brands from Catholicism through the major Protestant denominations into such offshoots as the Church of Jesus Christ of Latter-day Saints, Seventh-day Adventist Church, and Jehovah's Witnesses. But we know that versions of the story also have been carried to desuetude. Witness the Episcopal plight. No one (except Episcopalians) much cares about it.

What caused the demise of the top-heavy Episcopal system is the same marketing development that is accounting for the new explosion in what is called the megachurch. In my lifetime there has been a massive sea change in demand and supply. One of the first rules of marketing is never, never compete on price. Because there is always someone who can eat less, sleep less, spend less, and provide more than you. When offering an interchangeable product, *always* stay away from price cutting, even if it means you have to eat your inventory. It may be that Willow Creek will rue the day it dedicated itself to the demands of seekers, to the unchurched, to the will-o'-the-wisps who are essentially just passing through, just switching chairs after raiding the refrigerator. Sometimes consumption can be too easy, too passive. Sacrifice is an important generator of value. That's why Evian costs what it does and you have to take out a loan to go to college.

Who knows if this comfy brand of religion lite can do the job and hold the consumers in place? But it's also true that Willow Creek is not just competing with other denominations; it's competing with all other forms of entertainment, especially television. Why shouldn't the seekers hit the remote control clicker? What will happen if competitors offer still more horizontal rewards of community while also providing the vertical payoff of redemption *and* promise the penalties of exile? Beliefs, like purchases, are made to be witnessed, as well as consumed. Willow Creek, however, makes anonymity not just possible but unavoidable. No matter, this much seems clear: The consumerist church, intensely focused on the felt needs of its audience, by using narrative, sophistication, and electronic transmission, can make the process of doing church incredibly compelling. It can gather a huge audience. How long it can hold them remains to be seen.

3.

School Daze

We have an autocracy which runs this university. It's managed. We asked the following: if President Kerr actually tried to get something more liberal out of the Regents in his telephone conversation, why didn't he make some public statement to that effect? And the answer we received—from a well-meaning liberal—was the following: he said, "Would you ever imagine the manager of a firm making a statement publicly in opposition to his board of directors?" That's the answer! Now, I ask you to consider: if this is a firm, and if the Board of Regents are the board of directors, and if President Kerr in fact is the manager, then I'll tell you something: the faculty are a bunch of employees, and we're the raw material! But we're a bunch of raw material[s] that don't mean to have any process upon us, don't mean to be made into any product, don't mean to end up being bought by some clients of the University, be they the government, be they industry, be they organized labor, be they anyone! We're human beings! [Applause]

—Mario Savio

www.lib.berkley.edu/MRC/saviotranscript.html

In the early afternoon of December 2, 1964, Mario Savio took off his shoes and climbed onto the hood of a car. He was a junior majoring in philosophy. He was upset that the administration of the University of California at Berkeley had forbidden student groups to set up recruiting tables to promote various political and social causes. In addition, the administration had arrested a handful of students. So he put himself "upon the gears" of the machine.

For the first time in American academic history, students were in control of a premier university. I was in college at the time on the east coast. But I heard every word Savio said. I was paying attention. Here was the beginning of the cleverly named Free Speech Movement, which spread onto almost every campus in the country. It was a cauterizing moment, truly modern and deeply ironic. The event even had star power and, in a term much praised at the time, *synchronicity*. Joan Baez led a rousing chorus of "We Shall Overcome" and in so doing made going to school somehow analogous to being black.

Savio's point was well taken. The university was nasty business, all right, but it was, before all else, a *business*. Higher Ed, Inc., has since become a huge and very successful business. And, as is typical of absorbent capitalism, it does not deny its struggles as much as market them. Mario Savio died in 1996. To honor his activism and insight, the academic senate agreed to change the name of Sproul Steps, the site of many political speeches, to Savio Steps. In this interesting bit of corporate assimilation, Mr. Savio became a lasting part of his own observations: he himself was branded.

Although Mario Savio didn't mention it, the success story of Higher Ed, Inc., is based foursquare on the very transformation that had allowed him access to Berkeley. Since the Second World War, each generation has found that doors opened wider and wider. Unquestionably, university education is the key component in a meritocracy, the sine qua non of an open market. And increased access to university life has succeeded beyond anyone's wildest expectations. In fact, the current dilemma is the price of success. There is simply too much supply, too many seats, not enough Marios. The boom is over. Now marketing begins.

Counting in everything but its huge endowment holdings, Higher Ed, Inc., is a $250 to $270 billion business—bigger than religion, much bigger than art. And, although no one in the business will openly admit it, getting into college is a cinch. In fact, in 2002 two reporters, Janet MacFadyen and Dick Teresi, wrote a piece for *Forbes FYI* detailing how tough it was to get into a good college. What did they find? "After a few months of digging, we discovered the source

3.

HIGHER ED, INC., IN AN AGE OF BRANDING

of the confusion: Everybody is lying." The problem, of course, is that too many students want to get into the same handful of nameplate colleges, making it seem as though the entire market is tight. It most certainly is not. Here's the crucial statistic: there are about two thousand four-year colleges in this country. Only about a hundred refuse more students than they accept. Most schools accept 80 percent or more of those who apply. The remaining 20 percent of students either are accepted later or decide to postpone or forget about higher education.

The frenzy at the top is creating a marketing nightmare for all. That frenzy is not just caused by anxious kids and their protective parents but is abetted by admission directors at both colleges and high schools. The College Board, ever eager to juice up the SAT stats, goes along for the ride. All parties act in concert to stoke demand. And in so doing they foster the very situation that invokes competitive branding. Marketing 101, Rule 1: Storytelling as differentiation happens when too many suppliers are producing too many interchangeable products and peddling them to an audience too eager to listen.

The Statistics

One can see the explosion in Higher Ed, Inc., from many points of view—increasing enrollment, new construction, expanding statewide university systems, more federal monies, and changes in the professorate. Let's just focus on the last example. The 1950 census reported that there were 190,000 faculty members in the United States. A decade later, when Mr. Savio took to the hood of the car, there were 281,000. In 1970, when I entered the ranks, there were 532,000 and in 1998, the latest figures we have from the U.S. Department of Education, some 1,074,000. Is there another group which has so exploded and at the same time is so unable to shrink? For remember, what distinguishes the academic world is a lifetime hold on employment. Even ministers are eventually furloughed. Museum directors get canned. But make it through the tenure process, and you are there forever.

No one has paid much attention to the intractable bloat at the upper levels of American schooling because there has been so much churning at the entry levels. At the turn of the twentieth century, 1 percent of high school graduates attended college; that figure is now close to 70 percent. This is an industry that produces a yearly revenue flow of some $200 billion, more than six times the revenue generated by steel. Woe to the state that does not have a special funding program (with the word *merit* in it) to ensure that middle-class kids, who graduate in the upper half of their classes, get a pass to State University. Getting a college education is now a birthright, at least to some. It's become what high school used to be.

When you look at the numbers, you can see what's coming down the demographic pike. College enrollment hit a record high of 14.5 million in fall 1998, fell off slightly, and then reached a new high of 15.1 million in 2000. How did this happen when the qualified applicant pool remained relatively stable? Despite decreases in the traditional college-age population during the 1980s and early 1990s, total enrollment increased because of the high enrollment rate of newer students, ones who had previously been excluded.

To protect our market, academic administrators and the professorate essentially lowered the bar and broadened the consumer base. We had to. There were so many of us and our numbers couldn't contract. Rather like the Protestant denominations, we couldn't make Heaven harder to get into; we had to make it easier. So, like commercial marketers, we lowered the price and extended the brand. As we will see, we had help from the College Board, and, for a while at least, state legislators and private donors eager to see us grow.

Why Affirmative Action and Diversity Are So Important

What really has helped Higher Ed, Inc., has been our ability to open up new markets. As Bill Hybels targeted men, so Higher Ed, Inc., targeted women and minorities. Although affirmative action was certainly part of court-mandated fair play, it was also a godsend. It insulated us from the market shocks suffered by other cultural institutions.

If real estate is location, location, location, then higher education is enrollment, enrollment, enrollment. The engine that has until recently turned the gears has been a steady flow of what are called in the trade *FTEs* (full-time equivalents). Enrollment in degree-granting institutions jumped between 1978 and 1988, slowed a bit between 1988 and 1992, slightly declined from 1992 to 1995, and then spurted in the late 1990s. Much of this growth was in what was previously called *minority* (female and racial) enrollment. In addition, we have been able to extend our product line in graduate and professional schools upward. Our current growth market? Foreign students. No one talks about it much, but this market has been profoundly affected by the events of September 11, 2001. They've stopped coming. There are enough rabbits still in the python that we haven't been greatly affected yet. But we will be.

As could be predicted, the economies of scale have rewarded the bulk suppliers. "Get big fast" has been the writing on the blackboard. Despite the sizable numbers of small degree-granting colleges, most students attend the larger colleges and universities. As with the megachurch and the blockbuster museum, the future of Higher Ed, Inc., is clear. In fall 1998, 40 percent of institutions had fewer than 1,000 students; however, these campuses enrolled 4 percent of all college students. Meanwhile, 10 percent of the campuses enrolled 10,000 or more students and accounted for 49 percent of total college enrollment. This is eerily like what's happening at church: half of all churchgoing Americans are attending only 12 percent of the nation's churches.

What makes this explosion interesting from a marketing point of view is that Mr. Savio's observations ("the faculty are a bunch of employees, and we're the raw material") have been confirmed. In fact, Savio's insight may allow us to understand the nature of branding and social institutions when they approach the condition of oversupply. What he didn't appreciate is that instead of eating up raw material and spitting it out, Higher Ed, Inc., has done something far more interesting. As it has exploded, the content of higher education has been profoundly changed; some would say dumbed down, but that misses the point. As with our sister gatekeeper institutions in religion and the arts, at the undergraduate level we are in the business of delivering consumer satisfaction. Thanks to grade inflation, it's almost impossible to flunk out. Room and board have improved drastically. To survive, we imitate our cousins in retail. The commodified product is what I call *status satisfaction,* and the competition to supply it is occasionally fierce.

Where the Money Is Now Being Made in Higher Ed, Inc.

I teach at a large public university, the University of Florida. As I leave the campus to go home, I bike past massive new construction. On my distant left, the student union is doubling in size: food court, ballrooms, cineplex, bowling alley, three-story hotel, student legal services and bicycle repair (both free), career counseling, and all manner of stuff that used to belong in the mall, including a store half the size of a football field with a floor devoted to selling what is called *spiritware* (everything you can imagine with the school logo and mascot), an art gallery, video games, an optical store, a travel agency, a frame store, an outdoor outfitter, and a huge aquarium filled with only orange and blue (the school colors) fish. On a normal day some 20,000 patrons pass through the building. Like the university, the Student Union looks eerily like a department store.

On my immediate left, I pass the football stadium. One side of it is being torn apart to add a cluster of skyboxes. Skyboxes are a valuable resource, as they are almost pure profit. The state is not paying for them; the Athletic Department is. They will be rented mainly to corporations to allow their VIPs air-conditioned splendor high atop the hoi polloi. They have granite countertops, curved ceilings, and express elevators. In the skybox you watch the football game on television. Better yet, the skyboxes allow what is forbidden to the groundlings: alcohol. How expensive are these skyboxes? Well, it's complicated. There are 347 padded twenty-one-inch seats in the Bull Gator Deck. They run $14,000 a person, and you get only four games in the box. The other four you have to take out in the stands. Don't worry about figuring out the math. They are already sold out. The building I teach in is huge and looks like the starship *Enterprise.* It cost $10 million when it was built a few years ago and houses classrooms and faculty offices. These skyboxes are coming in at $50 million. Everyone agrees that the skyboxes are a good idea. They'll make money. Better yet, they'll build the brand.

Across from the football stadium, at the edge of the campus on my right, is the future of my institution. I pass an enormous new building with a vast atrium of aggressively wasted space. This building houses what is the center of much statewide activity: the headquarters of the University of Florida Foundation. This foundation funnels millions of dollars of private money into and through various parts of the university. I don't complain. Nor does the state. No one does. We know what's happening. However, when someone is caught embezzling huge sums, we are all aghast. Two decades ago, the foundation gave nothing to the English Department, but now about a hundred grand a year comes our way gratis. Out in front of the foundation, where a statue of some illustrious donor or beloved professor would stand at an elite school, is a bronze statue of the athletic department's trade-marked mascots, Albert and Alberta Alligator.

On this side of campus, "enrollment, enrollment, enrollment" is becoming "endowment, endowment, endowment." Americans donate more money to higher education than to any other cause except religion. And Florida, with its millions of retirees looking for "memorial opportunities," is a cash cow just waiting for the farmer's gentle hands. The residents of Florida have almost no interest in funding education, especially not K–12, which is in dire shape. But there are wads of money to fund bits and pieces of the campus in exchange for good feelings and occasional naming rights. As I write this, my university is planning a branch of the pharmacy school, to be called the Eckert Pharmacy Education Center of the University of Florida. The Eckert Corporation, a drugstore subsidiary of the J. C. Penney Company, is covering about half the cost.

American colleges and universities raise about $25 billion a year from private sources. Public universities are new to this game, but they have learned that this is where the action is—anywhere but in the legislature. Private dollars now account for about 30 percent of the University of Illinois's annual budget, about 20 percent of Berkeley's, and about 10 percent of Florida's. As tax monies are going elsewhere (not, alas, to where they are needed, K–12), large research universities are fattening up by moving to new fields, such as sponsored research or selling memorial opportunities. If you want autonomy from a whimsical legislature, you do best selling your brand to seventy-year-old donors, not to fifty-year-old legislators and certainly not to twenty-year-old students. To do this you have to change your story. You are selling to a new audience.

In a sense, tuition-paying undergrads are now the loss leaders in this new enterprise. Since the 1980s, student numbers and instructional costs have increased by about 10 percent, the costs of the professoriate by about 6 percent, and those of the administration by 45 percent. This is not bloat; this is the result of realizing where the money is and going after it. What used to be the knowledge business has become selling an experience, an affiliation, a commodity that can be manufactured, packaged, bought, and sold. Don't misunderstand, the intellectual work of universities is still going strong; in fact, it has never been stronger. Great creative acts still occur. Discoveries are being made. But the *experience* of higher education—the accessories, the amenities, the aura—has been commercialized, outsourced, franchised, *branded.* The professional manager has replaced the professor as the central figure in delivering the goods.

Here's How It Works

At second-tier schools, athletics are often the front door to this fundraising. I can't tell you how many times I've heard that "sports is our window to the world." That's the story behind my brand. For instance, the University of Florida receives about $130 million in *voluntary funds,* of which alumni donations account for only about $32 million. Many Floridians either love or hate the Fighting Gators. The lovers are passionate in part because of the haters. To them this is what the brand means. When Steve Spurrier was our football coach, he was derided as being haughty, arrogant, and dismissive. But during his reign, contributions increased. Why? Because he allowed expression of affiliation in much the same way that the New York Yankees gain fans by the obstreperous behavior of George Steinbrenner. Yes, he had a winning team, but he also had a galvanizing personality. He was, as they say, an easy identification. To some people he was an SOB, but he was our SOB.

As I was told by the head of the UF Foundation, Paul Robell, it's often not your alumni who care about your brand; it's the people who wish they could be your alumni. I remember once saying to the acting provost, wouldn't it be nifty if all the schools in our conference dropped the charade of the student athlete and just had students who also played football the way we have students who also play the oboe. I opined that fans would still appear in their orange-and-blue land yachts and still want to buy spiritwear irrespective of the quality of the game. He looked at me and said that tenure had been developed for people who thought like that. And he was right.

At first-tier schools, however, a different story is told. The brand at the winner-take-all schools is exclusivity. Having poor sporting teams sometimes even helps their story, although that has been rapidly changing. In both tiers, however, the money is to be made by franchising affiliation. What used to be a pyramid of mass culture reaching up to the upper levels of higher education has now flopped over into a kind of barbell market in which there is a massive bubble on either side. On one side are the richly endowed schools whipsawed by overdemand, who compete by claiming entering-class exclusivity; on the other side are factory schools with excess capacity, which compete by offering the economies of scale and spectator sports: Tiffany's versus Wal-Mart. In a way it resembles the peaceful kingdom of old-time Episcopalians and megachurch. But the middenominational schools, the schools that are neither big enough nor good enough—small, private, underendowed—are being crushed.

Church and School

The comparison of education and religion may be instructive. In both experiences we exchange a sense of meaning and place for attention and money. Historically, church and school came from the same place. In the eighteenth century they started to split but were still attached—if not at the altar, then in the vestry. They shared personnel, titles, common canon, congregational space, and, most important, a calling to proscribe certain behavior. The clergy and the professorate both came *ex cathedra,* wore black robes, spoke in a special language, and conferred various kinds of credentials. They were both, in a felicitous phrase from theology, "policers of the sublime." They also controlled the rituals necessary to punish and could invoke the penalty of shame, namely, shunning. Excommunication became the denial of commencement: you flunked. But if you passed you were saved—matriculation as secular salvation.

Until recently, matters were nicely divided into twos. Church and school were the teaching institutions: one concerned with sacred and the other with secular; one with the soul, the other with the soma; one preparing for the next life, the other for this one. These two capped-and-gowned arbiters had still more in common. Both callings were for males, and males only—Caucasian males from the middle class, to be more exact. In both cases the calling came from beyond the pale—either from above or from the past. You had your choice: high church or high culture.

It is tempting to say that these institutions have been transformed by a change in constituency: women and blacks have entered the ranks. It would be comforting to think that church and school have become more compassionate, kinder and gentler, more sensitive to the pain of others, because men are no longer in control. But the real upheaval has been in their relationship with their audience. Whereas once their parishioners/students came to them, now they have to go out to gather the audience. They have to, in a word, market a product.

Church and school now make their case not by wielding the shame stick but by promising the edutainment carrot. With some important exceptions (the most glaring being the Pentecostals and the University of Chicago), the dominant institutions now attempt to gather an audience by promising good feelings and fellowship, not fear and trepidation. No fire and brimstone, please. No harsh discipline. No shunning and no failure. Whereas they used to say, "You should be ashamed of yourself," they now say, "Be yourself, no matter what anyone thinks." It's as if Stuart Smalley, who delivers the Daily Affirmations on *Saturday Night Live,* had taken over the postadmissions management of Higher Ed, Inc. As we will see, preadmissions was taken over by the Marquis de Sade.

Once we understand the paradox that it's all about getting *in,* not getting *through,* we will understand, and even accept, such startling developments in the groves of academe as wholesale grade inflation; the outsourcing of services, including most of the teaching and even some of the library services; the selling of space—not just buildings and stadiums but cola-pouring rights and shoe contracts; admission

hijinks such as early admission and "tuition packages"; expensive propaganda such as viewbooks; and the gradual disappearance of need-blind admissions.

You can see this transformation by just glancing at the surface—at what in marketing is called *trade dress* and *wordmarks*. Competitive marketing explains why Colorado State University at Pueblo changed its name to the University of Southern Colorado, Beaver College became Arcadia University, Regents College became Excelsior, Hollins College became Hollins University, and the Penn State/University of Pennsylvania confusion is still a nightmare. Ohio University and Ohio State University have been in court about who owns the Ohio name. Since the experience is essentially fungible, the brand—the literal word—is crucial.

In addition, market pressures lead to Kermit the Frog as a graduation speaker, the appearance of celebrity teachers who don't teach, the University of Houston employing the ad agency McCann-Erickson, the fraudulence of teaching evaluations (and a gradual decline in the importance of teaching), the irruption in many states (starting in California) of admission via complaint, the explosion of state-based preferential "scholarships," and the loss of a shared curriculum. In client-centered transactions it's not what is transferred that's important; it's how the consumer feels about the experience. Hence the elevation—or in cant, *privileging*—of what the student already knows (gender, race, pop cult . . .) as subjects of academic concern. Let's look at some specific venues of this transformation from teaching to marketing to see the effects of branding on Higher Ed, Inc.

The Development Office

The farthest-reaching changes in postsecondary education are not seen on the playing fields or in the classroom or even in the admissions office. They are inside the administration, in an area murkily called *development*. If you don't believe it, go into the administration building of any school that enrolls more than 10,000 students (again, 10 percent of campuses of that size or larger now account for a shade less than 50 percent of all students) and ask for the university development office. You'll notice how in this part of the campus the carpets are thick, the wainscoting is polished, and the lights are dimmed. Often this office has a new name picked up from the corporate model. Sometimes it's hidden inside Public Affairs, or, more commonly, Public Relations. My favorite: University Advancement. At my school some years ago, University Relations was changed to Public Relations. The driving force is now the University of Florida Foundation. This part of administration used to be concerned with how we spoke to one another and to our alumni; now it's concerned with how we present the story of the university to the outside world. In the business world, *development* is called *corporate relations*.

When I asked John Lombardi, erstwhile president of my university and wunderkind of academic branding, for a list of his important accomplishments, he listed *inter alia* the nifty logo, the standardization of letterhead, the uniform signage, the centralization of all PR, and the University Foundation. He was right. Getting all the various parts of the campus—athletic, medical, agricultural, educational, and developmental—to speak with one voice is a triumph. It's like herding cats. Ironically, one of the reasons he was fired was not because he understood how the new university worked, but because he was so candid about explaining it. Forget the legislature; you tell a story, then you make money by renting affiliation with that story. Almost no one on the faculty stood up for him, although many knew he was right. He knew that he could replace his entire teaching staff overnight, but getting a football coach took time. And the head of the foundation was even more important. (Lombardi went on to become chancellor of the University of Massachusetts, Amherst.)

Development is one of the fastest-growing sections of the institution and one of the most important. In both PR and fund raising, it's the intersection of getting the brand *out* and the contributions *in*. Every day this becomes more crucial. That's because schools like mine have four basic revenue streams: student tuition, research funding, public fiscal support, and private giving. The least important is tuition, the most prestigious is external research dollars, the most fickle is state support, and the most remunerative is what passes through the development office. Leaf through *The Chronicle of Higher Education,* the weekly journal of the industry, and you will see how much newsprint is devoted to the comings and goings of this enterprise.

A

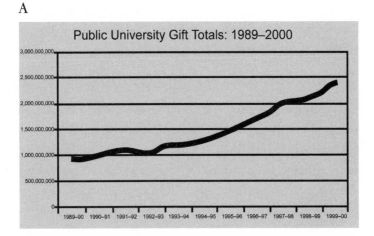

B

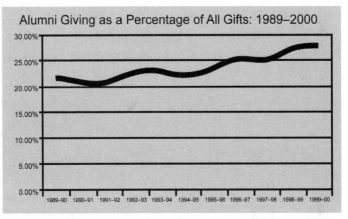

C

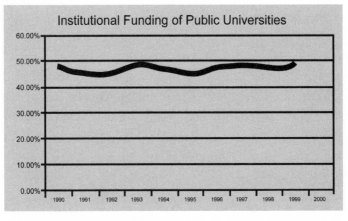

Where universities get their spending monies. (Source: Marts & Lundy, Inc.)

Look at where the development office is housed on most campuses, often right beside the president's office. Look how many people are in there. The boss is a vice president of the university. Ask people in the office if it should be called the Office of University Branding, and they'll know exactly what you are talking about. One informant at a first-tier school told me it's really the LSDM department. When I asked what the acronym stood for, she said, "Logos, Slogans, and Direct Mail." Then ask people in the office what they did before they started doing this. Most of them come from corporate marketing or finance. Ask them how much they get paid. They won't tell you. Frequently they are the largest employer of student labor on campus. Doing what? Telephoning you at dinner time. My favorite product? The marketing of named legacies. At the University of Illinois, for instance, they run from named chair ($1.5 million) to named professorate ($500,000) to named fellow ($250,000), university scholar ($250,000), research fund ($200,000), assistantship ($150,000), lectureship ($100,000), scholarship ($25,000), to simply the generic fund ($10,000). Every school does this.

At many schools there is also a buried pipeline that connects the development office with the admissions office. Most academic administrators prefer that it be buried deep, but from time to time someone digs it up. On February 3, 2003, Daniel Golden of *The Wall Street Journal* reported on how the formal practice of giving preference to students whose parents are wealthy—called "development admits"—has profound implications not just for affirmative action but also for the vaunted academic ideals of fair play. He picked on Duke University in part because Duke has been such an efficient user of this back-scratching between who gives a lot and who gets in. Say what you want; it's been successful in improving Duke's hardly Ivy League endowment. For the last six years, Duke has led all universities nationwide in unrestricted gifts to its annual fund from nonalumni parents. While 35 percent of alumni donate to Duke, 52 percent of parents of last year's freshman class contributed to the university—besides paying $35,000 each for tuition and room and board. In other words, the development office has done a far better job at gathering funds than has the alumni office. Here's how Golden says it happens:

The system at Duke works this way: through its own network and names supplied by trustees, alumni, donors and others, the development office identifies about 500 likely applicants with rich or powerful parents who are not alumni. (Children of major alumni donors are given similar preference in a separate process.) It cultivates them with campus tours and basic admissions advice; for instance, applying early increases their chances. It also relays the names to the admissions office, which returns word if any of [them] forget to apply—so development can remind them.

The development office then winnows the initial 500 into at least 160 high-priority applicants. Although these names are flagged in the admissions office computer, admissions readers evaluate them on merit, without regard to family means. About 30 to 40 are accepted, the others tentatively rejected or wait-listed. During an all-day meeting in March, [the admissions officer and the senior vice president for development] debate these 120 cases, weighing their family's likely contribution against their academic shortcomings.

Remember the scene in the third season of *The Sopranos* where Carmela has a lunch meeting with the dean of Columbia's undergraduate school? She thinks the lunch is going to be about her daughter Meadow, but it seems the dean wants a little development money. Carmela listens to his charming patter before being hit with the magic number of $50,000. She goes to Tony, who tells her that they're being extorted by the Ivy League and that he'll give only 5 G's. Alluding to some other problems, Carmela tells Tony he really needs to do something nice, and finally he reluctantly agrees. As a shakedown artist, he's met his match. The dean gets the cash. The scene works because we all recognize the academic hustle and the barely implied blackmail.

Why the Faculty Is Mum

At one level the corporatization of university life is easy to explain. For a while after Mario Savio, everyone got fat. But once the baby boomers passed through, once affirmative action had filled the ranks, once states had exhausted the financial rewards of continually expanding public education at the upper levels (often at the expense of K–12), and once every housing developer and city planner learned that building anything that smacked of higher ed changed the meaning of space, the inevitable happened. Postsecondary schools were overbuilt. The problem with higher ed is that you can't shrink it. There is hell to pay if you even try to talk about closing down superfluous, or redundant, or even incompetent departments.

Case in point: At the school where I teach, we spend about a third of our departmental money and time on graduate students. There are no university teaching jobs for our English Ph.D.s. A glance at the Modern Language Association job list shows that there are only a handful of entry-level jobs in non–affirmative action spots. The Modern Language Association's own data indicate that only about one in five newly admitted graduate students in English will eventually become tenure-track professors. Even that number may be too high. The number of open English teaching positions fell 20 percent from 983 to 792 in the first years of the twenty-first century and promises to continue to fall as the backlog of supply grows. And only about half of those jobs were tenure track. So the 977 doctorates produced in 2000–2001 will have to compete with hundreds of job seekers from previous years, to say nothing of all the adjunct faculty members who are looking for full-time, tenure-track work. What few jobs there are go to graduates of elite programs, the ones with the brand names.

So why don't we contract the program? In fact, why don't we shutter it until the market for our product improves? No, we expand it, thinking that if we want to be seen as a major university, we have to be *bigger.* We need more heft, we are told. Plus, we like having it. Although we are doing our best to outsource teaching by using our graduate students to do our most important teaching (of freshman writing), the graduate program is still terribly wasteful. But the point is this: would this graduate bloat be happening if truth be told and taxpayers understood what was happening?

Why the Battle for Bulk Has Become So Important

In some ways, schools like mine on the mass-supplier side of the barbell have no choice. From a marketing point of view, we know what happens when fungible suppliers clutter the market. Whether you are peddling bottled water or promised salvation, when you get fungibility, you'll eventually be distinguished via your storytelling. Those stories are brands, and the farthest-reaching development in education in my lifetime has been the competitive branding of higher ed. Although we may call ourselves names such as "the knowledge industry" or "the enterprise of the intellect," we are really in the business of retailing an interesting new product—the emotional credential—to consumers who have been taught to shop around. So far we have done an outstanding job.

The gatekeeper model lasted only as long as supply was tight. It's client-centered for the rest of us. We're ticket takers. An ad for New York University shows a young woman beside the headline "I am the president of me, inc." Meanwhile, Iona College jumps on the bandwagon with "Be the CEO of your life!" Mimicking our cousins in retail—you are what you buy—the promise of higher education is "Get your degree from me and $$ will follow." No one is making a case that Higher Ed, Inc., trains students for real jobs. Just the opposite. At the better mass-supplier schools, the one thing you are not being trained for is actual employment. At community colleges, yes, and at some of the low-ranking mass-provider campuses. So getting big is a protection. In fact, taking a lesson from banks, the goal is to be big enough that no one will let you go under.

What you buy at the premier schools, however, is something quite different. You buy a sense of place, literally *a* place, and the value of the place is determined by who is in the place next to you. You are buying, as they say, seat time en route to the next step: professional school. The elite school is protected by staying small and hard to enter. The diamond at Costco is the same diamond as the one at Tiffany. The baby blue box is different. You can give the rock away, but you protect the box.

One of the most intriguing products sold by the elite suppliers is called *peer effects*. The distinction is not made on the basis of curriculum, physical plant, sporting teams, teaching, or any such traditional marker. On this side of the barbell, rank is based on selectivity. That's why *U.S. News & World Report* rankings have become so wildly important. Don't ever let the amount of noise about how good

I am the president of me, inc.

At NYU's School of Continuing and Professional Studies we offer a unique learning environment with more than 2,000 different courses, each taught by today's real world professionals. And our students are the kind of people who know where they want to go – and know what it takes to get there.

We also understand what it takes to accommodate a busy schedule, so we offer classes days, nights, and weekends, at convenient times and locations. We even offer courses online through The Virtual College.™

Climbing your own corporate ladder? Start here.

· **Global Politics: Entering a New Era**
· **Finding Your Career Directions**
· **E-Marketing Seminars**
· **Chinese, Spanish, Arabic**
· **Digital Medical Illustration and Animation**
· **Hospitality Management**
· **Intensive Directing Workshop**
· **Philanthropy**
· **Screenwriting**
· **Designing Meetings and Events Websites**
· **Publishing Online**
· **Real Estate Opportunities and Techniques**

For a bulletin listing all our courses:
Phone: 1-800-FIND NYU, ext 34
Website: www.scps.nyu.edu/me
E-mail: scps.me@nyu.edu

NEW YORK UNIVERSITY
School of Continuing and
Professional Studies

The school as factory, the student as product, the graduate as ta-da! CEO.

IONA
*Profiling
Success*

"Be the CEO of your life!"

Al Kelly BA '80/MBA '81
American Express, Group President,
Consumer and Small Business Services

Major: Computer Information Systems/MIS

My greatest inspiration: I'd have to say it's my wife, whom I first dated at IONA and my four wonderful kids who inspire me every day.

Why IONA? I've always had a great level of respect for the Christian Brothers. Their teachings are in my blood and they constantly challenged me to broaden my perspective and approach any situation from all sides.

What makes it special: When you're there, you realize IONA has created a stimulating and comforting atmosphere that is truly student centered. The end result is the absolute best educational experience you could have.

To be the CEO of your life, call 800-231-IONA today.

Aspire. Achieve.

IONA COLLEGE
715 North Avenue, New Rochelle, NY/www.iona.edu

Celebrating 200 years of Christian Brothers' Education.

schools hate the rankings fool you. They depend on them. And peer effects are why the top universities either deeply discount or even give away their product in order to be assured that the entering class is the most select (not necessarily talented) they can find. They are the baby blue box.

Branding 101: How the Pyramid Became the Barbell

As enrollments exploded in the 1960s, what used to be a pyramid system with rich, selective schools at the top (read Ivy League and a handful of others) and then a gradation downward through increasing supply and decreasing rigor until it petered out in the junior and community college system, became a barbell, or an hourglass lying on its side. There is now a small bubble of excellent small schools on one side, really indistinguishable from one another, and a big bubble of huge schools on the other side, of varying quality. Since the most interesting branding is occurring on the small-bubble side as premier schools vie for dominance, that's where I'm going to focus. But the process is almost exactly the same for the big-box suppliers, albeit less intense.

The first matter to note is that good schools have little interest in the bachelor's degree. In fact, there's a direct ratio: the better the school, the less important the terminal undergraduate degree. The job of the student is to get in, and the job of the school is to get the student out into graduate school. The job of the elite schools is to certify that their students are worthy of further education in law, medicine, the arts, or business.

Premier schools have to separate their students by generating a story about how special they are. That's why good schools care little about such hot-button issues as grade inflation, teaching quality, student recommendations, or even the curriculum. These schools essentially let the various tests—the LSAT, the MEDCAT, and the GRE—do that kind of work for them. And, if you notice, they never divulge how well their students do on these tests. They have this kind of information, but they keep it to themselves. They're not stupid. They have to protect the brand for incoming consumers because that's where they really compete.

Elite schools are not threatened by what we on our side of the barbell fear—the much-ballyhooed "click" universities such as Phoenix and Sylvan Learning Systems—because these schools generate no peer effects. So too there is no threat from corporate universities such as those put together by Microsoft, Motorola, Ford, or even England's Open University and the Learning Annex. These industrial schools have not yet made their presence felt—but they will. The upper tier on the small side of the barbell is also not threatened by "learning at a distance" or "drive-through schools" because the elites are really not as concerned with learning per se as they are with maintaining selectivity at the front door and safe passage to still higher education at the back door.

The For-Profit School: Almost Brand-Ready

The University of Phoenix poses an interesting threat to the mass-supplier campuses not just by its service (all you need is a 56K modem, Internet access, and an e-mail account) but by its audience. The online school now accounts for more than 50,000 students, many of whom come from a market previously untapped: working people. Students are taught by some 7,000 faculty, most of whom have full-time jobs elsewhere. Tenure? No such thing. The University of Phoenix has stripped faculty members of their central role in higher education and replaced them with instructional design consultants. The American Association of University Professors has balked at granting accreditation, but it's a feckless position. After all, mainline universities have online courses that count toward degrees, so why shouldn't online schools offer mainline degrees?

Compared with community colleges and state universities, the University of Phoenix, for instance, is a pricey alternative. One of its most popular degrees, the MBA, retails for about $25,000, almost double what you'd pay at State U. Some spoilsport critics contend that the school takes in millions of federal student loan dollars that could go further in helping minority students were they spent at less expensive public institutions. No matter; once Phoenix is recognized as a going concern, as a brand, it will succeed. The school has been growing at about 70 percent a year, and if the price of its publicly

The University of Phoenix has more trouble finding qualified faculty than paying students.

traded stock is any indication, it has a bright future. Why? Simple: it claims to place 80 to 90 percent of its graduates in jobs within three months. Compare that with your Megauniversity and Unemployed Junior, and you may see the future.

Thanks to government-insured loans, the day is almost at hand for one of these "for-profit universities" to make its way through the clutter by aligning itself with an extant school and gaining real distinction. Here Phoenix may run into stiff competition. For instance, Disney has teamed up with Valencia Community College as well as the California Institute of the Arts, and the Detroit "big three" automakers have joined forces with the Michigan university system to form

Michigan Virtual Automotive College. In both cases, these schools draw faculty and talent across lines into private enterprise. The number of such pure busine-versities are exploding, from about four hundred fifteen years ago to more than two thousand today. You don't hear about them, but you will.

The temptation to give up the charade and join the corporate world is hard to resist. After all, if you use the model, why not reap the profit? Schools already have a toe in the water when they create chairs called the Yahoo! Professor of Computer Science or the Kmart Professor of Marketing. Sometimes the line is crossed because a university can't bring an innovation to market, and so it partners with a private corporation. For instance, Stanford University banks millions in royalties from inventions as disparate as synthesizing music or the technique that underlies genetic engineering. In so doing, however, Stanford is weaving its future in unpredictable ways. Acting in a businesslike way often leads to thinking like a business, making choices in terms of making money. MIT is getting $25 million from Microsoft as part of a partnership to develop educational technologies. Columbia University reported royalties from commercial licenses of $129,895,000 in 2001. Nobody used to pay much attention to this cross-pollination, but it is growing like Topsy as schools are realizing they can "marketize" their expertise and companies are realizing they can essentially rent schools to do some of their research and training. As Derek Bok, president of Harvard from 1971 to 1991, notes in *Universities in the Marketplace: The Commercialization of Higher Education,* it was during his tenure that schools started to move what they had learned about franchising athletics to renting out other parts of the campus, especially the medical schools. When a drug company promises to underwrite a cardiology department, even Harvard has trouble saying no. When a sneaker company promises to publish your syllabus, who can resist?

All right, it's doubtful that Yale Inc. or Harvard Corp. will ultimately give up the arm's-length charade and sell shares to the public. But not so with State U. The nonelites are especially at risk because they sell a product, not an experience, and that makes them vulnerable to the siren song of what looks like free lunches for all. While the good schools sell selectivity, the rest of the producers are sensitive to anyone who may lend a hand and a fistful of money. So what can mass-provider State U. do? Ironically, not much other than continuing to do more of exactly what they did that got them into this mess; namely, keep on bulking up, hoping to benefit from the economies of scale and the generosity of dangerous strangers.

The Classification Game: How It Happened

How did universities divide themselves up into pricey boutiques and huge department stores? How did the groves of academe become canyons of industry? With the rise of higher education in the late 1940s, institutions sorted themselves out into a dozen or so categories ranging from research universities to comprehensive campuses to private liberal arts and community colleges. By midcentury, the famed Carnegie Corporation tried to name and classify all the various forms of higher ed. These distinctions were to be based on academic mission, not marketing niche, and Carnegie thought this was important because it would make the distribution of funding logical and fair. You could save time if you knew that Such-and-Such U. was dedicated to the future of science and technology while This-and-That College was interested in undergraduate teaching.

Carnegie would build a taxonomy to resolve ambiguity. Ironically, the reverse happened. Carnegie developed four different categories of research and doctoral institutions, which they have now collapsed into just two. From the start there were problems. Programmatic anomalies such as having Boston College, Caltech, and the University of Idaho in the same grouping were an embarrassment, but you can see from the philanthropy's point of view how such a system was worth the price. Carnegie was trying to be objective and fair. But once it put the categories into place, it essentially forced the schools to become interchangeable suppliers—and that, as we know from observing the soap aisle, leads to competitive branding. Those low in the cohort have to generate narrative differences in order to distinguish themselves.

Wannabe schools allocated resources to be sure they had exactly what was needed to be considered a member of a higher subset. It's not important from a teaching perspective to draw a line between a school that grants, say, fifty Ph.D.s in only twelve disciplines from one that grants the same number in fifteen disciplines, but it is exactly those lines that separate Research I institutions from Research II schools. How ironic that as Carnegie was trying to make distinctions for such matters as foundation and government funding as well as for bond-rating services, it was also forming the template necessary to remove differences. The University of This State was becoming a lot like the University of That State. I remember hearing serious conversations in the 1970s that all we needed to do at the University of Florida was get hold of the budget of the University of Michigan and copy it. Thus began a slipstreaming in which schools isolated the top of their cohort and essentially said, "I'll take whatever they're taking."

And, from a marketing point of view, it was precisely this taxonomy that was hijacked by *U.S. News & World Report.* To fit into the proper classification, universities dropped programs and eccentricities that set them apart. The magazine then essentially made the similarities the basis of their concocting minute differences. If you didn't fit a simple category, like Reed College for instance, you got lost in the shuffle. Anxious customers went along for the ride—after, of course, buying the magazine. So in a way, the schools asked for exactly the treatment they got. They were branded whether they wanted to be or not. The second-tier schools, such as my university, were really squeezed. We claimed we were offering unique products, but we were all scurrying around to make sure we were not. In other words, in order not to miss out, we dismantled whatever singularity we had and did exactly what we should have avoided—namely, we became just like everyone else.

Meanwhile, there were better systems of ranking schools, but they lost out on what in marketing is called the *first-to-market advantage.* For example, the National Center for Postsecondary Improvement at Stanford has devised a more appropriate taxonomy:

- **Brand-name campuses:** These are the highly selective, high-status schools whose allure is that they are what they claim to be, names to conjure with. They are separated not by Ivy League or by conference, but by depth of story. Hence Berkeley, Duke, Amherst, Stanford, Harvard, and even NYU are in this slot. They act like a religious denomination—high church, as it were—immediately recognized not just by true believers but by the general public. They have a pronounced and easily decoded social standing. They are name brands, literally, and that is how you know them. The name is not "University of California at Berkeley"; it's just "Berkeley." Ditto Chapel Hill. UCLA is the acronym and the school name, as is Virginia's UVa or Washington's UW. The universities of Michigan and Illinois are simply called by their state names. Students are called first friends and then donors. Allegiance is deep. The value is not intramural but extramural, not in the experience but in the shared perception of others about the experience. Acceptance is crucial, yes, but denial is more important because the value in these schools is in exclusivity.

- **Mass-provider campuses:** Here are the hundreds of schools enrolling millions of students granting diplomas in factory fashion. Move 'em through. Second-tier state universities and perpetually anxious private schools keep one eye on the bottom line and the other eye on generating flow-through. The names are usually not shortened. It's the University of Florida, not Florida. Worse: it's the University of Florida at Gainesville. It sells credit hours. Convenience is all. Athletics are central because they are one of the few ways of generating brand distinction. At these schools the football coach *should* make more than the university president, because he is adding more to the brand. Commonality is the key to efficiency. Students are FTEs (full-time equivalents), and acceptance is usually by some kind of numerical system, such as being in the top 10 percent of your graduating high school class.

- **Convenience institutions:** Here is a mix of public, nonprofit, and proprietary institutions whose promise is exactly what the elite schools never mention: employment. Beauty school and truck-driving school are the pure forms. Students are customers, pure and simple. Convenience means cheap. But ironically here the curriculum is taken seriously because it matters. An employer asks if you have certain skills, not if you attended some named school.

From a survivalist point of view, the fault line in Higher Ed, Inc., lies right down the center of the mass-provider campuses and accounts for much of what has happened. Do anything, but don't end up too deep in the middle category or you'll go under. Paradoxically, it sometimes makes more sense to continue to fund hopeless endeavors such as graduate schools in the humanities than run the risk that you will be demoted into competing with the convenience suppliers.

What Happens to the Marginal Provider?

If you are a lower-echelon mass provider, you are forever in marketing limbo. You can never really take chances. First, there is the never-ending pressure to fill seats. As I wrote this in summer 2001, about three hundred mass-provider schools were still looking for students to fill up seats that fall. Which schools? According to the National Association for College Admission Counseling (NACAC), the list includes such mass providers as Georgia State, Colorado State, Eureka College in Illinois, and Marquette University. These are very different schools, but they all have the same problem: the baby-boom "echo" is not loud enough. There are not enough women, minorities, or foreign students clamoring to get in. The schools are good, but their brands are anemic. If you look at their acceptance criteria, you will see that they accept nine out of ten applicants, which essentially means that they exclude an insignificant number, a number made even less striking when you realize that some of the excluded were not planning to attend even if accepted.

Anyone who doesn't think there is a serious oversupply of university classroom space should check the Web site of the NACAC (www.nacac.com). It's an education in brand manipulation. If you ever wonder how the high school college counselor just happens to know which school Junior should be applying to after he's been refused repeatedly, here's how. Every May 1, member schools report to NACAC's Space Availability Survey. This date is significant because applicants who have received acceptances from colleges and universities have to decide by this date. After May 1, colleges and universities know if they are fully booked. The word as to where space exists then goes forth from NACAC's Alexandria, Virginia, headquarters to more than 7,900 school counselors, independent counselors, college admission and financial aid officers, enrollment managers, and other organizations that work with students. At this level of Higher Ed, Inc., there's a lot of excess capacity.

Admittedly, not all schools respond. Why should the premier ones cooperate? They're perpetually overbooked, thanks to their marquee brands. But of the 338 institutions of higher education (220 private and 118 public) that responded to the survey in 2002, 91 percent reported freshman space available. Nearly all (99 percent) of respondents reported space available for transfer students. Financial aid was still available at 94 percent of responding institutions, while housing was available at 88 percent of responding institutions. What do these schools have in common? They are relatively small. They usually have fewer than 10,000 students. But note this: they are not bad schools—just schools with no story.

Small private schools with little endowment are in perpetual distress. All they can hope for is the lucky death of a generous and not very savvy benefactor. As ridiculous as it is to give to an overendowed school such as Harvard, it is equally ridiculous to give to a small private school—that is, unless it is a brand-name school in the Williams-Amherst-Wesleyan-Claremont-Oberlin category. The no-name small schools are going under. You can bank on it, which is why banks don't. They can't expand because they can't float bonds because they are too small to expand: Catch-22, higher ed style.

While the good state schools subsidize their product with all kinds of state-based subventions that attempt to keep in-staters at State U., and the few rich private schools can do it with endowments, the small privates can't cope. So these schools often end up as convenience institutions with special dorms for single mothers or even day care. Or, more likely, they fold. And they do so in a particularly terrible way, in slow motion. It's here that tenure is being dismantled. Just give us one more year, pretty please, say the retiring faculty.

At least 27 of the nation's 1,600 private colleges closed between January 1997 and 2002—a 35 percent increase from the previous five-year period. Often this has nothing to do with the quality of service. Often they are doing an excellent job. The problem is not that Mom-and-Pop University can't compete with Wal-Mart U. on the basis of quality. It's that these small schools can't command the brand power to charge even baseline prices. Good schools *want* to discount prices; it often makes them more illustrious. But mediocre schools *have* to discount; they have no choice lest they tumble into the convenience school category.

Second, the product offered by the low-range mass provider is increasingly recognized as dubious. What used to be an article of faith—namely, that a bachelor's degree from Anywhere U. promised an economic advantage—is no longer the case. True, a degree from a prestige institution was worth every penny that it probably didn't cost (thanks to its usually discounted price). But it's iffy that you'll come out ahead if you receive a B.A. from one of the middle-level suppliers and pay the full fare. Once everyone has the same credential, a new separation degree is needed. Hence the explosion in such markers as graduation with honors, with departmental honors, with distinction, cum laude, magna cum laude, and notifications such as "honors in research," which means you wrote a paper, as well as entire new degrees, such as the MBA, or the surge in advanced teaching degrees, such as the MAT.

Here's what happens: as the average diploma from an institution with little name recognition loses economic value, competition stiffens for entry into prestige universities. Hence the bimodal distribution of attendance, with elite institutions at one end, convenience schools at the other, and the middle levels struggling to make a name for themselves. The Neiman-Marcuses and Price Clubs both will do fine in their market niches. Sears and Penney will be adrift in red ink. Montgomery Ward and Spiegel go under.

It is precisely this barbell market that has transformed not just retail (*adiós*, Kmart; hello, Costco) but suppliers of other cultural capital as well. We have seen the same horizontal hourglass in religion, in which the traditional denominations languish on one side (*adiós*, Presbyterians) while the aggressive suppliers of high-takeaway values thrive on the other (hello, megachurch). The intense innovation and attention to customer satisfaction occurs as schools follow luxury retailers in realizing that it is in their self-interest to continually push to the upper edge of their niche lest they become subsumed in the interchangeable world of middle—or worse, fall into the land of the no-names.

The Elites Have Their Own Arms Race

So what's it like at the upper end where Harry Winston competes with Tiffany, where Louis Vuitton elbows Prada, where Lexus dukes it out with Mercedes? What's it like among the deluxe brand-name schools? In a word, it's brutal. In some respects, it's worse in a marketing sense than for the mass suppliers. What looks like eternally overendowed and underutilized resources is instead the battleground of a winner-take-most contest described by some as an academic arms race. In fact, in two words, it's brutal and stupid. And it's not going away.

In 2002, one of the more curious stories was how the Princeton Admissions Department had hacked into Yale's admissions files. *Hacking* was really a misnomer, for all the Princeton admissions officer did was check on eleven students who were thought to have applied to both schools. He figured that Yale would not use passwords when social security numbers would do, and he was right. But it's not that he did it or that it was so easy to do; it was that the competition is so fierce in the luxe market that just a glimpse of what Yale was doing was enough to alert Princeton to the package it would have to offer to capture a few customers.

How did the competition become so intense? How did these customers get to be so important? Until 1991, the Ivy League and MIT met around a conference table each April to fix financial aid packages for students who were admitted to more than one school. That year, after the Justice Department sued the schools, accusing them of rampant antitrust violations, the universities agreed to stop the practice. Rather like Major League Baseball after the television contracts made the teams rich, bidding pandemonium broke out. Finite number of players + almost infinite cash = market bubble.

Here's the staggering result. Over the last three decades, especially recently, tuition at the most select schools has increased fivefold, nearly double the rate of inflation. Yet almost nothing can be seen for this price explosion. The money is going somewhere, yes. It's essentially going into paying a small number of players exorbitant salaries, and I'm talking not about the faculty but about the students. Go to an Ivy League school, and you'll see precious few students paying the full fare. The war is fought over who gets in and how much they are going to have to be paid to attend.

Admittedly, there are a number of other reasons for this inflation. Brand-name schools are getting incrementally better departments as they compete for top rankings. When queried, the brand-name schools usually invoke some variation of Baumol's disease, the observation made by William Baumol of NYU that productivity gains in service industries such as education tend to lag behind those in manufacturing. Tweak the astronomy department to jump a few notches in the *U.S News* ratings, and you find a flood of subsidiary expenses caused by library funding, personnel, and even in other departments.

The simple fact of the matter is that tuition price has become unimportant in the Ivy League. Now, like grade inflation, it's uncontrollable, and no one really cares. As with other luxury providers, the *Veblen effect* takes hold, and willy-nilly the higher the advertised price, the longer the line. Ask yourself this question: Could you sell Evian water at 20 cents a bottle? Could you sell a Harvard education if it were priced below $20,000? As Thorstein Veblen first noted in *The Theory of the Leisure Class,* sometimes the retail price in luxury goods works in direct proportion to value. Keep the value the same, but increase the sticker price: strangely, the value increases. This is a characteristic of the exotic and the luxurious. In brand jargon it's called the *Chivas Regal effect,* and nowhere does it work better than in Higher Ed, Inc.

The other nifty irony is that here among elite schools the more the consumer pays (or supposedly is charged), the less of it he gets. The mandated class time necessary for a degree is often less at Stanford than at State U. As a general rule, the better the school, the shorter the week. In many good schools, Friday classes have gone the way of what used to be Saturday (morning) classes. The weekend starts on Thursday. Often the putative reason for the shorter week is some special event like a field trip that was once taken but now is no more. But the real reason is that there is no reward for the top-line schools to cut costs or enforce class time requirements. They make up their own rules. Demand is essentially inelastic, and value is achieved by super-selecting consumers and then essentially paying them to consume. That's how you know you've gotten to the Land of Deluxe. A Prada baguette handbag retails for $2,000, costs a few hundred dollars to manufacture, a few hundred more to market, and holds less than the one you get at Kate Spade. But that's just the point.

Harvard: Top Dog in the Brand Kennel

Ask almost anyone in the education industry for the most overrated brand, and he or she will tell you "Harvard." This is one of the most timid and derivative schools in the country yet it has been able to maintain its reputation as the *über*-brand. Think of any important change in higher education from Mario Savio and free speech, to affirmative action, to multiculturalism, to women's studies, to cultural studies, and the one thing you can say is that (1) it didn't happen at Harvard, and (2) if it's central in popular recognition, Harvard now owns it.

When Harvard's president, Lawrence Summers, has a problem with Cornel West, it's national news. Other schools have had the problems of not knowing what African-American Studies was about and how to treat faculty whose work was unconventional, but only at Harvard does this make the nightly news. When its English Department invites a poet who has slurred the Israelis to come to read a few poems to a handful of people, *The New Yorker* carries an article about it. Harvard's grade inflation problems are well known, when in truth the problem is all over higher education. When Harvard students go on strike for custodial pay and working conditions, it's front page; when it happens at Yale, it's inside news. When an administrative board at Harvard decides not to hear alleged sexual misconduct cases unless there is "sufficient" evidence, it is national news. At other schools, it has been old news for a while. A phallic snow sculpture in Harvard Yard is commentated on. At Dartmouth winter carnival, it's ho-hum. Summers was on the cover of *The New York Times Sunday Magazine* (August 24, 2003) not so much because of doing anything different but because he's not Mr. Congeniality. Don't get me wrong, it's not that such subjects are not important; it's that only when they occur at Harvard do they become *really* important. Harvard is the megaphone of American education. When those in Cambridge whisper, the rest of us cup our ears to hear.

Harvard is synonymous with the ne plus ultra, the end of the road, the home of the best and the brightest. But why? Because although very little of importance comes out of Harvard, a great deal goes in:

namely, the best students, the most money, and, most important, the deepest faith in the brand. Everyone knows that Harvard is the most selective, with a refusal rate of almost 90 percent. But more important, the school is obscenely rich, with an endowment of almost $20 billion. Never forget that number. It's key to the brand. The endowment is greater than the assets of McDonald's, the GDP of Ecuador, the net worth of all but five of the Forbes 400, or the holdings of every nonprofit in the world except the Roman Catholic Church. This school is so rich that it was national news when an influential group of alumni suggested that if the school would just use competitive bidding it could save as much as $225 million annually. In a marketing sense, the value of the endowment is not monetary but psychological. Any place with that many zeros after the dollar sign has to be good.

Why would people give money to Harvard when they know they are getting almost no bang for the buck? Because endowment is at the heart of the power of a brand. It defines everything. In the late eighteenth century, some French economists seriously proposed that every twenty or so years all institutions should put their monies back into the pot and start again. Doing this once a century might well be a tonic to Higher Ed, Inc. This might be salutary not just because, in a sense, the rich get richer but because the rich are anathema to education. It is the huge endowments of the nameplate schools that force the other schools, the second-tier schools, to spend themselves into penury. Ironically, your gift to Harvard, in a marketing sense, does more harm than good to the general weal of Higher Ed, Inc.

It does, however, maintain the Harvard brand. When Interbrand, the worldwide advertising conglomerate, assembled the most powerful brands in the world, Harvard was the only school included, ranked with such names as Coke, Kodak, and Kellogg. In *Brands: An International Review*, the agency says about the depth of Harvard's brand as it migrates to the markets of the world:

> *Harvard's brand licensing program is particularly interesting. The items which the University will license include sportswear [excluding protective headgear], scarves, desk accessories, watches, jewelry, school supplies, etc. Those they will not license include ashtrays, shot glasses, butane lighters, weapons of any kind, food and beverages.*

No other university is able to make such distinctions because no other school has such brand power. When Interbrand looks for Harvard's cohort, it places it in a telling context; it goes into the world of leisure and culture. However, the Harvard brand also belongs in the luxury category, among Chanel, Rolex, Louis Vuitton, Rolls-Royce, and the Ritz Hotel.

Why Is the Harvard Brand So Powerful?

In the summer of 2001, I went to Cambridge to find out how this brand had gotten to be so powerful. On one level the answer is simple. Harvard's been around for a long time. It has what in marketing is called the *pioneer advantage*. It got there in 1636, well before number two, William and Mary, and more than half a century before Yale and all the other Ivy League schools. But the real reason Harvard is the ruling story of American education is because it never stopped, even for a second, telling everyone that it was Harvard. The school has taken great care in knowing not just how to tell its story but how

LEISURE & CULTURAL								
BRAND	LEADERSHIP	STABILITY	MARKET	INTERNATIONALITY	TREND	SUPPORT	PROTECTION	TOTAL
BARBIE	O	O	□	□	□	□	●	□
BERLITZ		O	□	O	⊡		●	O
CLUB MED	O	□	□	□	□	O	●	□
FINANCIAL TIMES	O	●	□		□	□	●	O
FISHER-PRICE	□	O	□	□	□	□	●	□
HARVARD		●	●	□	□	O	●	O
HILTON		O	□	●	□	O	□	O
HOLIDAY INN	O	□	□	●	□	O	●	□
LEGO	□	□	□	●	□	●	●	□
MATCHBOX	O	□	□·	□	□	O	●	□
MONOPOLY	O	□	O	O	O		△	O
PLAYBOY	O	□	□	□	O		●	O
READER'S DIGEST	□	●	□	●	□		●	□
SCRABBLE	O	O	O	O	□		□	O
STEINWAY	□	●	□	O	O		●	O
TRIVIAL PURSUIT	O	O	□		O	O	●	O
VOGUE	O	□	□	O	□	O	●	□
WALT DISNEY★	□	●	□	●	●	□	●	□

KEY ★★ Top Ten brand ★ Top Fifty brand ● exceptionally strong □ very strong O strong △ problem area

Harvard is one of the world's greatest leisure and culture brands, at least according to the Interbrand Group.

to make sure no one else edges on to its turf. It also knows when to shut up and let others do the talking.

I went to see Sara Wald, who is one of a cadre of lawyers who oversee what Harvard says about itself. She is also in charge of the literal colophon: color, badge, and motto. As is typical of Harvard, she is called not a "lawyer" but the Assistant Provost for the President and Fellows of Harvard College. If you ever try to use the Harvard name, the crimson color, or the Veritas badge without asking, Ms. Wald will want to have a little talk with you.

The Harvard Corporation controls every possible use of the Harvard wordmark. Outside the school, it copyrights each instance of every use. More important, it controls every mention inside the school as well. So if you are a Harvard professor and you think that it would be nifty to publish a little magazine, or if you have a news story, or if you want to have a conference and you are thinking of invoking color, crest, initial, or name, think again. This place speaks in one voice, and that voice is the voice of Father Harvard. No other school has taken such pains to make sure that its brand is univocal and unambiguous.

As an example, Ms. Wald told me that when Jane Fonda wanted to give $12.5 million to establish a Center on Gender and Education (to put forward the sometimes questioned views of Carol Gilligan, at that time a celebrated professor in the School of Education), Ms. Fonda shrewdly insisted that the new center have "Harvard" in its name. Harvard resisted but finally gave in. "When Harvard takes a step, it's noted," Ms. Fonda rightly said. But what she really meant is that if you can get Harvard to take a step for you, you're golden. So even though Ms. Fonda later withdrew half the donation, saying the school was dragging its feet, she had already harvested its value. Harvard, in Harvard fashion, said that it was returning the money because of "new rules regarding research centers." Perhaps it also realized that it had been too lenient in diluting the brand.

When a Web site called notharvard.com went on line to sell class notes, the assistant provost for the president and fellows was on the case. The use of *notharvard* was doing the brand "irreparable harm." In fact, the school argued in court, the Web site acted to "cheapen and tarnish the esteemed HARVARD mark." The judge agreed. When an HMO had the temerity to call itself Harvard Pilgrim Health Care, the crimson

No other university is able to make such distinctions because no other school has such brand power. When Interbrand looks for Harvard's cohort, it places it in a telling context; it goes into the world of leisure and culture. However, the Harvard brand also belongs in the luxury category, among Chanel, Rolex, Louis Vuitton, Rolls-Royce, and the Ritz Hotel.

Why Is the Harvard Brand So Powerful?

In the summer of 2001, I went to Cambridge to find out how this brand had gotten to be so powerful. On one level the answer is simple. Harvard's been around for a long time. It has what in marketing is called the *pioneer advantage*. It got there in 1636, well before number two, William and Mary, and more than half a century before Yale and all the other Ivy League schools. But the real reason Harvard is the ruling story of American education is because it never stopped, even for a second, telling everyone that it was Harvard. The school has taken great care in knowing not just how to tell its story but how

LEISURE & CULTURAL								
BRAND	LEADERSHIP	STABILITY	MARKET	INTERNATIONALITY	TREND	SUPPORT	PROTECTION	TOTAL
BARBIE	○	○	■	■	■	■	●	■
BERLITZ		○	■	○	■		●	○
CLUB MED	○	■	■	■	■	○	●	■
FINANCIAL TIMES	○	●	■		■	■	●	○
FISHER-PRICE	■	○	■	■	■	■	●	■
HARVARD		●	●	■	■	○	●	○
HILTON		○	■	●	■	○	■	○
HOLIDAY INN	○	■	■	●	■	○	●	■
LEGO	■	■	■	●	■	●	●	■
MATCHBOX	○	■	■	■	■	○	●	■
MONOPOLY	○	■	○	○	○		△	○
PLAYBOY	○	○	■	■	○		●	○
READER'S DIGEST	■	●	■	●	■		●	■
SCRABBLE	○	○	○	○	■		■	○
STEINWAY	■	●	■	○	○		●	○
TRIVIAL PURSUIT	○	○	■		○	○	●	○
VOGUE	○	■	■	○	■	○	●	■
WALT DISNEY ★	■	●	■	●	●	■	●	■

KEY ★★ Top Ten brand ★ Top Fifty brand ● exceptionally strong ■ very strong ○ strong △ problem area

Harvard is one of the world's greatest leisure and culture brands, at least according to the Interbrand Group.

to make sure no one else edges on to its turf. It also knows when to shut up and let others do the talking.

I went to see Sara Wald, who is one of a cadre of lawyers who oversee what Harvard says about itself. She is also in charge of the literal colophon: color, badge, and motto. As is typical of Harvard, she is called not a "lawyer" but the Assistant Provost for the President and Fellows of Harvard College. If you ever try to use the Harvard name, the crimson color, or the Veritas badge without asking, Ms. Wald will want to have a little talk with you.

The Harvard Corporation controls every possible use of the Harvard wordmark. Outside the school, it copyrights each instance of every use. More important, it controls every mention inside the school as well. So if you are a Harvard professor and you think that it would be nifty to publish a little magazine, or if you have a news story, or if you want to have a conference and you are thinking of invoking color, crest, initial, or name, think again. This place speaks in one voice, and that voice is the voice of Father Harvard. No other school has taken such pains to make sure that its brand is univocal and unambiguous.

As an example, Ms. Wald told me that when Jane Fonda wanted to give $12.5 million to establish a Center on Gender and Education (to put forward the sometimes questioned views of Carol Gilligan, at that time a celebrated professor in the School of Education), Ms. Fonda shrewdly insisted that the new center have "Harvard" in its name. Harvard resisted but finally gave in. "When Harvard takes a step, it's noted," Ms. Fonda rightly said. But what she really meant is that if you can get Harvard to take a step for you, you're golden. So even though Ms. Fonda later withdrew half the donation, saying the school was dragging its feet, she had already harvested its value. Harvard, in Harvard fashion, said that it was returning the money because of "new rules regarding research centers." Perhaps it also realized that it had been too lenient in diluting the brand.

When a Web site called notharvard.com went on line to sell class notes, the assistant provost for the president and fellows was on the case. The use of *notharvard* was doing the brand "irreparable harm." In fact, the school argued in court, the Web site acted to "cheapen and tarnish the esteemed HARVARD mark." The judge agreed. When an HMO had the temerity to call itself Harvard Pilgrim Health Care, the crimson lawyers were there to make sure it didn't happen. A beer company in nearby Lowell brewed Harvard beer, but only for a short while. When a South Korean school attempted to call itself Harvard English Academy and a Japanese school attempted to use Harvard Cram School, they were suitably discouraged. The Harvard Corporation is even trying to trademark the graduate programs as well as the medical school and the law school curriculum, so that class material, even in student note form, cannot be published for profit. Although it's been rumored that many people have asked the provost's office to please get Alan Dershowitz to refrain from using his academic affiliation when he's introduced on endless television chatter shows, he knows better.

How and Why Schools Advertise

With the possible exception of Harvard, the really good schools are essentially as interchangeable as the second-tier ones. All premier schools have essentially the same teaching staff, the same student amenities, the same library books, the same wondrous athletic facilities, the same carefully trimmed lawns, the same DSL lines in the dorm rooms. Their geographical locations differ, yes; they may have slightly different missions, management, ideology, size, curriculum, church affiliation, and whatnot, but in the main they are fungible service suppliers. They are brand-ready by necessity if not by desire.

Look at the Web sites of the most selective schools, and you will see almost exactly the same images irrespective of place, supposed mission, church affiliation, et al. True, they will attempt to slide in some esoteric fact such as, if you are using our library you may well notice that we have a Gutenberg Bible or that the nuclear accelerator is buried beneath the butterfly collection, but by and large they are quite like the soap aisle at Safeway.

If you really want to see the indistinguishability of the elites, find some National Merit Scholar and monitor the paper tsunami that comes cascading through her mailbox in the early spring. Most elite schools mail about ten items to various groups—rising juniors, rising seniors, various prize winners, and class rank holders—as well as to guidance counselors. Of this paper torrent of "permission marketing," the newest genre is bigger than a prospectus and smaller than a catalog—it's the so-called viewbook. The viewbook sets the brand—or at least that's the claim—so it's worth looking at.

At one level, the viewbook is just a glossy come-on that most schools now produce at a price of more than $100,000 (between $2 and $10 a copy!) a year. As with the Web sites, what you see in almost every "view" is a never-ending loop of smiley faces of diverse backgrounds, classrooms filled with eager beavers, endless falling leaves in blue-sky autumn, and lush pictures of lacrosse, squash, and rugby (because those sports imply an intimacy and distinction of people who know that football, basketball, and baseball characterize the mass-supplier brands)—and, most important, a voluntary collection of students whose interests are *just like yours.*

At the upper levels of academic marketing, no one takes chances. These luxe providers are just like Gucci, Fendi, and Prada. They all have the same heavily inscribed purses, scarves, and key rings. But go a bit lower, and chances are taken. Of all the Web sites/viewbooks I've seen, only schools such as USC, Reed College, Hobart and William Smith Colleges, Harvey Mudd, and MIT are the least bit daring. They are like Target, caught between Saks Fifth Avenue and Wal-Mart. Often these schools are daring because they have a particular problem they have to address. Ironically, they have too much distinction of some sort, so they use viewbooks to tone it down. Here, have a look at USC, a party school trying to be serious, or Hobart and William Smith Colleges, a good school in a difficult location. Both use the viewbook to resettle the brand story.

From a branding point of view, the viewbook is additionally interesting because here one sees how repeating a claim is the hallmark of undifferentiated producers. In ad lingo, it's called the unique selling proposition, or USP. However, once a school catches on to it, others quickly follow. Here's what Nicolaus Mills, an American Studies professor at Sarah Lawrence, found a decade ago just as the viewbook was starting to become standardized. Each school had the same glossy photographs proving its same claim to diversity:

> *What this idealized picture means in 1990 begins with the college code word of the 1980s—diversity. "Diversity is the hallmark of the Harvard/Radcliffe experience," the first sentence in the Harvard*

The viewbook not just confronts the stereotypes but exploits them: USC and Hobart and William Smith Colleges turn weakness into strength.

UNIVERSITY OF SPOILED CHILDREN?

A favorite stunt of rival football fans from UCLA, Stanford and Cal is to wave their car keys and credit cards in cadence as the Trojan Marching Band as it plays "Tribute to Troy," a march our opponents love to hate. This amusing ritual is meant to symbolize their contention that USC is the "University of Spoiled Children."

If you have heard the myth promoted by students at other colleges that USC's student body is rich and spoiled, consider this:

• USC has one of the world's largest financial aid budgets; over 60 percent of our students receive assistance.

• The average family income of students at California's flagship public universities is higher than the average family income of USC students (source: California Student Aid Commission).

• Over 60 percent of USC students volunteer in community service programs in neighborhoods around campus and throughout L.A. On the other hand:

• The student-to-faculty ratio is 14-to-1;

• The average class size is 26;

• Full-time faculty teach the vast majority of our courses;

• Students can get all the classes they need in order to graduate in four years;

• USC grads get jobs, attend the best graduate and professional schools in the country (including our own) and are supported by the Trojan Family, a network of nearly a quarter million alumni.

So, maybe we do spoil our students— and we intend to keep it that way.

USC

Study Abroad

the Expert with a Global World View

W

145

University register declares. "Diversity is the virtual core of University life," the University of Michigan bulletin announces. "Diversity is rooted deeply in the liberal arts tradition and is key to our educational philosophy," Connecticut College insists. "Duke's 5,800 undergraduates come from regions which are truly diverse," the Duke University bulletin declares. "Stanford values a class that is both ethnically and economically diverse," the Stanford University bulletin notes. Brown University says, "When asked to describe the undergraduate life at The College—and particularly their first strongest impression of Brown as freshmen—students consistently bring up the same topic: the diversity of the student body."

Such linking of fad and fashion with a school is not without occupational hazard. Like their colleagues selling soap, university brand managers often show a kind of mindlessness about their task that is inadvertently revealing. You can watch them staking the claim almost as if they were selling light beer. "Tastes great." No, "Less filling."

Misleading or not, recent glossy college recruitment catalogs have been filled with such clichéd pictures that resemble Benetton billboards. The problem is, as Benetton found out, that politically correct concerns are by their very nature unstable. You see this when a brand backfires. The University of Wisconsin admitted that it had inserted the face of a black alumnus into a picture of an all-white crowd at a football game on the cover of a viewbook. At the University of Idaho a graphic artist altered a photo of two students that appeared on a university Web site, replacing their heads with the heads of black and Asian students, and at Auburn University in Alabama, an ethical debate cropped up over the school's practice of purposely including more black students in viewbook photos than can be expected to be seen on campus. As is typical of fungible suppliers, in each case the schools were attempting not separation from cohorts but inclusion. In this kind of marketing, Higher Ed, Inc., is like the crowd in *Monty Python's Life of Brian.* Graham Chapman as Brian, mistaken for the Messiah, exhorts the crowd of devotees, "Don't follow me! Don't follow anyone! Think for yourselves! You are all individuals!" To which the crowd replies in perfect unison, "Yes, Master, we are all individuals. We are all individuals. We are all individuals."

If your school is really desperate you can always try to do what corporations sometimes attempt: advertise your way into Brandville by brute force. It usually backfires. The schools are anxious, and it shows. The problem is that since we never see the elite schools do it, other than in occasional ads for various summer schools, we assume that doing so is to admit you are desperate for customers or trolling for whimsical donors. Most advertising budgets would be better spent paying National Merit Scholars to attend. Look at these ads from *The New York Times* and *The Wall Street Journal:*

Savvy marketing or a waste of money?

147

How Did U.S. News & World Report *Get to Control Higher Ed, Inc.?*

This surplus of interchangeable suppliers is the context in which to appreciate one of the most spectacular acts of brand hokum in higher education—the *U.S. News & World Report's* annual "America's Best Colleges" issue. Forget the content for a moment; what this magazine franchise shows is that if you yourself are in a market of interchangeability (the newsmagazine) and if you are an also-ran (behind *Time* and *Newsweek*), you had better find a niche and mine it. Just as *Money* magazine mysteriously locates a totally different list of ten cities in its "Best Places to Live" issue and *People* magazine discovers a different "50 Most Beautiful People" each year, so too does *U.S. News* rank schools. Like most of the entertainment industry, magazines are in the business of gathering a crowd to sell to advertisers. The magazine content is the means, not the end. Higher Ed, Inc., is their content. And the crowd is to die for: intelligent, deep-pocketed, hyperanxious, and not willing to settle for last year's issue.

Since its inception in 1983, this issue not just raises a yearly firestorm but makes a pot of money for real estate developer and publisher (New York *Daily News)* Mortimer B. Zuckerman, who is sole owner. The school ranking is one of the few profitable things *U.S. News* does. That's why *U.S. News* brings out two main versions and then a handful of specialized issues during the year as well as a stand-alone book. And that's why these two issues have almost twice the circulation of the typical issue.

The college issue is an example of a symbiotic brand; it depends on the uniformity of other brands to survive. The education issue is a brand remora. Little wonder the magazine has applied the same formula to such other suppliers of fungible services: "Best Graduate Schools," "Best Values" ("Get the most for your money at these great schools with great prices"), "America's Best Hospitals," "Best College Sports Programs," and the once-remunerative "Best Mutual Funds." One look at the categories, and you see the intimate connection between interchangeable goods and the market for narrative differences.

What makes the branding of Higher Ed, Inc., a bit more complex is that it appears so rational. Of course, as I've mentioned, if consumers were truly logical, they would think of a product they wanted, go to the library and get *Consumer Reports,* then buy the best-rated version of the object. When you go to the grocery store, you would see just a few brands of toothpaste, a few shampoos, a few brands of dog food. Clearly, this doesn't happen. But in higher education that is precisely what we do. We read a certain magazine. Nothing comes close. And this accounts for the amazing stability of the top schools. While we like to see them moved around a bit, we don't want them churned up.

Take a trip to a library or Barnes & Noble, and you'll see an explosion of almost identical surveys. These surveys are uniform in their mimicking of the rankings. Their only difference is that they proclaim a unique point of view, a USP. Here are the *U.S. News* wannabes:

Princeton Review: The 300 Best American Colleges
The Fiske Guide to Colleges
Peterson's Guide to Four-Year Colleges
The College Handbook (The College Board)
Barron's Profiles of Colleges
Looking Beyond the Ivy League
Barron's Best Buys in College Education
How to Get into College (Kaplan/Newsweek)
Peterson's Competitive Colleges
The Best Buys in Higher Education (Times Books)
The Best College for You and How to Get In (*Time* and the Princeton Review)
American Universities and Colleges (ACE)
Money Magazine's College Issue
Choosing a College (Sowell)
The College Comparison Guide
The National Review College Guide
Lovejoy's College Guide
Insider's Guide to Colleges (*Yale Daily News*)
The Right College (Arco)
Making a Difference College Guide
The GIS Guide to Four-Year Colleges
Lisa Birnbach's New and Improved College Book
Comparative Guide to American Colleges (Cass and Birnbaum)

And this is to overlook the specialized guides that come from *Kiplinger's Personal Finance* magazine ranking, as well as the business school rankings of the *Financial Times, Forbes,* and *Business Week.* Even *The Atlantic,* usually above the fray, joined the ranking ranks. Such profusion of similar guides says three things: ingredient differences inside specific cohorts are minimal, customers are hyperanxious, and *U.S. News* has created the dominant brand in branding schools. Like Harvard, it got there first—the *pioneer effect*—and, like Harvard, it clearly protects its brand by subtly encouraging the churning of its competition. After all, the best the others can be is not quite Harvard, not quite *U.S. News.*

I've never met an academic administrator who didn't love to hate this issue of *U.S. News & World Report.* Read what Richard Beeman, dean of the College of Arts and Sciences at the University of Pennsylvania, had to say on the op-ed page of *The New York Times.* It's a commonplace of those that rank well:

> *When the* U.S. News & World Report *annual rankings of undergraduate programs at American colleges and universities appeared this week, I breathed a sigh of relief that my university continued to appear among the top 10 in the "national universities" category. But I certainly felt no joy upon the appearance of the annual rankings, for, like so many college administrators, I believe these rankings are flawed in their conception and pernicious in their effect on prospective students and their parents. . . .*
>
> *Even if the methodology were foolproof, the very idea that universities with very different institutional cultures and program priorities can be compared, and that the resulting rankings can be useful to students, is highly problematic. But perhaps even worse is that the rankings further exacerbate the rampant consumerism that is now so prevalent among entering students and their parents, encouraging an attitude that admission (and payment of tuition) to one of the "top 10 schools" is somehow a guarantee of a "top 10 education."*
>
> *Rankings both underestimate the amount of work it takes to get a college education and overestimate the importance of a univer-*

*sity's prestige in that process. In that way, they may do consider-
able harm to the educational enterprise itself.*

What the dean does not say is that in a way he is responsible for creating the hole that *U.S. News* fills. The rating issue exists precisely because of the absence of self-evident, intrinsic differences inside each
cohort. The schools have worked to remove those differences. Those
"institutional cultures and program priorities" are kept to a minimum
lest such eccentricities detract from the rankings. He also neglects to
point out that his school had been a perennial laggard in the Ivy
League and made up ground by being one of the most aggressive users
of early decision, a contrived method to improve yield figures.

For the elite schools, ED, as it is known, is marketing nirvana. If you
are a senior and promise to attend the school that accepts you, the
school graciously reciprocates by pushing admission forward so you find
out in December rather than April. Sounds great for the student, right?
No messing with extraneous applications. No preemptive refusals. You
can get some sleep. And so can your parents. But it's far better for the
schools. They are the ones who rest easy. By the end of autumn they can
fill up to one third of their slots with motivated (read full-paying) and sophisticated students. Their yield figures jump because they will get almost 100 percent acceptances. Remember, the kids promise to attend.
They are outcasts if they don't. Or so the schools trumpet. Of course, the
kids privy to these kinds of shenanigans are precisely those middle-class,
high-achieving kids who are going to attend the elite schools anyway. In
fact, this is essentially a new version of legacy acceptance, as a dispro-
portionate number of alumni children apply.

Although some of the Ivys have repudiated ED, Penn is currently its most vehement defender. If administrators wanted to destroy these rankings, all they would have to do is separate their
school from the common herd by establishing real differences—or,
even easier, refuse to submit data. But like sheep the schools patiently line up, submit their mildly massaged numbers, then wait to
be sheared and branded by the magazine. Then they bleat. "Oh,
how we hate these rankings," they moan as they furiously struggle to
best their cohorts.

There is no doubt that the newsmagazine's issue highlights the difference between the brand-name schools and the mass providers, but that's only because such a difference really exists. Remember the image of the barbell. But the guide does little to illuminate differences within the two classes. Yet the illusion of difference influences not just applications but also donors' contributions and, even more important for the also-rans, credit ratings for bond issues. This framework might have real consequences if the rankings stayed frozen. Some good schools would lose out, but thanks to the ceaseless churning, it's really a zero-sum game. Every few years a hot school cools and a cool school gets hot. But rarely, if ever, does a school on one side of the barbell make the big jump across into the other category. The top twenty has not budged in decades.

Ironically, the criteria—the very things no one really cares about—are revealing. U.S. News chooses such things as SAT scores, endowment, size and growth, the achievements of entering students, student retention, graduation rates, faculty pay, and number of Ph.D.s employed. It also includes (and bloats to an amazing 25 percent) the opinions of 4,200 college and university presidents, deans, and admissions directors, who rank peer institutions. Pleeease! does anyone think that those opinions are not tainted with unenlightened self-interest? Why would anyone believe them? Newsweek even reports that there is a flood of mail among administrators designed to influence this crucial judgment. So Elisabeth Muhlenfield, president of Sweet Briar College, reports getting a letter from Hobart and William Smith Colleges announcing its speaker series, while Middlebury College happens to send a book of campus photos unbidden.

The criteria also include rates of alumni/ae giving, which is why your phone rings at dinnertime with calls from some sophomore at your alma mater asking you not to give a lot but to give anything at all. That's because the amount doesn't matter to U.S. News; the percentage of giving does. A donation supposedly indicates a happy customer. But does it mean an educated one? A challenged one? Do you know who is the biggest employer of students on most large campuses? The phone bank of the development office, from which the kids are making those calls.

Although many of the methods used by Higher Ed, Inc., to build brand value (massaging the yield by refusing qualified applicants who are likely to go elsewhere, using early acceptance or early decision to increase the illusion of selectivity, and invoking the category called *value added,* which predicts graduation rates—as if they were important) are now at least murkily understood by the consumer, from time to time *U.S. News* comes forward with a real howler that shows what's going on behind the curtain in Oz. For reasons that have to do with making sure the schools get jumbled up (lest the consumer settle for last year's issue), the magazine decided to privilege a category called *expenditure per student.* This criterion covered how much money goes to fund the equipment used by each typical student. So what happened that year, 1997? Caltech shot up to number one. Number two? MIT. Why? Simple. The big-ticket, high-tech items for these schools gave them a huge advantage even over such schools as Yale and Harvard, which have small engineering departments. Caltech spent $74,000 per student for lab equipment; Yale spent $45,000. Needless to say, the next year the criteria were rejiggered so that the Heavy Iron schools could assume their rightful places.

The Jewish "Problem"

Although it's fun to blame the magazine, sometimes it's the schools that do strange things. Occasionally the rush to be branded has unintended and curious consequences. Here's an example. In the old-style, nondiversity world, where getting into Groton meant getting into Harvard, certain groups of high achievers, such as Jews, had their enrollment capped. In the modern world, the world driven by SAT scores and industrious achievement, Jews are in demand. In fact, as a group, they improve your numbers. So while only about 2 percent of the general population is Jewish, more than 22 percent of Ivy League students are.

In the spirit of these ecumenical times, a few years ago *U.S. News* started reporting about religious diversity on campus. They consulted the College Board, which drew data from the SAT bubble-in boxes. What did they find? *Mirabile dictu:* Jews are at the elite schools. Since having a Jewish population is now perceived as a brand necessity, schools like Vanderbilt have had to scurry to increase Jewish presence on campus. In a front-page article, *The Wall Street Journal* reported on Vanderbilt's bizarre problem and its more bizarre solution. This school, once a popular destination for southern Jews, had seen its Jewish enrollment dwindle from about 8 percent in the 1970s to about 3 percent. That's the second lowest Jewish enrollment among the nation's top twenty-five universities. Only Notre Dame, a Jesuit institution, has a lower percentage of Jewish students.

But what was especially important was that Vanderbilt lagged behind two of its main rivals in its cohort, Emory University in Atlanta and Washington University in Saint Louis. In part this is because of lower average SAT scores. Vanderbilt stands at number twenty-one in the 2001 list, three spots behind Emory and seven behind Washington. At least 35 percent of Washington students and about 30 percent of Emory students are Jewish. What to do? Recruit Jews to Nashville, Tennessee.

Because of its genuine regional nature, almost a quarter of Vanderbilt freshmen identified themselves as born-again Christians, nearly twice the average proportion as at elite private universities. If the desire for more Jews were ecumenical, that would be one thing. But it's not. "Yes, we're targeting Jewish students," Chancellor Gordon Gee told the local affiliate of Hillel, the Jewish campus organization. "There's nothing wrong with that. That's not affirmative action. That's smart thinking." Mr. Gee, who left the presidency of Brown University for Vanderbilt (and a big pay raise) in 2000, says that niche marketing to Jewish students is part of his "elite strategy" to lift Vanderbilt to Ivy League status. "Jewish students, by culture and by ability and by the very nature of their liveliness, make a university a much more habitable place in terms of intellectual life," the *Journal* quotes him as saying.

No matter how strange and curious the machinations of the evaluators or the evaluees are, the fact remains that none of these shenanigans would be happening if schools spent time and energy *really* differentiating the product, as Richard Beeman contends he so badly wants to do. Vandy is a unique school trying to efface differences but only in the service of improving its rank. Ironically, as we have seen, when suppliers make themselves and their services interchangeable, exactly this kind of trumped-up fictionalizing will occur. Rather like steers mooing and pawing the ground, Higher Ed, Inc., patiently stands in line, submits the yearly numbers, eats what it is fed, and waits for a crafty newsmagazine to stamp "premium grade," "flank steak," or "hamburger meat" on its public flanks. In a way, they get the treatment they deserve.

The Study the Schools Don't Release

When I was interviewing Alvin Sanoff, the second managing editor of the ranking issue of *U.S. News,* he started to chuckle about how the schools could easily put the ranking institutions out of business. The schools know how they stack up according to their own customer surveys. After talking to a number of academic administrators, I've since found out it's not a secret, but it's in no one's self-interest to promulgate what he or she knows. Remember how academic administrators howl when the issue comes out? That is, they howl once they see all their counterparts scampering around, trying to pump up their relative positions. For years, the Pew Foundation has been supporting a National Survey of Student Engagement, called NSSE but pronounced "Nessie." This produces data about the "takeaway value" of the educational experience from the point of view of the graduating student.

In one of the few candid assessments of the branding of Higher Ed, Inc., Robert L. Woodbury, former chancellor of the University of Maine system, explains the folly of the current rankings. In the thoroughly refreshing "How To Make Your College No. 1 in *U.S. News & World Report* . . . and Lose Your Integrity in the Process," he points out what seems so obvious:

> *When* Consumer Reports *rates and compares cars, it measures them on the basis of categories such as performance, safety, reliability and value. It tries to measure "outputs"—in short, what the car does.* U.S. News *mostly looks at "inputs" (money spent, class size, test scores of students, degrees held by faculty), rather than assessing what the college or university actually accomplishes for students over the lives of their enrollment. If* Consumer Reports *functioned like* U.S. News, *it would rank cars on the amount of steel and plastic used in their construction, the opinions of competing car dealers, the driving skills of customers, the percentage*

of managers and sales people with MBAs and the sticker price on the vehicle (the higher, the better).

All administrators agree that "exit" data are much better than "entry" data. But schools have this information! The magazine would use it if it could. Sanoff and others have asked for it. Why can't they get it? The schools in the study—some 617 of them and mostly the cream of the crop—will often not let the information become public. Why? They say that such student information cannot be made public because it's confidential.

Balderdash! If the students were told the information was going to be made public, they wouldn't bat an eye. In fact, they would *want* the information made public. They could have used it themselves when they were planning to go to college. Clearly, the elite schools don't release this information because it would have a profound effect on the top twenty schools rankings. The better the students, the harsher the comments. I've taught the same course to random undergraduates and to honor students. The honor students invariably complain more. They have higher standards not only for themselves but for me. And while we are on this subject, why does no school publish the test scores of its graduates: LSATs, GMATS, GREs, MCATs? Wouldn't those numbers be more revealing than SAT scores?

What Good Schools Sell Is Sell-Back

What the schools on the elite side of the barbell have to produce is an entering class that is not just the best and brightest they can gather, but one that will demonstrate an unbridgeable quality gap between themselves and the schools on the barbell's other side. They need this entering class because it is precisely what they will sell to the next crop of consumers. And it is this annuity that gives them financial security. In other words, what makes Higher Ed, Inc., unique and unlike other industries is that its consumer value is almost entirely based on who is consuming the product. At the point of admissions, the goal is not money. But it will be. The goal is to publicize who is getting in. That's the product. In Economics 101 this is called *peer effects.* The person who sits next to you generates value. In a sense, this is just an extension of what in advertising is called *celebrity value*.

Here's how it works from a marketing point of view: since there is a finite supply of talented students, the best schools must first establish brand dominance. This leads to what Gordon Winston, codirector of the Williams Project on the Economics of Higher Education, calls "an arms race," fought yearly to make sure your school prevails. In Professor Winston's words:

> *Competition among schools is, after an enrollment threshold, competition for student quality. Among selective schools, warm bodies—applications—are of interest because they translate into student quality by allowing selectivity in admission; indeed, those schools restrict enrollment* in order *to be able to be selective on student quality.*
>
> *Colleges and universities care about student quality—about who they sell their education to—primarily because of the (strange) "customer-input technology" by which higher education is produced: those who buy the product also supply the college with a primary input into its production in the form of student peer effects. A student's education will be better the higher the quality of the students with whom she is educated. (It's as if the Taurus you bought would be a better car ride, get better gas mileage and hold the road better—the better were the other people buying cars from that dealer. If they were Grand Prix drivers, your Taurus would become a Mercedes.) This is not a production process we're widely familiar with, but it's one that's long been understood at some level by those running colleges and universities—and those choosing them.*
>
> *So the quality of the education that any college produces will be improved if it can be sold to better-quality students.*

Since value depends not on intrinsic characteristics as much as on who is buying, a good school is advantaged by exploiting customers' *merit*, not *need*. But how to pay for this competitive largess if tuition is not the income spigot? At four-year private colleges and universities, fully three quarters of all undergraduates get aid of some sort. In fact, 44 percent of all "dependent" students—a technical term that refers to young, single undergraduates—with family incomes of $100,000 receive aid. What elite schools lose on tuition, they gain back elsewhere. Take Professor Winston's school, for instance. While the average school spends about $11,000 a student and takes in just $3,500 in tuition and fees, Williams, a superbrand, spends about $80,000 and takes in net $22,000. Why? Because Williams figures that to maintain its brand value, to protect its franchise, it can superdiscount fees and make up the difference with future cash flow into endowments, gifts, and perhaps even some government funding. Here's what the breakdown looks like:

Category	Cost per Student
Capital costs	$20,000
Faculty salaries and benefits	14,300
Financial aid	8,100
Room and board	5,900
Libraries and technology	5,300
Buildings and grounds	4,900
Administration	4,000
Athletics	2,400
Other (research, alumni relations, health services, etc.)	15,100
Total	**$80,000**

Professor Winston makes a telling point when he says, "A college is a firm that acts simultaneously like a car dealer and a church—it sells its product but does so at charitably subsidized prices that don't really cover production costs." But it gets curiouser and curiouser as the school gets higher and higher rankings. Conceptually, if an elite school could get the right student body, it would be in its best interest to give the product away: no tuition in exchange for the very best students. This approach is not without risk, as Williams recently found out when its credit rating was lowered by Moody's Investors Service in 2003 after it dipped too deeply into its endowment to fund its extraordinary incoming class.

Aspiring second-tier schools in almost the same cohort with really deep pockets mimic Williams with their undergraduate education, with varying short-term results. Emory University and Rice University, savvy beneficiaries of bulging endowments in the 1990s, have come very close to charging zero fees in exchange for upping their selectivity ratios. In the early 1980s, Trinity University in San Antonio bid for its place by offering free tuition to all National Merit Scholars. With freshman SAT scores averaging 1400 and more than 5,000 applications for 544 slots, Williams has promised to freeze tuition, room, and board at $31,520. But who cares? That figure is academic, both literally and figuratively. What counts is: Will they cap the tuition aid packages? No way. The aftermarket stakes are too high.

If you have plenty of time and curiosity, you can mine university Web sites for revealing data about this arms race. Schools often report the percentage of students receiving aid. The problem is that the number doesn't distinguish between loans and grants, or between federal money (which isn't considered in calculating the discount rate) and university money. But many of the sites also list the size and number of grants the schools offer and the qualifications—grade averages, arts accomplishments, and intended majors—which makes nosing around a bit intriguing. They are almost begging you to negotiate with them—that is, if you are in the top percentiles. If your numbers are really good, you are worth more to them than they are to you.

Sometimes a site will really spill the beans and show you the pressures a university is currently under. At the DePauw University Web site, enter an SAT or ACT score, a grade point average, and a class rank, and a computer program will immediately tell you what kind of "award" the college will offer. A student with an SAT score of 1020 and a 3.25 GPA, for example, will get $3,000 off the top. With a 1200 SAT and a 3.75 GPA, the award grows to $10,000. You're not going to them; they are going to you.

And sometimes you can see the brand pressures by watching the positioning battles fought between schools for shelf space. Look at Manhattan: there Columbia and NYU are waging a classic branding battle, complete with shades of the battles between Coke and Pepsi or McDonald's and Burger King. In the economics departments, these schools are acting like Cold Warriors, each laying in supplies of $300,000 professors like ICBMs. When a brand war gets down to a twosome—and that is what almost inevitably happens in a brand war—the also-rans can get run out of town if they are not careful. Think RC Cola or Burger Chef.

In 2003, Mark Levine, a frequent contributor to *The New York Times Magazine,* wrote a piece on NYU's mastermind, John Sexton, new president and self-styled "mythmaker." Levine reports that he asked Sexton whether or not the enterprise might be considered just "an elaborate marketing strategy, a way of selling NYU by positioning it as a hipper alternative to the better heeled schools with which it wishes to compete for talent and money." "Exactly!" Sexton shouted and then continued:

> *I think branding is just another name for the story we tell of ourselves, and I want our story to be told. Yes! Mythology, salesmanship, branding—it's all the same thing. There's a pejorative sense to that word* branding, *but there's a sublime sense as well. NYU had no mythology. We had no way of knowing who we were, what we were here for. The greatest power of a university president is to be the Homer of the community.*

Pity poor City University of New York (CUNY). In a desperate attempt to get back into the running with its more savvy brand brethren it had to start an expensive new honors program to pump up selectivity: free tuition, a laptop computer, $7,500 in an academic expense account, tickets to theaters and museums, special seminars, and personal academic counseling. In 2002, more than 2,500 students applied for the 235 slots on five of the CUNY campuses. The 743 students CUNY accepted had average SAT scores of 1325, about 135 points higher than the regularly admitted students. The program costs the publicly funded school about $1.2 million a year. This would never happen if NYU and Columbia were not in town, slowly but methodically eating CUNY's lunch—that is, what lunch CUNY hasn't already squandered with its profligate admissions policies.

Essentially, CUNY had no other choice lest the onetime "Harvard on the Hudson" slide down to convenience-level school. Its ill-advised open admissions program wrecked its numbers and reputation, to say nothing of the curriculum and teaching staff. All CUNY had to do was look over at other schools whose brands had gone up in smoke. Here's how poor Adelphi University, in almost the same market, tries to position itself:

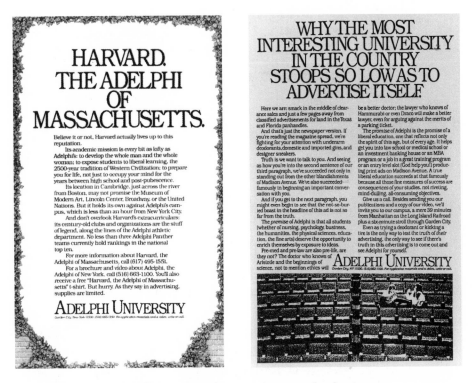

Adelphi University plays a mug's game and it shows.

Like megastates piling on more and more weaponry in the name of self-protection, brandname schools battle it out with "merit-based aid" and "preferential packages." What has happened to the "need-based aid" that Higher Ed, Inc., so proudly proclaimed a generation ago? Forgettaboutit. Since most of the high achievers come from the same demographic, and since most of them have the same in-demand talents (athletic, musical, organizational . . .) instilled by Mom and Dad, the misty vision of financial aid helping the really disadvantaged is just that. In a report from the Lumina Foundation called "Unintended Consequences of Tuition Discounting" (and available at the foundation's Web site) comes this disquieting statistic: in 2001, the average tuition discount rate for four-year private colleges was 38.2 percent, with nearly eight out of ten students getting discounts. Beginning in fall 1995, the study of data from the U.S. Department of Education found that the average dollar amount of institutional award was rising much faster for higher-income undergrads than for their lower-income peers at both public and private four-year colleges. In other words, aid was progressively moving away from need to merit.

In the Ivy League only about 10 percent of the students receive Pell Grants, one of the federal government's main financial aid programs. Yet most students from families with incomes near the national median, namely about half of all families, qualify for Pell Grants. Economic and racial diversity is mostly just eyewash, irrespective of the tub pounding of editorial pages and viewbook scenes. In a system driven by ratings, real diversity can be anathema.

More than one third of the money that private colleges spend on aid goes to students distinguished by merit, not need. This "every school for itself" syndrome has produced some unique results. Certain schools, such as Carnegie Mellon and the University of Rochester, have gained relative position by systematically upping whatever the competition is offering, and they won't quit doing this. They can't, lest they plummet in the rankings. The term *financial aid* now means the best negotiated discount a kid's parents can wrangle. The result is that savvy, achieving students who can afford the fare travel at the reduced rate.

Graduate schools, incidentally, are under no such free trade restrictions, so a special kind of waste occurs. The best schools buy the brand recognition at what seems ridiculous prices. Presumably they are producing a superior product. But what if there's no market for the product? To cite a typical example, Yale's English Department gives all its grad students a free ride—in truth, pays them to attend with stipends in exchange for getting a *crème de la crème* class. But for what reason? Not so that it can staff other grad departments with Yale Ph.D.s, because there are not enough jobs for English Ph.D.s. No, Mother Yale gets the best class she can because she is the brand that needs protecting. Now, what does that do to the second-tier supplier? All the graduate students in the University of Florida English Department—all of them!—now have their way paid by the taxpayers. Every single one of them is either on assistantship or fellowship, which includes tuition. We don't even ask if they can afford to pay. There is even a bit of academese to describe such a department. It's called being "fully funded."

The taxpayers are essentially being asked to underwrite the future inevitable unemployment of our product, all in the name of keeping us somewhere in the top hundred schools. And it's only a matter of time before some disciplines become totally unnecessary, like some form of Dewey decimal library science, yet the premier schools will continue to produce instructors solely as a way to maintain their standing among peers. "We're number one!" they chant, conveniently forgetting to ask, "Number one of what?" And, more pathetically, the secondary suppliers will be dragged along for the ride. "We're number seventy-five!" we chant mindlessly.

Is a Branded Education Worth It? Well, Yes and . . . No

We know the risk/reward ratio from the suppliers' side. What about the consumer? Is it worth it? "Getting in" is a $500-million-a-year industry complete with magazine rankings, prep courses, and limitless guidebooks. Parents can easily spend a few grand lining up Junior to be shoved into a slot just like the one next to it. Here's the bottom line. It's probably worth the monetary sacrifice *if* he has a shot at one of the top-tier schools.

As a *Fortune* magazine article appropriately titled "Is Harvard Worth It?" concludes, if you are accepted at a nameplate school and if the school is paying at least part of the tab—and chances are it will—you should head to the top. The self-selection of students based on brand recognition will make the experience richer and more rewarding. Forget the extra earning power; it may not be there. Plus, heading to the elites makes parents happier and increases their social status. After all, as rear-window car decals attest, a lot of the experience is for them. If you decide to buy generic, however, don't lose any sleep. As Alan B. Krueger, an economics professor at Princeton, and Stacey B. Dale, a researcher at the Mellon Foundation, found, the specific choice in the midrange makes no predictable difference. In other words, the qualities that get you into an elite school are more predictive of success than the specific choice of school. The irony is that the best school that turned you down is a better predictor of your future success than the school you actually attended.

A brand conundrum of a *queue-and-cascade* market explains why the premier schools don't do what logically might be expected by market forces, namely, expand enrollment until they have maximized returns. Ironically, that might be disastrous because exclusivity is what they sell. Part of the brand value of the premier schools is that there are never enough to go around. Luxury stores have learned that they always need to be running out of certain items. In fact, they often pretend to be out of stock. Rejection is part of what they sell. Not so for State U., where expanding inventory is exactly what the second-tier school creates in the hope of bulking up its offerings to get as many good students as possible while harvesting the economies of mass production. You rarely see an empty slot on the shelf at Wal-Mart.

The pressures on a "public ivy" such as Berkeley, UVa, UCLA, Colorado, UNC, or Michigan are intense because they are state schools and the "Accept me! Accept me! I'm a taxpayer" argument is most vociferous. But be careful. If such state schools just barely on the elite side of the barbell do heed the market's call and do the logical thing—namely, expand—they may pay the price. Witness the plight of school systems such as SUNY and Wisconsin and even California, which took good systems and diluted them. Rather like commercial branding, it sometimes makes more sense to create a new brand than to extend the home brand until it runs out of story—or worse, runs out of audience.

What does this brand sensitivity of the elites mean about the quality of the experience for the rest of us? How dangerous is it that schools follow the corporate model of marketing? Higher education is either a great deal or a rip-off. The Ivy League universities, for instance, in order to get the proper entering class (and build brand value), require only a handful of students to pay more than $20,000. As we've seen, forget tuition. The prestige school has other money pots. Every two weeks Harvard's endowment accrues enough cash to cover all undergraduate tuition. But what happens on the other side of the barbell? Mass suppliers also have to discount their sticker prices deeply to maintain their perceived value. What this means is that competition at the top essentially *raises* costs everywhere, but only certain schools have deep enough pockets to compete.

The lower you go, the worse things get. To get the students needed for better ratings, which draws better students, who boost external giving, which finances new projects, raises salaries, and increases the endowment for getting better students, which gets better rankings, which . . . , the second-tier school must perpetually treat the student as a transient consumer. That's why good schools, really good schools, have all that stuff, all those *things*, that have nothing whatsoever to do with their oft-stated lofty mission. There is even a term for these things inside the industry, *competitive amenities*—things such as Olympic-quality gyms that few students use, Broadway-style theaters that are empty much of the time, personal trainers, glitzy student unions with movie theaters, and endless playing fields mostly covered with grass, not athletes. Just take a tour of an Ivy League school and observe not just the facilities but how much use they get.

This marketing madness is now occurring on the other side of the barbell with the mass suppliers getting into the act. So the University of Houston has a $53 million wellness center with a five-story climb-ing wall, Washington State University has the largest Jacuzzi on the West Coast (it holds fifty-three students), Ohio State is building a $140 million complex featuring batting cages, rope courses, and the now-necessary climbing wall, and Southern Mississippi is planning a full-fledged water park. These schools, according to Moody's, are sell-ing billions of dollars of bonds for construction that has nothing what-soever to do with education. But it's all about generating difference, about branding.

Freebies are especially rampant wherever they can be made part of recruiting. So Duke gives out free cell phones, Middlebury sup-plies Ben & Jerry's ice cream gratis, Emory takes freshmen to the At-lanta Braves games, and Northwestern has cable movies in the dorms. Needless to say, food service has improved—no more mystery meat. *The Wall Street Journal* even dedicated one of its "Weekend Journal" stories to Phi Beta Cafeteria, showcasing the gustatory delights of Higher Ed, Inc. The winner? Berkeley College Dining Hall at Yale. What's cooking in the future? An all-organic "sustainable-foods" menu with the help of celebrity chef Alice Waters. Clearly, whatever eighteen-year-old is already interested in this kind of food is the same kind of serious student who may well blow the lid off the SAT. This kind of amenity also helps tamp down a particularly annoying statistic that *U.S. News* foregrounds: upper-division transfer rates.

The escalation in competitive amenities is especially acute in venues in which there is a wannabe school next to an elite. So NYU has been spending lavishly on undergraduate dorms (whoops! they are called *residence suites* or *living/learning centers*) as part of its repositioning. Boston University is doing the same. When the Princeton Review foregrounds this extravaganza, it does it under a new rubric: "Dorms like Palaces." These four-star dorms have central air-conditioning, wireless Internet, a private bathroom for every two students, and great views. But, in a sense, these alphabet schools—NYU, BU—are acknowledging the presence of Columbia and Harvard.

From the pedagogical point of view, it would be nice to think that better teaching or better research was separating the top-of-the-line schools from the midline ones. But let's face it: most research, most of the tenure-earning stuff, is really unimportant fluff. Sturgeon's Law, that 90 percent of everything is crap, is never truer than in academic publishing. Plus, ironically, the big names that you find at the luxury schools, the so-called marquee instructors, seldom dip a toe into undergraduate waters. They got on the masthead for a reason: they don't waste time teaching undergrads. They are just a continuation of competitive amenities, the professor as celebrity endorser.

Ironically, in Higher Ed, Inc., the goal of the top-level professorate is to do as little teaching as possible. The higher you get on the academic food chain, the more time you have to teach, yet the less you are rewarded for doing it. Of course, in the viewbook, the celebrity prof is shown lovingly lending a hand to the struggling student. If a celebrity professor does deign to teach undergrads, it usually happens in a large class with the TAs doing all the hand holding and paper grading. Old-style teaching is the least important part of higher education and that's why so much of it is being off-loaded to adjuncts. Now you know why so few good schools want to release the Nessie numbers. Teaching adds nothing to the brand. Can you name a school distinguished by great classroom teaching? In fact, one of the best predictors of tenure denial at the elite schools is the winning of teaching awards. Why? You must be spending too much time with students and not enough on research. Once again, Harvard famously leads the way.

"If everyone agreed to cut physical plant and amenities by half, could we still provide the same education?" asks Professor Winston at Williams College. He knows the answer is *yes*. But understanding the marketing machinery operating Higher Ed, Inc., may explain why this doesn't happen. Plus it may explain some recent developments at universities, such as (1) the predictable and supposedly uncontrollable eruption of grade inflation and the concomitant charade of teaching evaluations, (2) the single-minded outsourcing of almost every conceivable aspect of Higher Ed, Inc., (3) the selling off of academic space as the campus becomes commercialized: Georgia Tech put McDonald's golden arches on the floor of its coliseum, Columbia University lent its name to a for-profit company offering distance learning classes over the Internet, The University of California accepted a research grant from a pharmaceutical company to research new drugs and give the corporation the right to get the first look at the results, and faculty members have titles such as Weyerhauser Professor of Forestry, (4) the loss of any shared nationwide curriculum, (5) the collapse of good schools at the low end of a cohort, and, of course, (6) the impact of shopping for branded education not just as a way to enter the institution (early admissions, negotiated tuition) but as a method of choosing a course of study. What looks like dumbing down is in reality a predictable effect of competitive branding.

The Last Thing a Good School Cares About Is . . . Teaching

From a branding point of view, what happens in the classroom is beside the point. I mean that literally. The old image of the classroom as Socratic ideal, with Mark Hopkins (future president of Williams) at one end of the log and the student at the other, is no longer even an invoked idea. Higher Ed, Inc., is more like a sawmill. A few years ago Harvard started a small department called the Instructional Computing Group, which employs several people to videotape about thirty courses a semester. Although it was intended for students who unavoidably missed class, it soon became a way of not attending class. Any enrolled student could attend class on the Web, fast-forwarding through the dull parts or not watching at all. And with grade inflation you can be comforted by the fact that it really makes no difference. This is "distance education" from a dorm room at an advertised $37,000 a year. The professors didn't complain. From their point of view it's okay: next semester, just cue the tape. Roll in a new log.

Elite schools are no longer in the diploma business; that's for the convenience schools. And they are no longer in the cultural literacy department; that's for the mass media. Higher education is in the sponsored research and edutainment business; what colleges and universities offer is just one more thing that you shop for, one more thing you consume, one more story you tell and are told. Not by happenstance do you hear students talking about how much the degree costs, how much it is worth, what a credit hour is going for, as if they were trying to decide between watching TV and going out to the movies. And that is very much how the schools themselves talk as they look for new sources of research or developmental funding.

In many schools there is even a period called *shopping around* in which the student attends as many classes as possible, looking for a "fit," almost like channel surfing. Then there is a drop-add period, after which the student is locked into a schedule. But not to worry; in most schools you can drop a course with little effort, especially if you are not doing as well as you would like. What do you lose? Only your money, and as we have seen, at the prestige schools even that is not really your money.

So we "do college" as we do lunch or do shopping or do church. That's because for most students in the upper-tier schools the real activity is getting in and then continuing on into the professional schools. No one cares what is taught in grades 13 to 16, certainly not the professorate or the students. Not by happenstance is one of the favorite words on any campus today "whatever," usually delivered with a shrug. To some degree this observation is the result of an education that teaches the equality of not just points of view but subjects of study. I'm not really judging here, for this *whateverness* may just as well be the result of emancipation from rigidity, as it is from being overstimulated, as it is from perhaps just being really tolerant. I only point it out because it may be the appropriate response to a pattern of learning by consuming.

Understanding this sangfroid also explains why no one on either side of the lectern cares much about the curriculum. To the outside world this coolness may be perplexing, but not to those of us in the academy. How many times have I heard my nonacademic friends complain that there is no coherence in the courses their kids are exposed to? It is perfectly possible to have a sophomore survey in American literature taught in a handful of schools of comparable value and not cover *any* of the same selections—in fact, not read any of the same writers.

Back in the 1950s, introductory courses used the same textbooks, not just intramurally but extramurally. So Introduction to Writing (Freshman English) used the same half-dozen handbooks all across the country. No longer. The writing courses are a free-for-all. Ditto the upper-level courses. Here are some subjects my department covers in what used to be English 101, the plain-vanilla composition course: attitudes toward marriage, business, best-sellers, carnivals, computer games, fashion, horror films, *The Simpsons*, homophobia, living arrangements, rap music, soap operas, Elvis, sports, theme parks, AIDS, play, and the ever-popular topic of the marginalization of this or that group. Even when the title of the course is something like Postcolonial Studies in British Commonwealth Literature of the Caribbean, chances are that the real subject often will be politics. And if you come across a title such as Theory of Gender, dollars to doughnuts the real subject is homosexuality, homophobia, and oppression studies.

I won't bore you with the list of what else is taught other than to say that, as consumer satisfaction has become central in the marketing of higher ed, the elective has become the core curriculum. And not just at the elite schools, where perhaps this makes sense, but all the way across the barbell. Take Shakespeare, for example. At places such as Amherst and the University of Michigan, his works have disappeared as a mandatory subject of study. When the National Alumni Forum (NAF) studied the curricula of brand-name schools, it found that more than two thirds of them allow English majors to graduate without studying a word of the Bard. In *The Shakespeare File: What English Majors Are Really Studying*, the NAF listed what each name-brand school required to graduate. Only a few schools require what used to be standard shared and assumed knowledge. To paraphrase the old Oldsmobile ads, "This is not your father's education." And as older faculty retire, it's going to be less and less so. The process has been going on for thirty years now, with the result that an English major at UF today can graduate without taking a course in literature before 1960—in fact, can graduate without taking a single course in literature! We are not unique.

If you want to see what's making its way into the undergrad curriculum, have a look at what is currently on the bill of fare at graduate schools. Again, take my school as an example. We are a typical midrange mass supplier. I am in a $10 million department with sixty faculty and two hundred graduate students. The University of Florida is not going to populate the upper reaches of academia with the next generation of instructors. We all know that. In fact, we place only a few of our grad students a year in what might be called real tenure-track teaching jobs. The grad students are here because we have to have this program to be considered a Research I institution. So in exchange for underwriting *all* their tuition, regardless of ability to pay and regardless of any future employment, we employ them in what amounts to voluntary serfdom. They do much of the undergrad teaching, especially composition courses, which are difficult and time-consuming to teach. In fact, most of the sixty full-time faculty have withdrawn from the lower-division writing program so that we can concentrate on our graduate students. We know that most of the students in our graduate program will never even finish the program, so we wink and say "Let's get on with it." Most are here between jobs, so to speak. Here's how we really feel about them: a first-year M.A. teaching three courses a year receives about $12,000 in gross pay per year and gets zero benefits. Now you know why TAs all over the country are struggling to become unionized. They know they are not apprentices—there are no jobs: they are mules.

And what do they study in grad school while teaching writing to freshmen? Here are a few examples from the publicly posted descriptions of course offerings, quoted verbatim, from the last few years. The full descriptions, as well as many others I've not included, are on the department's Web site. Recall, this is an English department in a mass-supplier university. Along with standard fare, we teach courses in:

ENG 6075 Queer Theory and Cultural Politics: This course provides a graduate-level introduction to major concerns, methodologies, and texts in queer theory. The first part of the semester will be devoted to discussion of field-defining texts. . . . In the second part of the course, we will situate queer theoretical approaches in relation to specific sites of cultural engagement, seeking to illuminate both the cultural implications of queer theories and the theoretical insights of queer cultural work (including community organizing, activism, and institution-building, as well as writing, films, and other forms of artistic production).

ENG 6075 Theory: Issues: Hauntologies (Spectrality, Materiality, Representation) What can we speak of, in the name of the ghost? What articulations does the revenant come to authorize? Can we think of a "materiality without matter," and what material effects (politically, historically) might the spectral trace bring about in the act of representation?

LIT 6855 Disney and Its Discontents: This seminar will focus on Disney—the man, the corporation, the global phenomenon. And on its discontents; for many intellectuals anyway, Disney has become nearly synonymous with a conservative, patriarchal, heterosexual ideology linked with American cultural imperialism.

LIT 6358 Womanist Intellectual Thought: Objective: The obscuring position of African American women in the record of American intellectualism has resulted in a consensus among the uninformed that the phrase "black womanist intellectual" is an oxymoron. This seminar disputes that assumption by focusing on black women's intellectual traditions and challenging imposed boundaries that define intellectual thought.

ENG 6075 Introduction to the Geographies of Culture: Theorizing Space and Spatiality. In this course we shall navigate the complex terrain of a conceptual field that has come to take a central place in the debates in literary and cultural studies: that of space and spatiality.

ENG 6137 Introduction to Film Theory: History and Heterology: This seminar will consider fundamental issues in the current theorization of film and video, from poststructuralism, gender theory and postcoloniality to historiography and heterology. Part of its purpose is to introduce multiple approaches to film criticism and theory at a graduate level. As a result, we will engage with film as a mode of inscription where conceptual and propositional capacities intersect with figural, productive and libidinal economies.

LIT 6934 Studies in American Culture: Sex and Citizenship: This course will re-examine core concepts within the U.S. political imagination from perspectives informed by attention to sex, sexuality, and, in particular, sexual deviance. Bringing to bear the insights of feminism and queer theory, the course seeks to complicate key terms such as "privacy," "public," "citizen," "freedom," "rights," "choice," "democracy," "politics," "property," and "consent"; and to reconsider their role in structuring both sex and society.

ENG 6077 Pragmatism and Performativity: This course will explore the intersections of pragmatic and performative accounts of meaning production, subject formation, and political agency, attending in particular to their engagements with speech act theory.

LIT 6856 Postcolonial Theory: This course is an introduction to the enormously influential field of postcolonial studies. We will study the ways in which postcolonial theory has intersected with and impacted diverse areas of inquiry such as feminism, historiography, culture, and ethnography. At the same time, this course will stress the importance of historicizing postcoloniality.

ENG 6077 Holograph(em)ic Singularities: Romanticism, comics, film, and mathematical notation: "Textual transformation" is an operation that is implied by and inferred from graphic signs, but in at least one important sense there's no such thing as narrative transformation per se as such in the texts to be considered in this course.

ENG 6076 Theorists: Deleuze: "What got me by during that period was conceiving of the history of philosophy as a kind of ass-fuck, or, what amounts to the same thing, an immaculate conception. I imagined myself approaching an author from behind and giving him a child that would indeed be his but would nonetheless be monstrous."— Gilles Deleuze. This statement by Deleuze is one oft quoted, although translations differ. It is a limited statement, limited to what might be called the philosophical period that Deleuze never abandoned.

This is pretty heady stuff and, I think it safe to say, not at all like the graduate curriculum of a generation ago. Remember that the grad students now taking these courses will, if they are immensely lucky, find jobs in the lower tier. They will not end up teaching in the Ivy League or even in mass-provider schools. Remember as well that these grad students teach our lower-division writing and literature survey courses. Given this as part of the course of graduate study, one can see how undergraduate courses on "Homer Simpson and Derrida" get into the teaching schedule with quicksilver speed. No one raises a peep. No peep because we all know one thing: teaching is not where the action is. The classroom in Higher Ed, Inc., is a marketing dead end. Thus a number of English departments have become self-styled philosophy or political science departments. The teaching of writing and reading of canonical literature has all but disappeared.

That said, every once in a while a firestorm does erupt. Here is a description of part of an elective section of freshman English, a required course in the English department at Berkeley.

> *English R1A: The Politics and Poetics of Palestinian Resistance (4 credits): The brutal Israeli military occupation of Palestine [ongoing] since 1948 has systematically displaced, killed, and maimed millions of Palestinian people. And yet, from under the brutal weight of the occupation, Palestinians have produced their own culture and poetry of resistance. This class will examine the history of the [resistance] and the way that it is narrated by Palestinians in order to produce an understanding of the Intifada. . . . This class takes as its starting point the right of Palestinians to fight for their own self-determination. Conservative thinkers are encouraged to seek other sections.*

Now, what is fascinating is *not* the course. As you have seen, it's standard fare; it could have been offered at Florida. What is noteworthy is that after Roger Kimball, a perpetually outraged conservative and editor of *The New Criterion*, lambasted the school, Robert M. Berdahl, the then-chancellor, responded. In a letter to *The Wall Street Journal*, the chancellor found the course much like Claude Raines found Casablanca: shocking, just shocking. In the spirit of

173

Mario Savio, Berdahl made it clear that the university really cares about protecting free speech and that the problem with this course is that the graduate student who was teaching it was throttling dissent. He concluded his defense by saying:

> *Universities should not avoid presenting controversial material. At the same time, it is imperative that our classrooms be free of indoctrination. Indoctrination is not education. Classrooms must be places in which an open environment prevails and where students are free to express their views.*

The chancellor never second-guesses the appropriateness of such a class of Freshman English: only its student policies—the problem was only that it discouraged "conservative thinkers" from attending. Mario Savio *über alles.*

To be sure, the nonacademic world may be momentarily aghast. Is this the place to be catechizing or teaching how to write a sentence? But cries of dumbing down or politicizing the classroom miss the point. No one cares about what is taught because that is not our charge. We are not in the business of transmitting what E. D. Hirsch would call *cultural literacy,* nor are we in the business of, as Mark Twain said, teaching the difference between the right word and the almost right word. We are in the business of creating a total environment, delivering an experience, gaining satisfied customers. The classroom reflects this. Our real business is being transacted elsewhere on campus.

Does Anyone Care Who Is Teaching?

If, as it seems clear, no one really cares what's being taught, does anyone really care who is doing the teaching? Clearly, no. And it's easy to see why. Since what top universities on both sides of the barbell produce is a brand story generated by incoming selectivity and, to a lesser degree, on corporate affiliation in the sciences, everything else can be outsourced. And it is. Just as Nike has its manufacturing plants in faraway places and uses the home office to sell the story, so too the modern university pushes the manufacturing aside to concentrate on

generating brand value where it counts—in the development office, on the playing fields, in research, and in public perception.

And, as with its non-academic cousins in industry, the privatizing or subcontracting out of university services happens in many places. Here are some obvious ones that no one fusses about: health care, bookstore, financial management, security systems, event management, campus cleanup, alumni relations, and, most lucratively, fundraising. Also, the food services at most schools are independent, the cola-pouring rights are sold to Coke or Pepsi, printing is outsourced, and student housing has been increasingly absorbed by companies that build on campus and lease back space (a nifty way to resolve *in loco parentis* liabilities). Not only have schools been able to achieve the economies of scale by off-loading these services, they have been able to immunize themselves from bad publicity and legal actions.

There is even an organization called the National Center for the Study of Privatization in Higher Education, which can tell schools of some two thousand companies offering at least a hundred different types of services. The next step is to outsource the one nonacademic service most schools have guarded: admissions. If you look at the various job lists for academic administrators, you'll see that the admissions office is always in turmoil. If you ever wonder why, just consider this observation from someone who has done the job. As Rachel Toor of Duke University's admissions department puts it in her refreshing book, *Admissions Confidential: An Insider's Account of the Elite College Selection Process:* "I travel around the country whipping kids (and their parents) into a frenzy so that they will apply. I tell them how great a school Duke is academically and how much fun they will have socially. Then, come April, we reject most of them." Her job is to generate a buyers' frenzy.

This same phenomenon is reported on by Jacques Steinberg in *The Gatekeepers: Inside the Admissions Process at a Premier College,* where he makes the analogy between executives cooking the books to inflate company earnings and admissions officers doing the same to impress the ranking industry. From his study of Wesleyan, he concludes that a "premier college" can rocket to the top of lists with very little number crunching. Having a high rejection rate is like a restaurant having a long line outside. After all, if there are so few intrinsic differences, what better way to generate value? So in a sense, part of what the good school sells is contrived frenzy and intense anxiety. And this is all generated by the sweet people who are so eager to show you around their school.

In a few places, usually among the also-rans, admissions work has been outsourced. The fast-growing field is called *enrollment management* and firms do the job from generating market surveys to mailing promotional material and finding an entering class. For instance, D. H. Dagley Associates handles recruitment and admissions for about forty schools. To be sure, no first-tier school would be willing to risk its brand to outsiders, even though most of those schools' viewbooks and Web sites are produced by private hands.

From a management standpoint, much of this outsourcing makes sense. In its desire to standardize Higher Ed, Inc., the Carnegie Commission on Higher Education even encouraged schools to divest themselves of peripheral activities, so they could pay attention to "core competencies." Why shouldn't a city outsource its garbage pickup to Waste Management? And why shouldn't a university outsource its food service to Marriott? Or its bookstore to Barnes & Noble? And why shouldn't a university outsource its entertainment? Or even its athletics?

Whoops! Now things get a bit more complex, but you can see this happening already. My school, like many large state universities, has resolved the "sports problem" by cutting the Athletic Department completely loose. We are connected, as they say, only by the phone lines. The Athletic Department has its own autonomy, answering not to the provost but to the president, and really not to him but to the trustees, and really not to them but to the deep-pocketed tithing fans. The football program essentially has its own internal curriculum with its own teachers and classes. When the athletes have to come out of their special dorms and take courses in the regular school, a staff of counselors plans their schedules by cherry-picking sympathetic instructors and courses such as Wildlife Issues, Math for Liberal Arts Majors, a music-listening lab, Recreation Studies. . . . What used to be Rocks for Jocks or Physics for Poets has become Commercial Recreation, Corporate Communications, Adult Fitness, and Residential-Property Management.

The sporting teams are no joking matter, as they are at the heart of the mass-supplier brand. These "unpaid professionals," as sports economist Andrew Zimbalist dubs them, are forever in need of careful academic and social management. At my school, for instance, the athletic department has been able to insinuate many of its players into the classification of *learning-disabled*. Of the regular student population, 295 of 46,055 are in this category—0.6 percent. Of the athletic population, it's 70 out of 460—15 percent. What's the advantage? If you are in the LD category, you can have a note taker, your reading material is put onto audiotape, you get extra time on tests, and you receive preprinted copies of the instructors' overheads and PowerPoint presentations. The Athletic Department spends about $1.93 million on such academic management—about $4,200 per scholar-athlete. The Fighting Gators take in about $34 million in ticket sales, TV revenues, and assorted sports income, and hundreds of millions more in brand awareness. So for the university it's a good deal; maybe not so good from most of the players' points of view. Many don't graduate.

By far the most interesting outsourcing has occurred not in athletics but in the place least expected but most sensible from the branding perspective, namely, around the classroom. Recall that the core of the modern university is not telling stories *in* the classroom (education) but telling stories *about* the classroom (marketing). When I interviewed John Lombardi, former president of my school and now chancellor of the University of Massachusetts, he was nothing if not candid. At Florida he had founded the Lombardi Program on Measuring University Performance, which publishes an annual report, *The Top American Research Universities*, ranking research universities according to nine criteria, such as the amount of federal research money received, incoming students' SAT scores, endowment totals, and number of doctorates awarded. So, I asked him, what generates brand value for Florida? Big research money? Important degrees? No, he demurred, it is the medical center, the Fighting Gators football team, and the idea of the school. The "idea" of the school? Yes, the story of the university, the story that the school tells about itself, that generates the best quality of incoming student. I asked, "You mean the brand?" He said yes. The job of the modern university president, he said, was to manage the brand. And if you tell your story well you retroactively improve the quality of every degree you have previously granted. And that is often the path to increased contributions—not just from alumni but from those who wish they were.

So from a cost-accounting and storytelling point of view, it makes good business sense to trim those parts of the endeavor that don't add to the brand. In the area of learning, research adds to the brand, yes, but teaching does not. The danger with pruning is that you will end up with what in the trade are known as *marquee programs* that drain money away from other departments. The result is "steeples of excellence surrounded by tenements of mediocrity." As Lombardi told me, really awful programs can hurt a school, but no one knows about mediocre teaching. Can you name a school with really bad teaching? In truth, at most schools the teaching is pretty good. It should be. The teaching faculty has plenty of time to do a good job. The average faculty member at a midlevel school teaches two courses a semester, about six contact hours a week. Plus, no matter how bad the university classroom experience is, it's going to be better than that at most high schools.

Forget departments, he told me; if you want to build the brand, focus on such unique curricular experiences as an honors program. At UF, he did just that. Lombardi greatly expanded the University of Florida Honors Program, which offers smaller courses, exclusive residence halls with a big arched sign out front, special advising, and, most important, an Associate of Arts Degree with Honors. It's a school within the university, essentially the school that delivers what the brand story promises—a school dedicated to achievement and learning. Students clamor to get in. Ditto the faculty.

The Adjunct Faculty

With the bulk of teaching, it makes sense to outsource it to the cheapest supplier. And Higher Ed, Inc., has. The number of part-time faculty members and those who work full-time without tenure-track status has increased dramatically in the past two decades. According to the U.S. Department of Education's American Council on Education's report "The New Professorate: Characteristics, Contributions, and Compensation," the number of part-time faculty members increased by 79 percent from 1981 to 1999, to more than 400,000 out of a total of 1 million instructors. The biggest growth spurt occurred between 1987 and 1993, when 82 percent of the 120,000 new faculty members hired during that period were for part-time positions. During the period from 1981 to 1986, fewer than 30 percent of 90,000 new faculty members had been part-time. The adjuncts are all over Higher Ed, Inc., on both sides of the barbell.

How we treat this shadow faculty tells much about the branding process. We have an insider's lexicon that explains the degree of their imposed ephemerality. Here's just a bit of it. *Annually renewable* means that no matter what follows these words, you are disposable. *Gypsy scholar* is a Ph.D. who has traveled around through adjunct positions and now knows what annually renewable really means. *Independent scholar* is a euphemism that implies you have another life, and there is even a National Coalition of Independent Scholars to give it an eerie sense of credibility. Whenever you see *adjunct* as an adjective, reach for your hat because it overwhelms anything it modifies, as in *adjunct professor.* It really means you will get no benefits and no security. Also watch out for the little preposition *in*, as in Senior Associate in . . . or Master Lecturer in . . . , because it registers a nonrenewable position. *Tenure-track* is the crucial adjective if you are in the second-tier schools, because your job may well become permanent. But if you are at a prestige school, it means about the same as *adjunct.* So if you know someone who is an assistant professor at an Ivy League school, the one thing you know is that he or she will not be there for long . . . about eight years. The elites prefer to hire at the top, where they can be assured of celebrity value. They rarely promote from inside. And if you ever see the term *lecturer, instructor,* or *visiting assistant professor,* don't bother to unpack your bags.

Adjuncts have become so much a part of Higher Ed, Inc., that they even have their own column in the vade mecum of the industry, *The Chronicle of Higher Education.* "The Adjunct Track" addresses such topics as "How can adjuncts build collegiality with other adjuncts given the highly competitive nature of the adjunct job market?"; "How to Be One of the Gang When You're Not"; "Your Eggs Should Be in More than One Basket" (in which adjuncts are informed that they should "spread themselves out over as many different hiring institutions as possible in order to not be overly dependent on any one of them); "Time Is Money" (in which adjuncts can improve their hourly earnings rate by building time management skills); "Being a Professional in an Unprofessional Climate" (how adjuncts should maintain professionalism even if they're not paid well or treated as professionals); and "Office Hours Without an Office" (suggestions for how adjuncts might fulfill their commitments to students given that their hiring institutions often don't provide them offices). On the Web, take a look at "Workplace: A Journal for Academic Labor" (www.workplace=gsc.com) for more of the same. Or just enter "adjunct teaching" into a search engine and see what comes geysering up.

What this language shows is the depth of subterfuge and the corporate doublespeak invoked so as not to tarnish the brand. The teaching system, especially in the humanities, is so oversupplied with qualified teachers that only an idiot manager would not harvest a bumper crop of adjuncts and pay the lowest wage. Remember, we have brought this on ourselves by encouraging second-tier producers to continually flood the market with freshly minted Ph.D.s. We have met the sorcerer's apprentice, and he is us. Barry Munitz, former chancellor of the California State University System, estimated that more than half of all his classroom hours were taught by "disposable workers." Since Mario Savio, the California system has been a model for the rest of the country in this as in much else. During the 1990s, more than half of all California hires were to people with no hope of secure lines. From a branding point of view, it makes sense.

Evaluation of Teaching and Inflated Grades at Lake Woebegone U

Once you realize that there is little interest in what's happening inside the classroom or in who is doing the teaching, you can safely conclude that no one really cares about how it's being done. And you can see this in the paradox of evaluating teaching. As the curriculum has lost coherence and the teaching staff has become increasingly adjunctified, the student evaluation "instrument" (as it is often called) has become an important marketing charade—not important as a way to improve teaching, but important as a sign that the school really cares about ped-

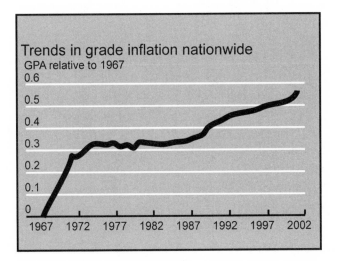

Up, up, and away: a composite of mean GPAs from twenty-nine universities relative to a 1967 baseline. (Source: www.gradeinflation.com)

agogy, cares so much that it is forever pestering the customers in much the same way that your automobile dealership is forever asking you if you had a good time while your car was being lubed and vacuumed.

As there are occasionally members of the flat-earth society, there are those who maintain that grades have not been systematically inflated or, if they have, it's only because the quality of students has improved. Those of us in the trenches know better. It's not that it happened; it's how it happened and especially why it can't be stopped. In a recent report prepared by the American Academy of Arts & Sciences, again sponsored by the Carnegie Corporation, Henry Rosovsky and Matthew Hartley observe that since the early 1960s there has been an upward shift in the grade point average without a corresponding increase in student achievement. And while it is a national phenomenon, Rosovsky, a former Harvard dean, and Hartley, a lecturer at the University of Pennsylvania, say the phenomenon is "especially noticeable" in the Ivy League.

How else to explain how in the 1960s, Harvard called the select students invited to join Phi Beta Kappa the "Junior Eight" and the "Senior 16"; today it has the "Junior 24" and the "Senior 48." The University of Pennsylvania in the 1960s identified 40 seniors annually who were eligible for its chapter of Phi Beta Kappa; in 2001, 450 students were on the same list—about one third of the graduating class. The term "graduation with honors" has become a joke as the average grade in the Ivy League is a high B or low A. At premier schools such as Harvard, half of all the grades in arts and sciences are A– or above. More than 90 percent of Harvard graduates in 2001 graduated with honors. Starting with the class of 2005, Harvard is using percentage caps in each honors category to control the bloat. In typical complexity, the new policy mandates that summa and magna cum laude degrees will together comprise up to 20 percent of the graduating class while summa, magna, and cum laude degrees in fields will together account for up to 50 percent of the graduating class. Go figure. Some schools, such as Brown University, even drop low grades from transcripts, saying that the resume should record only accomplishments. "When you send in your resume, do you put down all the jobs you applied for that you didn't get?" asked Sheila Blumstein, a dean of the school. "A Brown transcript is a record of a student's academic accomplishments."

At a mass-supplier school such as the University of Florida, we take a slightly different approach. To those teaching in the Honors College, the director of the program sends a polite reminder each semester:

> *I'm sure you can understand that Honors students do not want to jeopardize their scholarships by participating in the Honors Program. Hence the Honors student should be graded using the same criteria as you would use grading a regular (non-Honors) student dealing with the same information. This does not mean that Honors students should be graded more leniently. But, by the same token, they should not be graded more severely. Additionally, please note that Honors classes do not use a grading curve.*

The language may be complex, but the message is clear. Just as the Ivy League is to the rest of Higher Ed, Inc., so the Honors Program is to the rest of the university. You are not grading these students relative to others in the program, you are grading them relative to all other students who might have taken your class. After all, the students in the Honors College should not be penalized for being in small classes with more attention and concern expended on them. The least they can be assured of is an A. That's one reason why students clamor to be included.

How is this tied to branding? Grade inflation is the tribute standards pay to the concept of a happy customer. In regular economic inflations there is usually a counteractive deflation that occurs as the market blows off a top. Statisticians call it *regression to the mean.* Not so in this case. Grade inflation is not a bubble but a ratchet. The situation is now dormant because there is nowhere higher to go and no turning back. A report by Valen Johnson, a statistician then at Duke, predicted that if the grade trend continued, the school would grant A's to all but 3 percent of its students by 2010. We have all moved to Lake Wobegon, where "all the children are above average."

When I was at Harvard trying to figure out how it nurtures and protects the most powerful brand in Higher Ed, Inc., I had lunch with Dean Henry Rosovsky. The now-retired dean is an avuncular man, an economist by training, and we had lunch at the Faculty Club. He seemed bemused that someone interested in commercial branding would think of Harvard as a luxury leader, but he wryly admitted that it made some sense. However, although he told me he was very concerned about grade inflation, he didn't seem to appreciate Harvard's role in sustaining the bloat. The fact that the rest of us know that this is an intractable problem for Harvard, and that even Harvard president Lawrence Summers can't control it, is really beside the point. Because it's happening at Harvard, it has the imprimatur of brand acceptability. Once again, Harvard is famous for what it didn't invent.

The process can't be stopped. Some years ago, I received a memo stating that the average grade in my department was B+. Many of my colleagues are giving almost all As. The younger members of the department have never known a C, let alone a "gentleman's C." George W. Bush went through Yale with a gentleman's C average. His youthful critics say that's proof he's not smart, but it's proof only of how deeply ingrained grade inflation really is. If he were at Yale today, he'd be a B+ student just like almost everyone else. When I tell my colleagues that this kind of grading is unfair to good students, I'm told that graduate schools don't know that my C is someone else's B+. And they are right.

But the real reason for the rampant grade inflation has to do with the rise of consumerism and the impact of branding. As long as post-secondary education is interchangeable at the upper levels, no one is going to risk being branded with the story of tough grading. Feeling bad is not a sign of customer satisfaction and course evaluations may reflect it, professors fear. With the exception of the University of Chicago, which prides itself on generating exactly that sensation and harvests the crop of consumers who like the idea that they are serious about studies, no one else is willing to let a C be average. Only at Chicago do students love to tell you about how they got 1600s on their SATs and now get Cs in their classes. The University of Chicago owns this intellectual territory. A few years ago it headlined its viewbook "The Life of the Mind." No other school in Higher Ed, Inc., would dare to do this. And now even Chicago is having second thoughts, fearing that it is getting a skewed entering class, ironically lowering the school in the rankings for doing what should elevate it.

The Solution to Inflation Is As Obvious As It Is Impossible

As long as competition for the best entering students is fierce, and as long as students are judged only as they enter, no school will be willing to rejigger the grades so that a C will again be average. Ironically, grade inflation really hampers the good students and makes their passage to graduate education more dependent on exactly what the faculty complain about—namely, standardized tests and overblown recommendations. It also hampers departments that have been laggards in inflating, such as the sciences. Given a choice to take an elective from sociology or botany, most students will go for the A in the hand rather than the C in the bush.

If the faculty is complicit in the branding of the academy by acts of omission, the administration is really culpable by acts of commission. All it would take to stop grade inflation is this: Let me hear from the dean that he wants a list from the department chairs of all those who are grossly misjudging their students. Let him publish the grade distribution of the faculty. Some instructors who now give a class of twenty-five students all As would soon stop and think: Is it logical that the distribution curves are being held in abeyance and all my students are equally excellent?

But no such memo is forthcoming, nor will it ever come. My dean, like his counterparts in business, is rewarded by productivity. The board of trustees, the legislature, the president, and the provost all know that funding is based on student credit hours. You increase revenues and market share by moving them in and moving them out expeditiously. *U.S. News* even rewards this efficiency under the rubric *value added.* The problem with the marketing model is that you can't apply it just here and there. It tends to be applied wherever possible. Expediency is an added value. And inflated grades are nothing if not expedient. They make life easier for all concerned—all, that is, except the best students.

Where Will Branding Take Higher Ed., Inc.? The Florida Example

The commercialization of Higher Ed, Inc., has had many salutary effects: wider access, dismantling of many discriminatory practices, increased breadth and sophistication of many fields of research, and, let's face it, an intense, often refreshing, concern about customer relations. There's no doubt that when my department was told to limit the class size of certain courses to nineteen students, it was because we were trying to increase the number of courses the university had below the magic twenty-student number favored by *U.S. News.* But the movement from considering our end users to be students, then FTEs, then clients, then customers has not been without certain sacrifice to both parties.

Again consider the University of Florida, because it's typical of the mass-provider campus. On one hand, the state of Florida doesn't have the resources, or willpower, or really the social need to have a premier system. Who cares about education in a state populated by people who come here to retire? Most Floridians feel they have already paid their dues. But on the other hand, Florida is one of the largest and wealthiest states, and it should have something at least presentable.

So to get the student body we need to compete in the rankings, we essentially give the product away. We have no choice. Other states will take our best students if we don't. So we rob Peter to pay Paul. Here's how it works. The state has a program called Bright Futures, primarily funded by the lottery money. In its five-year history, Bright Futures has

funded mostly white, middle-class students from families earning between $30,000 and $70,000, with about 30 percent of them earning
more than $70,000. While whites are 60 percent of the high school grad-
uating classes, they are 77 percent of Bright Futures students. Fully 95
percent of the entering freshmen are arriving with most, or all, of their
tuition paid by the program. All a high school senior has to do to qualify
is to get a B average and achieve a cumulative SAT score of 970 (a score
well below both the state and national average), and the state will pay 75
percent of that student's tuition. A student with a 3.5 GPA and a 1270
SAT gets a free ride: the state pays the entire cost, including a $600
stipend for books. These kids can help us stay just above the fold in the
U.S. News rankings because they really can go elsewhere.

So in a way, the mass-provider school is behaving just like the elite
school in terms of discounting product. The difference is that the elite
schools can afford it. We can't. Ivy League monies come from endowment and have the promise of replenishment if the school retains
its reputation. State university monies often come from the lottery
and have the promise of replenishment if the state continues to allow
this tax on ignorance. States without lotteries are forced to compete—
often, like Michigan and Nevada, using tobacco settlement monies or,
like Mississippi and Missouri, by using other state revenue. Miami
University in Ohio put forward and then withdrew a plan to charge all
students the same tuition but then grant in-state students special
scholarships equaling or exceeding the per-student subsidy received
from the state. The plan was just too complicated. About half the
states have been sucked into simple-minded plans such as Bright Futures, which are essentially a subvention of middle-class education.

Everyone admits that most of these kids would go to college anyway. But would they go to a school in the state system? No one wants
to find out. Our neighboring states have programs such as Bright Futures that advantage their relatively affluent students too, so, in a way,
we'll never find out. Georgia, for instance, has a program called
HOPE (Help Outstanding Pupils Educationally), which gives its state
university a competitive advantage for in-state students. To our west,
Alabama is contemplating such a program. So of course it's a wash,
with no school attaining anything other than a momentary advantage
and all schools attaining an inequitable advantage for the affluent.

What was an arms race for the elites is also an arms race for the mass providers.

The invocation of the feared "brain drain" is powerful, carrying with it the dreaded descent into convenience school category for both the University of Florida and our sister school Florida State University. So now we are involved in a sectional dustup of our own making. Meanwhile need-based aid falters, even though the whole idea of using lottery money was to loosen up monies for the financially stressed. We all know the answer: a sliding scale that rewards merit but also takes into consideration family income. But will it happen? Doubtful. When the state pols suggest reconfiguring Bright Futures, the students who are already funded howl that they are being discriminated against for working hard. Remember, every one of these students comes from a voting family.

We do some strange things in the name of competitive branding. Florida State University has even started an aggressive advertising

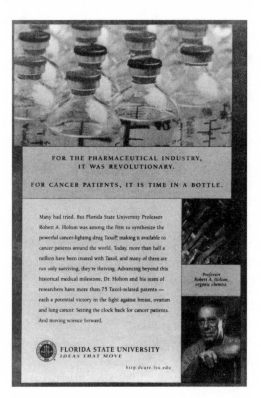

Florida State University advertises in The Wall Street Journal *not for students but for dubious prestige.*

campaign, shrink-wrapping a glossy magazine about itself and attaching it to various regional publications, as well as creating an ad campaign in *The Wall Street Journal* featuring its faculty and their discoveries. When asked why it spends almost a million dollars on such propaganda, FSU officials have been candid: they feel they have to do something (anything!) to improve their ranking. Do they think they are going to get students from the families of readers of the *Journal*? No. What they'll get is the illusion inside the state that they have an out-of-state presence—and perhaps influence the opinions of the 4,200 administrators who do the peer rankings for *U.S. News*.

The New U., Inc.

From any objective standard, programs such as Bright Futures for kids who have good prospects anyway and glossy advertising for a school that needs no presence on Wall Street may seem like a foolish way of doing business. Much the same thing is probably happening in your state. Face it, Mario Savio was correct. Before all else, the modern university is a business selling a branded product. Here is David Kirp, professor at the Goldman School of Public Policy, University of California, Berkeley, and author of *Shakespeare, Einstein and the Bottom Line: The Marketing of Higher Education:*

> *While the public has been napping, the American university has been busily reinventing itself. In barely a generation, the familiar ethic of scholarship—baldly put, that the central mission of universities is to advance and transmit knowledge—has been largely ousted by the just-in-time, immediate-gratification values of the marketplace. The Age of Money has reshaped the terrain of higher education. Gone, except in the rosy reminiscences of retired university presidents, is any commitment to maintaining a community of scholars, an intellectual city on a hill free to engage critically with the conventional wisdom of the day. The hoary call for a "marketplace of ideas" has turned into a double entendre, as the language of excellence, borrowed from management gurus, dominates in the higher-education "industry." Trustees, administrators, faculty, stu-*

dents, business, government—*everyone involved in higher educa-tion is a "stakeholder" in this multibillion-dollar enterprise.*

A few university presidents know this and are willing to admit it pub-licly. Here is Michele Tolela Myers, president of Sarah Lawrence, from an op-ed piece in *The New York Times*, under the title "A Student Is Not an Input."

Attend a conference of higher education leaders these days, and you will hear a lot of talk about things like brand value, markets, image and pricing strategy. In the new lingua franca of higher education, students are "consumers of our product" in one con-versation or presentation and "inputs"—a part of what we sell— in the next. It's easy enough to see why academia has gotten caught up in this kind of talk. We borrow the language of busi-ness because we are forced to operate like businesses. Higher ed-ucation has become more and more expensive at the same time it has become increasingly necessary. As we look for ways to oper-ate efficiently and make the most of our assets, we begin learning about outsourcing, for-profit ventures, the buying and selling of intellectual property. And as the public is well aware, colleges and universities are now in conscious and deliberate competition with one another. We "bid for student talent," as the new lan-guage would put it, because we know that "star value" in the stu-dent body affects the "brand value" of the university's name: its prestige, its rankings, its desirability, and ultimately its wealth and its ability to provide more "value per dollar" to its "cus-tomers."

As we in the academy begin to use business-speak fluently, we become accustomed to thinking in commercialized terms about ed-ucation. We talk no longer as public intellectuals, but as entrepre-neurs. And we thus encourage instead of fight the disturbing trend that makes education a consumer good rather than a public good. If we think this way, our decisions will be driven, at least in part, by consumers' tastes. Are we ready to think that we should only teach what students want or be driven out of business?

And this from Judith Shapiro, president of Barnard, on how commodification has even affected the parental role:

> *Confidently, with generosity and grace, most parents let their children grow up. They realize that the purpose of college is to help young people stand on their own and take the crucial steps toward adulthood while developing their talents and intellect with skill and purpose. But this truth is often swept aside by the notion that college is just one more commodity to be purchased, like a car or a vacation home. This unfortunate view gives some parents the wrong idea. Their sense of entitlement as consumers, along with an inability to let go, leads some parents to want to manage all aspects of their children's college lives—from the quest for admission to their choice of major. Such parents, while the exception, are nonetheless an increasing fact of life for faculty, deans and presidents.*

What none of these commentators is willing to acknowledge is that, in Max Weber's sense, the professionalizing of the academy has been something that both the professorate and administrators have not just allowed, but willingly, often gleefully, participated in. We have gone from artisanal guild to department store, from gatekeeper to ticket taker, from page turner to video clicker. The result has not been all bad. But when we cede control to the market we can hardly complain that somehow this has been done to us. This commodification, selling out, commercialization, corporatization, whatever it is called, is at the heart of such programs as Edison Schools, school choice, and even Channel One. Yes, it's what happens when learning and marketing become an end, not a means. But it's also what happens when you make your products interchangeable and then try to fit the top one hundred schools into the top twenty. When you act to improve ratings simply because you've "got to be perceived as a top-tier school," you are asking for exactly the kind of branding battle that is now occurring. Ironically, the more you give to your school when it has a capital campaign dedicated to upping its rank (as the University of Richmond recently did with its Top-Tier Initiative), the worse it gets.

As we will see in the last chapter, the future of Higher Ed, Inc., is to continue to exploit its brand equity by extending itself deeper into such areas as marketing consumer goods and even branding living space. Not by happenstance are universities finding revenue not just in selling their alumni lists, and their buildings for naming rights or their name to credit card companies, but in extending the very campus to include such things as retirement communities and even graveyards. Before complaining about how they are being treated by consumers, the participants in Higher Ed, Inc., might do well to consider what Mr. Savio said years ago: the university is becoming industrialized not by outside forces but by internal ones. Rather like the child who, after murdering his parents, asks for leniency because he is now an orphan, universities that have become plump feeding at the commercial trough now complain about how it's been done to them by the market. This contention of victimization is of course a central part of the modern Higher Ed, Inc., brand. The next words you hear are: Please give, we desperately need your support.

4.

Museumworld

The Art of Branding Art

Is the Guggenheim a brand? Yes.

— Thomas Krens, director of the
Solomon R. Guggenheim Foundation

I'm careful about using the word branding.
*I don't use it unless I have to. It's obviously
appropriate to use in the private sector, but it
raises concerns in the nonprofit world.*

— Maxwell L. Anderson, ex-director of
New York's Whitney Museum of American Art

So why is branding so contentious in the nonprofit world that most museum directors tiptoe around it? The answer seems simple enough. In a word, because the story—the home brand, if you will, of the nonprofits—is that the one thing they are is *not corporate*. The market, ugh, how vulgar. Churches, which historically developed modern-style marketing, are distraught when the word *branding* is mentioned. Higher Ed, Inc., becomes apoplectic, at least publicly. So too museums—most museums—claim to have a higher calling than competing for market share. They are not soiled by the workaday world. They don't sell a product. They are not an industry. They pay no attention to the turnstile. No merchants are in these temples. Here are only the custodians of, shhh, please be quiet, don't touch, the deep truth.

Ironically, however, the one thing most museums will be if they are not industrious about branding themselves is around for long. Unless, that is, your museum sits on a huge mound of endowment money or is dedicated to a popular subject, such as rock 'n' roll memorabilia. Only then can you afford to say the corporate model doesn't fit. Almost without fail, the museum curators who complain about the dumbing down of exhibits and the selling out of space are the ones tending a cellar full of old masters atop a mound of well-protected cash. For them, the museum is secular cathedral and art is Eucharist. They are the lucky few who can profit and exploit the museum brand the way some elite colleges can or the Episcopal Church once could. But what of the rest of the industry?

Their less-well-heeled brethren are not so sure. In fact, most museum directors are now remarkably like old-line denominational bishops and small-college presidents. They have the touch of panic around the eyes and mouth. That's because there has been a phenomenal explosion in museum construction and the concomitant need to fill them not with artifacts but with consumers. Four percent of American museums were founded before 1900, 75 percent since 1950, and 40 percent since 1970. If you drew a graph of museum growth, you would see something that looked like a slow-motion "J" with the straight-up jolt coming in our lifetimes. These things have been sprouting up all over the place. And, like country churches and private colleges, a lot of them are now closing down.

Museums are the most popular cultural institutions visited by Americans. More people attend them than sporting events. In 2000, more than a billion people attended at least one of these places. Problem is that, as with the megachurch or the state-funded university, the rich grow and the poor panic. The country's brand-name superstar museums (say, the Met, MoMA, the National Gallery of Art, the Art Institute of Chicago, the Guggenheim, and the Getty) are becoming rather like the Ivy League, putting intense pressure not only on one another but on the second echelon. They even have a consortium of eleven important museums that has done market research complete with focus groups and postexhibition questionnaires sponsored by the Getty Center for Education in the Arts. The venerable Met has been doing tracking studies of its shows since 1971, which it says is to convince the city that it should be given special tax breaks, but the studies also help determine what to exhibit. The camel's nose of market research is already well under the museum tent wall. And why shouldn't it be?

As we will see by looking at the Guggenheim, the nameplate museums put special pressure on competitors at the low end of the cohort. But the brand competition is epidemic. According to *The Official Museum Directory*, there are more than 8,300 museums listed by membership but, in truth, there are probably more than 11,000. Those 8,000-plus are just the accredited ones, the nonprofits who have a declared formal educational mission, one full-time staff member, a willingness to pay dues, and what passes for "a program of events." All you have to do is take a trip across the country to know that even the 11,000 figure is amazingly low. If you factor in the irrepressible Halls of Fame (as in the National Cowgirl Hall of Fame, the Country Music Hall of Fame, the Free Software Hall of Fame, the Poetry Hall of Fame, the Roadkill Hall of Fame . . .) the numbers explode. Places that memorialize stuff are everywhere. Think about it. There are museums all around you. From where I sit in northern Vermont, there are five bona fide museums within a radius of twenty miles. In number, museums are now more prevalent than colleges, a bit less popular than churches.

And they are having the same problems in almost the same places as churches and universities. That's because the one thing you can expect whenever three or more of any cultural institution are gathered together is that someone is going to start telling a story about what is offered. If you want to increase your competitive advantage and up the gate and fund-raising, you are going to have to separate yourself, tell a story, and establish a brand, or your neighbor nonprofits are going to squeeze you out of the market. Ironically, if you are going to survive, you are going to have to think of yourself, if only for a moment, as just another entertainment. To be successful you are going to have to think of yourself as delivering emotion, not just putting up things to look at and typing out a little explanation on the side.

Thinking this way causes consternation. A museum is not an entertainment, not an immersion environment such as the Rainforest Cafe, Sony Wonder Technology Lab, or Niketown, for goodness sake! Don't believe me? Just ask a museum director, and you'll catch an earful. "We will never compromise our integrity or our mandate to uplift culture," say the directors. "What we do we do for the betterment of the general weal." Then they will ask if you want your name entered in the donors' list as an individual, friend, supporter, contributor, sustainer, partner, patron, benefactor, fellow, or de' Medici. As opposed to Higher Ed, Inc., or the megachurch, Museumworld is one of the few places you can generally buy your way onto the board of directors, or at least become a trustee. Ironically, the world that owns not enlightenment or salvation but art is currently the world most susceptible to the siren sound of *ka-ching*. In the culture world, only the perpetually distressed symphony orchestras and ballet companies listen more intently.

Many museums currently live on the edge of bankruptcy. They understand the famous conversation between George Bernard Shaw and a dinner companion: "Would you sleep with me for a million pounds?" to which she replied "Yes, I would." Shaw then asked "How about for one pound?" to which the lady replied, "Do you think I am a prostitute, Sir?" He retorted, "We've established that, milady. We are simply haggling over the price." So too the quid pro quo world of the museum elite comes down to pricing. The real question is, which marketing techniques are permissible and which are off limits? Will there finally be two kinds of museums, the temples of high culture devoted to scholarly pursuits funded by individual largess and corporate affiliation, and the entertainment centers catering to popular taste and funded by the turnstile? It's beginning to look that way.

What? No Public Support?

American museums are unique in all the world in that they live almost entirely in the marketplace. The one kind of funding that we Americans have little of and expect to have even less is what the Europeans and Asians still enjoy: state funding. To make matters more competitive, as the number of museum sites has increased, the alternative sources of public cash have markedly decreased. Face it: museums are no longer unique. Once every city starts using the museum as an anchor store to bolster a gentrified downtown, the museum is well on its way to behaving just like another Sears or J. C. Penney. If cities cut museums loose from funding, as they certainly will do when monies become tight, the inner-city museum may well collapse. As it is now, according to the American Association of Museums, only about 60 percent of America's two thousand–plus art museums have enough income from their endowment to cover their operating costs. So competitive branding is inevitable. Just as inevitable is that it will never be called that.

The Europeans are facing the same dilemma, but with a difference. They have a long history of last-minute state support. Thatcherism, which cut loose English museums from what was sometimes 90 percent funding, has spread to the continent. Until 1993, the Louvre was entirely state-funded. Now the national museum must find 30 percent of its yearly operating costs on its own. The Louvre still has only four full-time fund-raisers on its staff, compared with fifteen at the various Tates in London and forty at the Metropolitan Museum in New York.

Although government subsidies to most of Europe's museums are less generous than they once were, they remain the primary funding source for these museums. From a marketing point of view, this makes sense. After all, most of the great European museums are "destination spots," *valent le voyage,* must-see points along a formatted tourist itinerary. So most of them charge only a low entry fee or none, hoping to make up for it with sales taxes on the goods sold in the museum store. The European collections of art also have a deep tradition of belonging to the citizenry. In most European museums you don't see omnipresent plaques memorializing donors' names. It still runs against France's instincts to name a wing or a room after a generous donor or even attach a patron's name to a gift. But if you pay attention to the I. M. Pei–designed entryway to the Louvre, you can see that one of its primary roles is to force visitors to move through the profit-generating shopping center that now guards the entrance.

The British are less squeamish about commercializing space. For instance, there is a Sainsbury Wing at the National Gallery and a

Sackler Wing at the Royal Academy of Arts—named, respectively, after retailing and pharmaceutical interests. Even after Thatcher, museum directors in Britain are certainly under far less commercial pressure than their colleagues in America. But although they ultimately rely on state coffers, their managers increasingly have to respond to the marketplace. Subsidies for museums have fallen in real terms: the government now provides 70 percent of the funding for the British Museum, down from 80 percent in 1993. In 2002, the subsidy came to more than a whopping $50 million. The venerable BM has to fill the gap with increased revenue from commercial activities, sponsorship, and donations. That's one reason why it has moved its books to the newly built British Library: to make room for its new two-story complex of stores and restaurants.

The Art Glut Is Part of the Problem

So why is there such a frantic hubbub filling the museum world today? Why are museums filling your mailbox with direct mail? Why are they filling their gallery space with motorcycles and movie posters? Is it just about the money? No. There's a supply problem. There's an awful lot of art sloshing around in an awful lot of places. Art has become common—too common. When you get museums expanding into erstwhile factories, as is now the fashion (think Mass MoCA in an old electronic factory in North Adams, Mass., MoMA QNS in a converted Swingline staple factory in Queens, Tate Modern in a former power plant in London, the Dia Art Foundation in an old printing warehouse in Beacon, New York . . .), you know something internal has exploded. And that something is simple: too much stuff.

All over the West, we have been furiously creating art. It's become a huge business, rather like in the Renaissance. So it is inevitable that, as financial pressures mount, more and more objects will be sucked into the museum not just to fill space but as a way to continually refresh and generate new meaning for the competing brands. After all, art is, in a sense, just a story we tell about an object, and museums are holders of these stories. We have become addicted to the shock of the new. The safe place to be is on the cutting edge. Pick any time in

Manhattan, and chances are that a major museum is showing something never before seen inside a museum.

Although you see this best in New York City, it's really pandemic. As I write this in 2003, more than twenty American art museums are in the process of constructing a new building, expanding gallery space, spreading their franchise. Just as the medieval church used the relic to expand the mendicant order, so the modern museum uses the objet d'art. The more you have, the bigger you can be. Predictably, the range of exhibitions is also broadening to supply the market of eager consumers. How nice to know that what we thought was entertainment is really art. When *Star Wars: The Magic of Myth* drew almost a million paying customers to the Smithsonian National Air and Space Museum in 1997, you knew not only that this exhibit would soon come to a museum near you but that Harry Potter and the Hobbits would be next. The Museum of Fine Arts in Boston will be turning over its gallery space in 2005 to showcase *Speed, Style and Beauty: Cars from the Ralph Lauren Collection.* In Atlanta, the World of Coca-Cola pavilion continually outdraws the High Museum of Art.

As might be expected, the real inventory glut is with modern and postmodern art. In fact, *postmodern* is a portmanteau term that allows art to range free of any received tradition. The oversupply is legitimate glut. Just pay attention to how often the phrase "I/He/She am/is an artist" punctuates our conversations without invoking any consternation, and you see the problem. Of course you are an artist. Almost everyone is. Is there anyone who isn't? Go to the mall. Look at the sales of art supplies. Almost every American town has an arts festival. The little college town where I live has two of them, and they are surprisingly good.

The supply will only worsen if the government ever gives in to a scheme put forward by museum directors to allow fair-market-value tax deductions for artists' donations of their works to museums. The current law allows artists who donate their own works to a museum to deduct only the cost of their raw materials. Museums, which now resemble vast storage sheds, will become flea markets. And who determines the fair value? The professional appraisal comes from, you guessed it, the museum.

In a slightly tongue-in-cheek op-ed piece in *The New York Times*, Joseph Epstein, author of a wry look at art called *Snobbery: The American Version*, had the temerity to suggest that the myth that art exists within every schoolchild is the cause of so much dreck. He explains:

> *There is something very American in the notion that almost everyone has a book in him or her. (In the survey of 1,006 Americans, sponsored by a small Michigan publisher, almost equal numbers of people said they wanted to write a novel, a nonfiction work, a self-help book or a cookbook.) Certainly, it is a democratic notion, suggesting that everybody is as good as everybody else—and, by extension, one person's story or wisdom is as interesting as the next's. Then there is the equally false notion of creativity that has been instilled in students for too many years. It was Paul Valéry who said that the word "creation" has been so overused that even God must be embarrassed to have it attributed to him. . . . Misjudging one's ability to knock out a book can only be a serious and time-consuming mistake. Save the typing, save the trees, save the high tax on your own vanity. Don't write that book, my advice is, don't even think about it. Keep it inside you, where it belongs.*

What happened next is instructive for the future well-being of Museumworld. For such effrontery, Mr. Epstein was peppered with irate letters to the editor. Here's a bit of what they said:

> *Thank goodness that Joseph Epstein is not my 9-year-old daughter's teacher, discouraging her creativity and dashing her hopes that she can write a story that others might want to read. Perhaps, Mr. Epstein, you should have kept your discouraging opinion "inside you, where it belongs." As for me, I'll keep on writing, and, yes, even trying to have my work published—starting with this letter.*

and:

> *I'd like to add to Joseph Epstein's plea to would-be authors. To everyone who ever thought he could paint, sculpt, weld, sing, com-*

pose, write poetry, direct a film or act: Forget it; you're no good. And to all of those people who thought that they might train for and complete a marathon or triathlon: Get over it; you won't win. Best that everyone just stays at home on the couch and reads all 15 of Mr. Epstein's utterly indispensable books.

and:

Joseph Epstein writes: "According to a recent survey, 81 percent of Americans feel they have a book in them—and that they should write it. As the author of 14 books, with a 15th to be published next spring, I'd like to use this space to do what I can to discourage them." I am so glad that my 16-year-old daughter won't ever have Mr. Epstein as a teacher. When she read that paragraph, she said, "How sad that there are people who don't feel they have a book inside them."

Clearly Epstein hit a nerve. And that nerve is near the heart of American self-esteem education and redemption-based religion, which is in turn the reason the *schlock pile,* as Mr. Epstein calls it, is so high. If everyone is an artist and art is everywhere, then it is not very important. No wonder there are so many museums so filled with this stuff. No wonder competitive branding is erupting. Have a look at this Ad Council campaign done for the jingoistic Americans for the Arts (as opposed to Americans Opposed to the Arts?).

We know a great deal about art. We probably know more about what high-culture art looks like than any generation before us. We certainly didn't learn about these images in school, where genuine art appreciation is pretty much neglected other than to certify that My Child Is an Artist. Oddly enough, we don't spend a lot of time *studying* art in museums. Museums have become either tourist destinations to rush through with a checklist (made expeditious by many museums' supplying little maps of the must-see objects) or just elegant places to meet others or wander around and shop. They have become places to go for cocktails and weddings and positive self-esteem. As one wag suggested, the main difference between church and museum is that in church you have bread and wine, whereas at museum

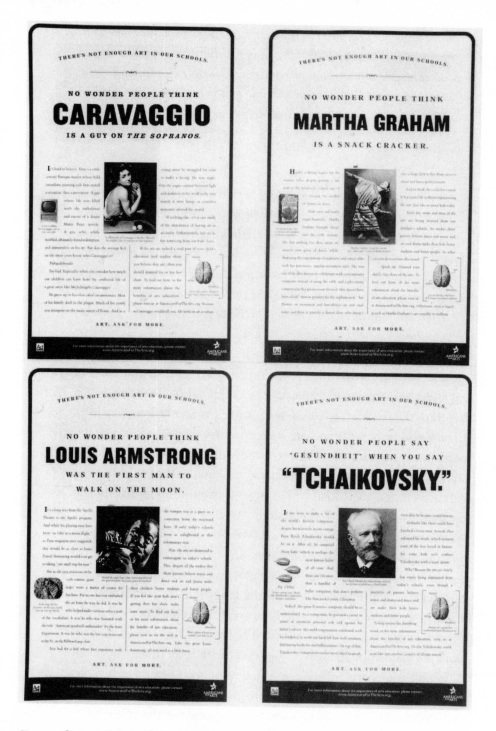

How can there not "be enough art in our schools" when everyone is an artist? The Ad Council doesn't ask a more interesting question: Is there too much advertising in our schools?

affairs you have bread, wine, *and* cheese. No, we've learned a lot about art because we see lots of advertising. The average urban American supposedly sees about three thousand ads a day, and I would venture that about 10 percent of them include a high-art image.

The Real Modern Museum Is the Magazine

Open any magazine. The repertoire of high-cult art used in advertising is limited to perhaps only a few hundred or so works we all recognize. But we see them over and over. The more middle-class the venue, the more common the invocation of high culture as value creator for brands. If the upper class owns the stuff and the lower class couldn't care less about it, the middle class imbues it with value. Art has become a central vocabulary for narratives now attached to fast-moving consumer goods, a competitive amenity, an aspect of design. And advertising, more than anything else, builds value for these destination pieces that are so much a part of the blockbuster exhibitions at the superstar museums.

Mass-market magazines are rife with not just allusions to works but the works themselves. In fact, magazines are what most of us have for starter museums. In a McLuhanesque observation in 1954, a copywriter from Young & Rubicam, the great ad agency, realized what was happening: "If we were to eliminate in any one issue of *Life,* all advertisements that bear the influence of Miró, Mondrian, and the Bauhaus we would cut out a sizable proportion of that issue's lineage." He neglected to say that knowing those images and seeing them *in real life* has become a central generator of cultural capital.

This has never been more true than today, even though *Life* is now moribund. Here is just a glimpse through the gallery of ads in the most middlebrow periodical of American culture, *People* magazine. To demonstrate, I have picked the November 18, 1991, issue because it comes from the early 1990s, when the art market exploded. Museums, galleries, and auction houses became oversupplied with product; hence the branding battles of the last decades.

We know the canonical works not because we really know the art culture, but because we have been inundated by commercial branding. *The Blue Boy* by Gainsborough is a stock image in advertising con-

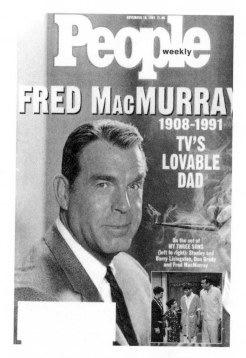

The November 18, 1991 issue of People *is a veritable museum of art inside advertising.*

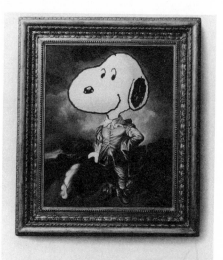

The only way to understand these ads is to first recognize the value of Lichtenstein and Gainsborough.

noting values inherent in eighteenth-century portraiture. We needn't know that Master Jonathan Buttall's fancy dress in the then-passé Van Dyck style and the very bluishness were more likely the result of Gainsborough's attempt to better his rival Sir Joshua Reynolds. All we need know is that the painting looks so opulent that setting anything near it raises the perceived value.

The Scoresby ad, however, takes a more circuitous route, from the comics of Milton Caniff to the benday dot art of Roy Lichtenstein and then back to the world of popular culture. If ever there was an apt example of the syncretistic nature of modern culture, here it is. Images migrate back and forth between Aesthetica and Vulgaria so quickly that if all the words were removed from this ad we would be hard pressed to identify the image as an ad. In other words, the brand image exists separate from the product. It is, I blush to say, art.

Moving a little farther away from invoking masterpieces to borrow value are images like these from the same issue of *People*. The Dole ad is visually layered over the medieval Garden of Earthly Delights. It is an image worthy of close reading. No art emblem is more resonant than that of Arcadia, the promised land of milk and honey. Arcadia has simply been replaced by Brandopia. We half expect to see the Pillsbury Doughboy, Ronald McDonald, and the Coca-Cola polar bears come running down the path. This ad also owes much to medieval painting in which the images of cornucopia are willfully and gleefully distorted to show the promise of the life beyond. Here is indeed a sun-kissed world (notice the bursting sun in the "o" of Dole), a world of prelapsarian innocence in which all choices are possible ("All Do's. No Don'ts," the headline tells us), and in which good health will be doled out to you all your livelong days.

The Buick ad, however, makes its evocation of a-r-t much clearer. The artist himself stands front and center as if his work, and by extension all art, endorses the car itself. In fact, if you read the text you even find in the head copy—near the opened paint cans—the artist's name. You haven't heard of Ed Lister of California? Well, you are not alone. Neither has LexisNexis, the database news service. But who cares? He is an *artist*. He has paint brushes and dirty pants just like important artists. He may even have received a grant to make art. Ed's stuff will be in a museum . . . somewhere, someday. Who cares that

The vision of Arcadia from Dole and an Impressionistic work from Buick.

the headline puns on the art-history period Impressionism while Ed's own painting is decidedly abstract? The text asks us to decide if the painting "capture[s]" the essence of the Skylark (even Shelley had trouble here), which is a nice touch of postmodernism.

Moving still farther away from the invocation of specific attributes of high culture, but still depending on our association of art and brand value, we might consider these ads, again from the same issue of *People*. The artist's studio/gallery is a common site to position your product especially if you don't know what you are doing. So in the Sony ad, which has the sepia colors and ragged edges of an art photo, we see

Art is everywhere in People—*in a gallery, on a watch, in a headline.*

the hardwood floor and framed works that tell us we are in a modern art gallery. In the middle ground a gentleman in rumpled suit is tied up in an old-style phone, victim of a passé technology. He is displayed in the kind of simple-minded imagery of new-style performance art. Had the gender roles been reversed, a brouhaha might have been occasioned. But in the foreground is the pert newcomer with her then avant-garde cordless phone, gleeful that she, at least, is no longer hamstrung. "Don't Be Bound By Convention" we are told in a thoroughly modern misunderstanding of the history of art. But then again we are told in the copy to the left of the telepixie that this mass-produced phone has a "design that expresses your individuality."

An equally ahistorical but thoroughly modern approach to art is the Anne Klein watch, important not because it is a pleasing or well-made object, but because it bears the artist's signature front and center on its faceplate. After all, in brand central you don't buy a specific painting, you buy a Picasso; you don't buy a pair of jeans, you buy Calvin Kleins; so why buy a watch when you can have the metonymic Anne herself? The Noblia campaign, in which "art & leisure" are "in time with each other," is another object/art cliché. As we have seen, just the mention of *art* is often enough to invoke value.

How to generate value by association? Make it invoke the inventory of Museumworld by putting it on a pillar, an easel, in a frame, or on a wall, or just copy an already certified masterpiece.

High-culture art floods advertising because putting your product near a piece of certified value causes the value to leak over into your object. Instead of guilt by association, it is value by association. Proximity breeds affiliation. Our unconscious connection with the museum as a touchstone of unquestioned value can be seen all through promotional culture. For instance, just placing a frame around an object transformed its value. Better yet, put your object in a museum, and you immediately hijack the value of high culture and put it into the service of your disposable product.

Art History and Branding

This interpenetrating value works only if the affiliated manufactured object has uncertified and ambiguous worth. As we know, the first law of branding is that when you have a surplus of something—anything! be it airline tickets, bottled water, computer chips, pew space, flour, classroom seats, painted images, sliced bread, B.A. degrees, redemption— the only way to distinguish your version is by telling a story. The circuit is simple: plenitude ⇒ consumerism ⇒ branding. You can tell this story in any number of ways: you can claim your product will make a person

sexier, younger, healthier, more sensitive, a deeper thinker, or whatever. But tell a story you must, or you will be overwhelmed by the stories of other interchangeable objects. In this context, art is just another story.

Modern branding has been so insistent and redundant that it has drained certain objets d'art of their value. Overuse has exiled once-startling works such as *La Gioconda* (generally known as the *Mona Lisa*), *American Gothic*, *Washington Crossing the Delaware*, *David*, *Whistler's Mother*, and *The Scream* into the limbo of poker-playing dogs and horses pounding the surf on velvet. Monet, Picasso, Degas, Cézanne, Gauguin, and van Gogh are just on the edge of becoming clichés. Soon, like the aural exhaustion of Rossini's *William Tell* overture, the "Summer" section of Vivaldi's *The Four Seasons,* the Fourth Movement of Beethoven's Symphony no. 9, Shostakovich's "The Gadfly," Strauss's "Blue Danube," Gounod's "Funeral March of a Marionette," or Smetana's "Dance of the Comedians," they will become set pieces. They will have become literal stereotypes, stamped out too many times, made kitsch by association.

Ironically, having these commercial clichés in your museum collection militates against shifting your inventory. Visitors have become habituated to consuming them as washcloths, mouse pads, paperweights, shopping bags, and key chains. And it's not just advertising that resettles works of art. Commercial culture of all kinds is simply too insistent. To return to the musical analogy, who can ever listen again to Sousa's "Liberty Bell March" without seeing that giant foot come down from above, squashing the cartoon figures from *Monty Python's Flying Circus,* or hear Liszt's Hungarian Rhapsody no. 2 without seeing that great piano virtuoso Bugs Bunny pounding it out with such wabbit aplomb? Therein lies the risk of haphazard approbation. Sometimes stickiness can't be controlled. If you ever want to experience human disillusionment, stand in the Louvre and listen to the murmur of the busloads of art pilgrims observing the *Mona Lisa:* "How small. How dark. How disappointing."

Superstar museums have to deal with this paradox of cross-pollination between Aesthetica and Vulgaria. "Destination pieces" generate traffic, yes, but they also tie up the gallery space. Like their cousins in retail, curators need to rotate inventory. To encourage repeat viewers these elite museums cannot put certain crowd favorites—such as, say, Monet's water lilies or haystacks—into storage because so many visitors come specifically to see them. Getting into the museum canon can sometimes be stultifying as the brandstory ossifies into becoming just another jingle. You are stuck with it.

In a sense, the invocation of connoisseurship is the brand meaning of the visual arts. And it's precisely that standoffishness that generates the value of commercial association. In this sense, perhaps Walter Benjamin was right. In "The Work of Art in the Age of Mechanical Reproduction" he famously argued that our desire to experience the authentic has been hampered by the engines of mass production. We no longer really know which twin has the Toni or whether it is real or Memorex. It's not the artifact that has changed, but our expectations. We prize originality not just because we don't have it; we wouldn't even recognize it if we did. We prize the specific original, the name brand if you will, because it makes us feel special and it is that experience that is at the heart of Museumworld.

In other words, art is the story we tell about an object and getting the object into the museum is an important part of the story. Perhaps, that's why the museum and the machine develop concurrently. They depend on each other. If the machine says, let's make the same thing over and over, the museum says let's not.

The Museum as Modern Reliquary

The museum experience, like the religious experience it mimics, is carried in an aura that implies the unique. There is no copy. That's its brandstory. In this sense, the first museums were the church strongboxes in which the bits and pieces of holy bodies were held in ornate containers called *reliquaries*. How relics got their value is revealing as it anticipates the museum experience. A relic was usually the dusty remains of a saint or a patch of fabric which, unlike a manuscript or a picture, had no intrinsic value. After all, it was just a fragment. Its value was *all* narrative.

Since each individual church needed to be built over some object (else how to differentiate the specific brand?), the mendicant orders of the Church would often splinter some already consecrated relic and then pretend that it had been stolen. For obvious reasons, there was no open market in relics. You couldn't buy and sell them. That would be sacrilege. Once "stolen," however, the Church order could construct what was essentially a franchise around the brand. The process was called *furta sacra,* or "relic theft," and the attached narrative was called the *translatio.* Relic transportation is the first instance of literal brand extension.

By the time of Chaucer's *Canterbury Tales* in the late fourteenth century, the deception has become industrialized. The Pardoner is making a market in selling pig knuckles. He is a despicable character, to be sure. But he knows, as does Chaucer, exactly what he is selling. He is selling a nondescript bone that carries a story, which delivers a feeling. The feeling is of forgiveness and redemption. Chaucer's wry approach to this charlatan has been often noted in literary criticism because he, Chaucer, is doing the same thing. The relic, like the story Chaucer himself is telling, carries an affect, a feeling. That's the basis of *genre,* the basis of narrative, the underpinning of the Canterbury *tales.* Want to laugh? Listen to comedy. Cry? Try sentimental drama. Shiver? Horror is for you. Want to be awestruck? Hold a relic. Or, today, go to a museum. Feel a sense of redemption.

Like a modern version of the Pardoner, museums essentially merchandise the sensation of a secular epiphany by conveying a story about certain things. The reason why museums are so interesting to study as marketing institutions is that we can see the process in operation. As opposed to churches, we can watch museums evolve because they are modern. When Henry VIII broke up the monasteries in the sixteenth century, a flood of once-sacred objects entered the marketplace. Now at last there developed a real barter market for relics previously moved through a market of contrived theft. These objects could be bought and sold. By the end of the seventeenth century, wealthy—and often eccentric—men collected bits and pieces of what was usually cast-off church memorabilia (what we now call *art*). Such collectibles were often put into storerooms called *cabinets,* a French word for a room of no specific use, and there they remained, often for generations.

Along with church artifacts, another collectible was oil paintings. Like relics, oil paintings were all over; there were tens of thousands of them. In fact, they were one of the first objects to enter the magical world of branding. We often forget that most oil painting done before the rise of Romanticism was done by journeymen who were told where to paint, how to paint, and especially what to paint. Then their works were often discarded or painted over because the canvas was often more valuable than the images. That's one reason why frescoes were so popular. They were cheap and easy to reuse. As the English critic/novelist John Berger argued first in his BBC television shows and the companion text *Ways of Seeing,* oil painting became so popular precisely because it was one of the few ways to tell stories about yourself (self-branding), and once you lost interest or were gone, the painting essentially lost value. Now, of course, just the opposite is true. The age of a painting often generates part of its perceived value. In fact, the patina itself is an augmenter of value as it testifies to weathered age.

Although the dominant consumer of oil-based visual stories was the Church of Rome, the medium was so popular that individuals got into the market, using painters to brand themselves, their families, or their guilds. Hence, the narrative of most pre-modern art is either the tales of Christian myth or stories of individual aggrandizement. Think of paintings such as Holbein's *The French Ambassadors,* in which the clear intent is to tell the world how successful the foreground figures are.

Please look at all our stuff, say The French Ambassadors, *1533, by Hans Holbein, the Younger. (Jean de Dinteville and George de Selve ["The Ambassadors"] by Hans Holbein, the Younger © The National Gallery, London.)*

213

An instructive etymology may show how commercial the process was. The phrase *objet d'art* originally meant any object worthy of being painted; that is, worthy of a narrative, of a brand. An objet d'art was whatever you chose to tell the painter to include in his painted publicity of you. Then it became what a collector wanted in his *cabinet*. Of course, now it means any object worthy of finding a place in a museum. The value has gone from the patron's choice to the connoisseur's to the curator's.

Such painted images went into the nascent collectors' *cabinets* along with rifled booty from the monasteries as well as all manner of stuff often drawn from their interest in the natural world. A piece of petrified wood was stacked next to a Quattrocento cherub, which was next to a stuffed dog. The general term to describe all the objects was *curiosities,* which originally meant things that were rare or hard to find—but not necessarily valuable. This was shortened to *curios.* Only in the modern world has *rarity* become a term of appropriation, a tribute to the fact that most things that surround us are machine made. In a sense, the machine has made possible the market for what the machine cannot make, namely, art.

So here are the two headwaters of high-culture art: (1) The Reformation in Europe and the sacking of the monasteries in England, both of which let loose a terrific supply of oil paintings and other once-sacred objects, and (2) secular oil painting, which became a method of aggrandizement and family memory but was valuable only as long as the subjects wanted to show off. All over Europe storehouses of curios appeared: the German *Wunderkammern,* the Italian *gabinetti,* the English *cabinets of curiosities.*

A better word was needed to describe this holding room because *cabinet* was also "a *small* container of precious objects." Predictably, cabinets started imitating the other places where valuables were stored: church reliquaries. And as learning moved from the Church to the university, so too did the cabinet/reliquary. From this alliance of precious objects and high-culture storytelling comes the now-common connection of the university and its collection of valuables, hence the library. So too the modern-day museum comes from this cross-pollination. The place sacred to the Muses, the repository of these objects, including books, is the *museum.*

The American Contribution: Peale and Barnum

We are not the first to be confused about what belongs inside the secular reliquary. We are not the first to be shocked by seeing motorcycles in the Guggenheim or *Star Wars* trivia at the Smithsonian. Have a look at an American example of such confusion in the *cabinet* of Charles Willson Peale in 1822. Peale saw his collection as representative of the world and initially filled his *cabinet* to the roof beams with undifferentiated stuff. Peale was the patron saint of the flea market. He finally had more than a hundred thousand things, some animal, some vegetable, and some mineral, all jumbled in together. His stuff was literally spilling out the doorway. Someplace was needed to warehouse them, yes, but what he really needed was a definer of space, a gatekeeper, a curator.

What early museums looked like before curators took over: Charles Willson Peale, The Artist in His Museum, *1822. (Courtesy of the Pennsylvania Academy of the Fine Arts, Philadelphia. Gift of Mrs. Sarah Harrison.)*

215

Look carefully at the peeking Charles Willson Peale. On his right side are display cases of stuffed birds, each in a reconstructed habitat, but on his left are the tools of his art: brushes and pallet. All that separates them is the tasseled curtain that Peale holds up as if to beckon us inside. This curtain is not to separate the pictorial from the natural sciences. Note that above the bird boxes are paintings, portraits of the heroes of the American Revolution. And note too that in the foreground are several mastodon bones, a skeleton, and a stuffed turkey. The visitors in the background are in both a picture gallery and a natural history exhibit. Make up your mind, the curator of the modern museum would surely say to Peale, your museum badly needs some "deaccession." Museumworld needs categories the way literature needs genres, the way an orchestra or an acting company needs a repertoire. Specialize. Exclude.

Peale charged admission to see his collection of curios. He was one of the first to realize you can make a living by exploiting human curiosity about rare things. But as you can see from the famous painting he did not tell stories about his collection. There were no labels. But the mere fact that he was able to make money from his hodgepodge proved crucial. What would happen if he were able to label, hence create a narrative for his objects? In other words, what would happen if he branded them, if he applied a *translatio* to his relics?

We would not have to wait long for the answer. At the same time that collectors were assembling their attics, as it were, of objects, other collectors were realizing that people would pay to see what they had assembled, especially if the objects came loaded with a narrative. These new stories were brain-spun and happened concurrently with the rise of the novel. They are works of a new kind of edutainment: fiction in the service of instruction. If you don't like them, they are *hype.* If you do, they are . . . *brands.*

The great entrepreneur of this kind of object *cum* story was an incarnation of Chaucer's Pardoner, Phineas Taylor Barnum. Oddly enough, P. T. Barnum learned the Pardoner's trade by selling lottery tickets. Private lotteries were common, corrupt, and thoroughly Darwinian. As an agent, Barnum knew that you don't sell the ticket, you sell the possibility, the story. The strongest story wins. And you told the story by promising the future at the same time you were insisting that

Lithograph of Barnum's American Museum, ca. 1850. The top four floors were a hodgepodge of freaks and curiosities, each presented with a narrative explanation—indeed, as Barnum said, a "great, pictorial magazine."

right here (right now!) is the time to buy—almost word for word the spiel of the Pardoner. Barnum's lottery office soon became one of the largest suppliers of tickets in New England. "My profits," Barnum humbly reported in his best-selling autobiography, *Struggles and Triumphs or, Forty Years' Recollections of P. T. Barnum,* "were immense."

It was only a hop and a skip before he was applying exactly the same selling techniques to his new endeavors: the selling of oddities to the curious, the merchandising first of hoaxes and then entire exhibits of the weird and dubious to a newly literate audience that prided itself on its savvy. That audience was the supposedly sophisticated urbanites of the New World, New Yorkers, and his venue was the supermarket of the strange, the commercial museum.

In 1841, Barnum purchased the building and contents of John Scudder's American Museum, a five-story firetrap on Broadway just north of the Battery. When Barnum was through with Scudder's collection, nothing in the building was what it seemed. Everything had a story attached. It was a temple to Humbug. In the same year he gobbled up Peale's collection of oil paintings and stuffed animals, mixing it in with Siamese twins, Tom Thumb, and various "mermaids." What held the hodgepodge together was the story, the narrative, the brand, and the devout and abiding interest of his customers to trust that brand, even if it meant being momentarily gulled. Curiosity may have killed the cat, but it made P.T. a rich man indeed.

Never underestimate the complicity of your audience. As Barnum knew, they were never passive. Supposedly no one complained when Barnum introduced the "inverted horse" at his museum. This "natural anomaly" had its head and tail reversed in position. The curious paid and then found an ordinary horse, tethered by its tail in its stall. His rhinoceros was advertised as a unicorn. The first hippopotamus seen in America was called "the Behemoth of the Scriptures." The alligator was the biblical Leviathan. In fact, the public loved it. When Barnum wanted to get people out of a crowded exhibit, he would post a sign proclaiming "This Way to the Egress" over the exit door. Customers expecting to see some sort of exotic waterfowl found themselves on the outside of the show, and they had to pay again to get back in. Most were not mad, however, but amused.

Although museum directors today would be loath to admit it, the blockbuster museum show comes directly from P.T. No matter what you sell, or when you sell it, Barnum knew that the first law is you must gather a crowd. Make traffic. Want to see the bee-utiful Mermaid from Feejee, a sight to dream of, "a bare-breasted, fish-tailed enchantress"? Thousands of people in the 1840s did. They lined up for hours outside Barnum's American Museum, as he renamed the emporium after a disastrous fire. They saw the head of a monkey crudely sewn onto the body of a fish. It may be sacrilegious, but it is true that the museum directors are not above observing the line in front of the tent. The great ones (or maybe it's the hungry ones) from Thomas Hoving to Thomas Krens even admit it . . . often gleefully.

Barnum mastered branding. He spun out stories not just around the Feejee mermaid but around Joice Heath (George Washington's supposed nurse), Charles Stratton (a midget who became General Tom Thumb), Eng and Chang (the Siamese twins, who fathered some twenty-two children), a microcephalic black dwarf (who was first advertised as the "What Is It?"—the missing link between man and monkey—and later as "Zip"), the Wild Men of Borneo, and Jo-Jo the Dog-Faced Boy. Barnum knew that you cannot anticipate, let alone understand, an event without a context, a frame, a story. Forget the object. You sell the story; you throw seeing the object in for free.

P.T. knew as well that in the hands of a master, the brand becomes more than claptrap that you jury-rigged around your product. When it worked, what you sold was both the product and the humbug, the steak and the sizzle. The commercial museum became so popular that Barnum was able to break it off and add it to the circus. Thus the sideshow, a predecessor of what is now the staple of museum fare, the special exhibit. See it now, it'll be gone tomorrow. Pay a little extra. Those crowds patiently lining up in front of the MoMA, and then patiently lining up again for a special exhibit, are very close to their great-grandparents patiently lined up in front of Barnum's museum. Best yet, very often inside the museum you pay again to see that really special show. Then you buy a memento in the gift shop.

Barnum was the first impresario to understand the bizarre ratios between the spending of money on advertising and the increasing of revenues. He understood the importance of creating occasions in which to tell the story and make the sale. In *Struggles and Triumphs,* Barnum humbly acknowledges his contribution: "I thoroughly understood the art of advertising, not merely by means of printer's ink, which I have always used freely, and to which I confess myself much indebted for my success, but by turning every possible circumstance to my account." Ever wonder why museums spend so much of their supposedly short supply of cash on advertising the "you'll never be able to see it again" exhibits? Check Thursday's and Friday's issues of *The New York Times,* and you'll see pages of advertising tribute to Barnum.

The Modern Museum

At the end of the nineteenth century, thanks to the necessity of formal and state-supported education, cultures got separated into high and low, good-for-you and bad-for-you, art and entertainment.

Barnum was shunned. Peale was spruced up and reorganized. Things got serious. The fun went out of museums. The panjandrums of the Land of High Aesthetica drove out the visigoths of Low Vulgaria. Shhhh, please, this is a library, this is art.

The modern, formal, self-conscious museum developed from the often obsessive but joyful collections of undifferentiated stuff. Often the modern collection was first assembled by an industrialist who hired a new type of intercessor, the heavily credentialed connoisseur, to be sure the dross was removed. Then it was cataloged, framed, pedestaled, and heroically lit. By the nineteenth century the deadening *catalogue raisonné* was a standard of appreciation and show-off value. Bloodline and heritage were foregrounded: *provenance.* Imitation, which was so much a part of early modern art, was abhorred. Authenticity prevailed. Forgery entered the art-historical lexicon meaning no longer an object crafted at a forge but one counterfeited. These aseptic collections were housed in the family mansion, which often consisted of multiple connecting rooms.

Hence the dreary template of the standard museum. Gallery space is housed in separate rooms connected by faux doorframes. In Museumworld, you are like a house guest being ushered from room to room, rather like being with the dreadful Duke in Browning's poem "My Last Duchess." The grid structure of parallel galleries and cross-connecting rooms with a specific itinerary for the visitor is a vestige of this homebound collection. Little name tags are all over, attesting to provenance. Go into the Frick Collection, a small museum in the former Manhattan mansion of one of these industrial collectors, and you can really experience the intimidating intimacy. Inch for inch, this is the greatest old-style museum in the Western Hemisphere. Thorstein Veblen was right. To the industrial Ozymandias, art was no fun, it was not decor—it was a weapon. "Look upon my works, ye mighty, and despair."

In the next step, the mansion, usually done up in Beaux Arts style, grew "wings" filled with the treasures contributed by other wealthy men. Increasingly women became involved, first as the inheritors of this stuff and then as collectors of it. To get to this next step of heft, however, a crucial event in the industrializing of museums had to occur. The federal government got involved. Never underestimate the importance of taxes in the creation of Museumworld culture.

First, in 1909, the Payne-Aldrich Tariff Act added works of art more than twenty years old to the list of duty-free import objects, and, second, in the 1930s new tax laws allowed duty-free passage of such works from an estate to a charitable institution. Those cabinets of curios were soon crossing the ocean in huge shipping boxes, all indirectly subsidized by the American taxpayer, often ending up in vast intimidating downtown mausoleums.

The Role of Government

As with Higher Ed, Inc., which continually adds value by dividing high and low, the charitable deduction in federal and state taxes made Museumworld possible by subsidizing the supposed high. Thanks to the boundless chicanery of lawyers, it soon became possible to "lend" works to these institutions and then get them back with a nifty increase in value. It still happens. In 1973, the Metropolitan showed the collection of paintings by the Victorian artist Sir Lawrence Alma-Tadema belonging to Allen Funt of *Candid Camera* fame. Mr. Funt was a smooth operator of more than a camera. Eight months after the show closed, he sold his entire collection. Thanks to the show, the market price had soared. It is common (although hardly trumpeted) for an artist to donate a work to a museum that is foregrounding his work. Quid pro quo. Both backs are scratched.

Take a stroll in the cellar of a museum such as the Met. See all those paintings just hanging there like slabs of meat? The superstar museums are lucky if they can display 10 percent of their holdings. Lending a painting to the Met is like donating money to Harvard. While neither can really use your largess, the museum can at least make your other holdings grow in value. Although no one has the exact figures, *The Economist*, the English financial magazine, estimates that even midlevel museums exhibit at the most about half their total holdings.

No wonder the current hubbub over the repeal of the estate tax. Museums, already overstocked with inventory, squeal that they will be cut off from their supply of new images. But donors squeal that their objects will decrease in value. And they are right. The abolition of estate and gift tax is the silver cross to the museum vampire. Museum directors are convinced that charitable giving would dry up if the "gifting" were no longer paid for by taxpayers. But what they are also concerned about is that perceived rarity will be unmasked for the charade that it is.

When was the last time you heard of a museum selling a work? In the rare instances in which it happens there is usually an elaborate explanation such as "We're selling the extra Blank so we can buy the Blank-blank to fill in a gap (and perhaps we can use a little of the excess to fund operating expenses)." Then there is the tattletale word *deaccession*, which entered Museumworld jargon in the 1970s. What makes the word interesting is that it generates a subterfuge. What it usually means is selling an object. Let a museum deaccess in order to meet expenses or build endowment, and the squeals of other museum directors crying foul is deafening. Often such sales make good sense. But the art industry—artists, donors, galleries, collectors—would suffer so the Association of Art Museum Directors expressly forbids it under all but dire circumstances.

The role of the government hardly ends with estate taxes. One of the more interesting aspects of Museumworld is how the government, which supposedly is removing direct funding either in the form of tax policy or drying up the National Endowment for the Arts (NEA), is allowing a certain tax haze in the clearly for-profit museum store, the museum dining room, and the museum Web site. The application of the unrelated business income tax is a curious and overlooked aspect of the corporatization of the museum. Talk to anyone in the museum business, and he or she will tell you that museums do a lot of business inside this haze. Even department stores, whose balance sheets are certainly affected by having museums in the trinket business, know better than to raise a ruckus. After all, many of them (such as Bloomingdale's) have commercial cross-marketing links to museums (such as the Met).

One bit of government largess that does need to be acknowledged because it has had such far-reaching effects is the underwriting of the insurance costs for traveling exhibits. As with elite universities, the value of art is in perceived selectivity. And how does your object get into this level? It travels inside a blockbuster exhibit. The transportation costs are small compared to the insurance. And who underwrites the hefty reinsurance? The government. Ever wonder how the heavily advertised megaexhibit has been a phenomenon of our times? How suddenly we have been flooded with treasures such as the tomb of King Tutankhamen or the seemingly endless paintings of Picasso, Monet, Matisse, Gauguin, and van Gogh?

The blockbuster traveling show, which is the Christmas season for museums, is the direct result of the NEA's Arts Indemnity Program, started in the 1950s. This Cold War program was a jingoistic way to expand Western European influence in the name of providing wider access to canonical works that just happened to be Western. After the terrorist attacks of September 11, 2001, the Arts Indemnity Program upped the insurance from $5 billion to $8 billion, increasing individual coverage from $500 million to $600 million and essentially guaranteeing that blockbusters will continue. But the elite museums, which are currently sitting on vast storehouses of unexhibited art, have done relatively little to send their own nonelite collections around to lesser places. Why? It's a hassle, and the lesser works will not increase the brand power of the museum. Very often private foundations such as the Knight Foundation underwrite the sharing of nonmarquee objects with smaller venues. Meanwhile, the superstar museums increase the value of their objects (and in so doing encourage tax-deductible donations) by cooperating primarily only with each other.

Museumworld, Inc.

Here is how matters stood in Museumworld, until recently. Big industrial cities such as Cleveland, Detroit, and Chicago had collections that rivaled those of the great museums of Manhattan, Philadelphia, and Boston. In a way, they were mimicked by Higher Ed, Inc.—the museums of Yale, Harvard, Chicago, and Princeton. And there was a comfy relationship between these suppliers of cultural capital. Art departments, especially Harvard under Paul Sachs, fed the curatorial ranks with careful men fully committed to the myth of the palliative powers of art. The museum was in control of this trained elite. They took the legendary course ("Fine Arts 15a: Museum Work and Museum Problems," which became simply "the museum course"), they monitored the canon, had two middle names, wore bow ties and horn-rimmed glasses, went to St. Grottlesex, twinkled like clerics in a Trollope novel, and were thoroughly sincere. Like the Episcopal Church (which they attended), art appreciation and ownership was a badge of social class.

But then, around the same time that Higher Ed, Inc., exploded and everyone had to go to college, every city decided that it too deserved a first-class museum, if not for the unwashed hoi polloi then for the kiddies. In the mid–twentieth century, the high-art museum started to ooze out everywhere. The Industrialization of Museum Culture was upon us. The Ivy League and elite schools, including tiny Williams College, a liberal arts school in the Berkshires, started pumping out graduates with MBAs and even Ph.D.s on the curriculum vitae. Seemingly all over Texas, as well as in L.A., San Francisco, Minneapolis, Richmond, and Kansas City, an art collection became part of civic pride, like an anchor store in the civic mall, a way to both enlighten and gentrify downtown.

The Williams mafia in particular were muscling in on the action, and people such as Thomas Krens were defining the new-new modern museum. Admittedly, Krens is the most audacious of this new generation, and his management of the Solomon R. Guggenheim Museum arched more than a few eyebrows. Members of this new generation are willing to take chances, realizing that they are competing not with each other but with every other entertainment venue. Compare his view of the modern urban museum with that of Philippe de Montebello, director of the Metropolitan Museum of Art, and you will see the shift. Here is verbatim what Mr. de Montebello put forward in descending order of importance when asked by Judith Dobrzynski of *The New York Times:*

- Great works of art.
- Intelligent and seductive presentation with good lighting and labeling.
- Highly accomplished, public-spirited curators.
- Substantial acquisitions funds.
- An endowment large enough to ensure integrity and independence from market-driven decisions.
- Fully committed trustees.

- Staff members who believe in authority and discrimination in judging and presenting art.
- Ease of access, physically through amenities, and intellectually, through programs that deepen the experience and understanding of art.
- Ease of access *fuori le mura* outside the walls of services and information through the latest technology.
- An unwavering belief in the primacy of the experience of art over that of "museum as agora," mindful of Hector's exhortation in Shakespeare's *Troilus and Cressida:* " 'Tis mad idolatry to make the service greater than the God."

This is almost pure Harvard "Fine Arts 15a," which Mr. de Montebello took from Paul Sachs. And here, from a 1999 lecture, is what Thomas Krens listed as "the components of a great 21st-century museum" (again in descending order):

- A great location, with urban interaction.
- Great collections.
- Great architecture.
- A great special exhibition.
- A great second special exhibition.
- Two shopping opportunities.
- Two eating opportunities.
- A high-tech interface via the Internet.
- Economies of scale via a global network.

If what is happening in the megachurch and Higher Ed, Inc., is any guide, Mr. Krens's version, in which the museum and the department store merge, will ultimately prevail. Reverence for the experience will replace reverence for the object. Here's why.

The Museumification of Shopping and the Shopification of Museums

In the 1960s, as our culture started moving from a gatekeeper to a ticket-taker culture, from a custodial culture to an entertainment culture, the museum was forced to compete for what became the modern patron, the shopping tourist. At the same time, the high-end retail marketplace was making its way uptown toward the museum, bringing with it the complementary form, the touring shopper. This new museum visitor was not just a consumer of the artistic experience, she was a customer of the thing itself. Museum mile was soon including such other outlets as opuluxe shops, elegant dining, spectacles of all kinds, even including the midcult department store, which sold pieces of things called *art*.

The modern department store and the art museum are now joined at the hip. They have always been close since they appeared almost simultaneously in London and Paris in the twilight of the nineteenth century. They are all about vaunting things, branding things. They both attempt not just to be with it, but slightly ahead of the curve. Structurally, they are dream palaces, Lands of Enchantment. The principle guiding the museum is the idea of singularity; the principle of the department store is abundance. The museum says, "Don't touch, you can't have." The department store says, "Please fondle, it

can be yours." Museum says unique, store says it's part of an ensemble. But they are both about consumption. The initial human behavior in both is scoptophilia. We gaze at the framed and floodlit objets d'art behind glass. We gawk at the decorated and elegant mannequin in the store window. We peer at the label beneath the painting just as we inspect the label on the object. We need to know provenance, the brand, *s'il vous plaît*, before we can consume.

Walter Benjamin, the moody Cassandra of modernism, was prescient. As he remarked in numerous essays and observations, the *flâneur* is both window shopping and gallery cruising. His eye lights on new things, but his "I" needs to know narrative in order to know value. He is a story hunter, if you will, the first modern cool hunter. He finds stories at the center of the new industries: retail and repository, store and museum, advertising and education. The narratives intertwine. "All department stores will become museums, and all museums will become department stores," said Andy Warhol of the impending amalgam. In fact, Pop Art was the party thrown to celebrate it.

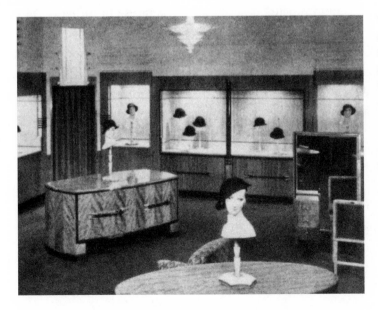

The department store floor starts imitating gallery space—the hat department at Meir & Frank Store in Portland, Oregon, before and after museumification in the 1930s.

How Inventory Is Built

We know how things get into the department store. A professional buyer predicts future taste. But how do they get into the museum? What gets them over the transom, up on the wall, behind the glass, and under the light? Who decides what to buy? What to exhibit? In artcrit this process is never called marketing; it is called "museumification." What gets in has become the hot-button issue of the industry. Who is in charge, the ticket taker or the gatekeeper? Who runs the mint of cultural capital? On one hand, museum space is the literal site for adding value to objects. A work is "privileged" just by being allowed on to the floor or walls of the temple. Value is added. Hence one of the raging battles in the culture wars has been what to allow in and especially what to keep out. How important is the line of customers out front? If you pretend that what is dense and unpopular is art, the line will be short. If you include commonly known objects, the line lengthens. University professors with tenure can foreground difficult art, but museum directors, who are fired with some regularity, need to be careful. For them, mild scandal is good marketing, complexity bad. Achieving this delicate narrative is at the center of museum branding.

The task of deciding what goes onto the floor is given to *curators*. The word is unfortunate because the job requires not caring for objects so much as choosing which objects deserve care. While such arbiters like to think they are putting shows together, in truth they are more like textbook or anthology editors. They don't work alone. They are usually the second to know. In the modern world of gate receipts, it is the audience who determines much of what is moved into and out of sight. Observe the classroom, for it has become strangely analogous to the museum walls. Allow women into the classroom, and sooner or later the anthologies will start foregrounding women writers. African Americans come into class, and you find that slave narratives become featured as literature. Allow Hispanics in, and—well, you get the point. Like the carnie of the sideshow, the curator who wishes to hold his job always has his eyes fixed more on the line in front of the tent than on what is behind the tent flap.

Jesse McKinley, a reporter for *The New York Times,* roamed the museums of Manhattan in mid-March 2003. For his piece "Art Is Long? So Are the Lines," he attended some typically contemporary shows in Museumworld. The exhibitions unfolded a process rather like the counter programming of commercial television. So at the Met there were two blockbusters: *Leonardo da Vinci, Master Draftsman,* covering old masters, and *Manet/Velázquez: The French Taste for Spanish Painting.* At MoMA QNS (MoMA moved to Queens while its new building in Manhattan was being prepared) was *Matisse Picasso,* a typical blockbuster drawing about five thousand visitors a day. The Whitney couldn't really compete and so was doing *Scanning: The Aberrant Architectures of Diller + Scofidio,* a retrospective of cerebral architecture from a husband-and-wife team, and *Elie Nadelman: Sculptor of Modern Life,* a rather spare, dull show of a rather spare, dull sculptor. These shows at the Whitney were also an admission that no one could compete with the Met and MoMA, especially not while the Guggenheim was superhip, showing the films, sculptures, and

Spring 2003 in Manhattan Museumworld is a Darwinian struggle at the turnstile.

photographs of a former J. Crew model in *Matthew Barney: The Cremaster Cycle*. This exhibition drew nearly 300,000 visitors. Was it happenstance that Maxwell Anderson, director of the Whitney, resigned during this shakeout? Although we usually don't like to admit this, art museums are behaving just like television channels, and directors are being treated suspiciously like programmers.

Note the number of combination shows. No one in Museumworld will admit this, but showing two artists together is good box office. See it now! Michelangelo versus Raphael. Competition is always implied, even if not overtly stated. What's more compelling than Matisse versus Picasso? Manet versus Velázquez? None of these events was cheap. The baseline experience cost about $15 a person, not including incidentals and souvenirs, but McKinley's observation was accurate: the museum experience is not just competitive and acutely aware of alternatives, it has a deep grip on the modern consciousness. These places, complete with Acoustiguides and reams of paper instructions, were playing to packed houses. Each venue was distinct and different, and each knew exactly how long the lines were out front of its competitors.

Given the intense competition not just with other museums but with other providers of take-away emotions, it is inevitable that museums colonize the extremes. So it makes programming sense that da Vinci, the Impressionists, the moderns, and the post-moderns are slugging it out at separate superstar venues. High-end retail works the same way. Go into Armani, Gucci, Louis Vuitton, Versace, or any other supplier of deluxe on Fifth and upper Madison Avenues in Manhattan (or on Rue du Faubourg St.-Honoré in Paris, Via Condotti in Rome, or Bond Street in London), and what do you see? An almost exact replica of what is happening on museum row. They all sell the same stuff, and so they counter-program designer fashion. Not by happenstance are luxury retailers cheek by jowl with museums, and not by happenstance does the designer's name function like the artist's—the brand literally.

Look carefully. In both museum and high-end retail, objects are reverentially lit from above, boxed into elaborate cases or set into frames. The spare and sometimes even brutal isolation of an object as mundane as a scarf or a pocketbook placed all alone as if it cannot be contaminated by other members of the same class is stock in trade for museums. Like the works of art they imitate, the window treatments are often edgy, even scandalous: think Gucci, Louis Vuitton, even Prada. The stack-it-high-and-pile-it-deep of Kmart is turned upside down in the world of museoluxe. Place it by itself and then flood it with white light. Put a label beneath it. Hide the price tag but make it available. As David Brooks has argued in *Bobos in Paradise: The New Upper Class and How They Got There*, taste in art and taste in fashion are the basis of a new kind of consumption community. Bobos (**bour**geois **bo**hemians) know consumption is the art of self-creation and that this activity is the highest form of modern shared creativity. In a sense, it's what we have for religion, the commodification of *felt needs*.

The luxury store window has now joined the museum wall in replacing the church fresco and reliquary as objects of the fervent gaze. People pausing by windows, doing what is dismissed as window shopping, bear an eerie similarity to spectators gazing in the museum, who are a modern version of the penitent adoring the icon, in turn, a variation of the *ur*-configuration: the believer and the ineffable Beyond. Little wonder we bow our heads as our hearts skip a beat. It's the commercialization of awe, the branding of epiphany.

231

The Prada Prado

Take a stroll in New York's SoHo district and have a look at Prada's $30 million "epicenter store." First, it's literally in space once occupied by a branch of its exhibitionistic cousin, the downtown Guggenheim Museum (now kaput). Second, the store even has the same architect as the Guggenheim's Las Vegas digs—the ultraslick shopper Rem Koolhaas. Third, it seems to have no signboard, no logoed label over the door. Just like the Frick. This is exclusive, for connoisseurs only. And, fourth, when it opened, the store issued a catalog that looked just like a *catalogue raisonné*.

That's because it's a museum, not a retail outlet! Or, at least, it's an art gallery. The one thing that it is not is what it is. What matters is what isn't matter. From the sidewalk, the 23,000-square-foot space looks like an industrial loft. But once inside, you know better. It's performance space. You are the performer. Suddenly, the floor you enter on, a broad sweep of exotic zebrawood, drops off like an Acapulco cliff. At the edge, you feel like Keats's "stout Cortez . . . silent upon a peak in Darien." As the Romantic poets and painters knew, precipices precipitate awe. Here and there on a dozen descending terraces, a few shoes are strewn to signal what? an avant-garde shoe department, perhaps. The floor then flattens out for a few yards in the basement before curving back up to crest at sidewalk level. This is the famous Wave. It really is awesome and a little dangerous. Shoppers of the aesthetic moment gasp and grab the handrail as art patrons did a century ago when looking at the paintings of American Luminism by the likes of Albert Bierstadt, Thomas Cole, or Frederick Church.

In retail jargon, going into this place is having an *immersion experience,* sort of like going to bike week with a bunch of Harley Hog owners, eating in the Rainforest Cafe, or shopping in Niketown. Forget the inventory, hell, it's just shoes, pocketbooks, and scarves: it's the gasp that counts. That's the brand experience. To make sure you don't forget the sensation, a massive soft cloud sculpture of Prada fabric swings overhead like a huge fisherman's net. A chunk of the Wave can be flipped down to become a stage. Sweep away the merchandise and the shoe terraces and the miniamphitheater seats two hundred patrons, just like the high school gym that doubles as the cafeteria and school theater.

The sales arena is theater, as though shopping were really a drama. Well, it is.

So where's the Pradaschmatte? The store seems to say, forget it. There's more important stuff than stuff. Such as art, for goodness' sake. At street level, the ugh! inventory is in movable cagelike display racks hung from the ceiling on industrial tracks. On the lower level, most of the clothing is shown on movable wall units in a series of painfully cramped spaces. The dressing rooms are really impossible to relax in. Whenever I have been there most of the people were just gawking, not daring actually to try anything on. How could they? The stuff is too intimidating and unfamiliar even to touch. High-tech sliding glass doors are controlled by foot pedals, one of which instantly changes the glass from transparent to translucent, supposedly to ensure privacy, but instead gives the eerie sensation that someone else's pedal may be reversing the action. Once inside the booth, you can see yourself in mirrors, and can check out your rump via a live video feed. But is anyone else watching? You're never sure. The experience of putting clothes on is bizarre. In the dressing room, video cameras and touch-screen monitors give you the impression *you* are an object being framed and hung for display. You are art. Measure up!

Every Museum/Store Show Needs a Catalog

If you want to find out what this mixup of deluxe and objet d'art is all about you should consult Mr. Koolhaas's *The Harvard Design School Guide to Shopping*. Publication coincided with the opening of the Prada store almost as if it were yet another *catalogue raisonné*, this time one to really settle the score. The chunky tome is every bit as curious as the title suggests, right down to the invocation of the Harvard brand in the title and an illustration etched into the book jacket. Etched in bas-relief on the jacket is an escalator surrounded by dollar signs. Go figure. The actual title appears only on the back of the jacket as if to tell you things are not as they seem. Inside, however, the treatise offers a reckoning and acceptance of the not-so-startling fact: It's all about consuming brands of sensation. That is what we have for modern art, well, for postmodern art.

Koolhaas has been here before. In the 1997 competition for the expansion of New York's Museum of Modern Art, he famously put "MoMA Inc." on his proposed design. He didn't get the job, but he made his point. Shopping is now "the defining activity of public life." We shop at the airport, we shop at church, at school, so what? Wanna make something out of it? Thus the train station is now a mall. McDonald's is also a toy store. The University sells "spiritwear." Freedom is just another word for time left to shop. Urbanization is commerce. Museumworld Inc. Get used to it. Brands 'R' Us. Art is just very expensive stuff.

And Koolhaas has a point. Why shouldn't the shopping experience cross-pollinate with the museum trip, which itself has overlaid the trip to church? Shopping is what we have for modern pilgrimage. Sales are crusades. A nifty pocketbook is a chalice. The eerie transformation of midtown Manhattan, where the luxury flagships are elbowing aside the great churches of mercantile Christian culture, shows the new colonization occurring. From Saint Patrick's to Saint Thomas to the Fifth Avenue Presbyterian Church to Christ Church all the way up to Saint James Church on Madison Avenue and Seventy-first Street, these hulking stores have gobbled up what was once prime liturgical space. Are the designer flagship stores becoming the new pulpits from which the word goes forth? Koolhaas certainly thinks so.

And if you look at these dreadnought stores you can see they have all self-consciously lifted the architecture of the museum to resettle it as the store-as-museum. And it's happening all over town. So in Tribeca, Issey Miyake's New York home-base store was designed by Frank Gehry, of the Guggenheim Bilbao (Spain) triumph. On the Upper East Side designer mile, Madison Avenue, Jean Paul Gaultier has a boutique designed by minimalist Philippe Starck. Hermès, Giorgio Armani, and Comme des Garçons have engaged modern architects Tadao Ando, Renzo Piano, and the Swiss duo of Herzog and de Meuron to design new stores, showrooms, and headquarters to showcase not just their designs but their designer personae.

Look at the new Hermès North American headquarters. It was designed by the Phillips Group. Hermès is acutely aware that the structure is going to be compared to the Manhattan headquarters of its archcompetitor, Moët Hennessy Louis Vuitton. The LVMH tower is as elegant as any museum, the epitome of controlled refinement. Walk by it at night, and you will be struck by its angled sections, columns of light slowly shifting, eerie reflections, a sense of magic. It glows. It's like unfolding origami. Walk inside and you think you are in a pocket-sized cathedral or minimuseum. Hermès knows it's not about scarfs and pocketbooks; like LVMH, luxe is all about generating excitement.

What this architecture makes clear is that if there was any doubt about the distinction between high and low, art and commerce, it's no more. In fact, the distinction was nicely done in by the museum itself. The 1990–91 MoMA show called cautiously *High & Low: Modern Art and Popular Culture,* assembled and glossed by Williams mafioso curator Kirk Varnedoe and *New Yorker* writer Adam Gopnik, may have been lambasted by academic critics, but it was welcomed by everyone else. It told the truth. The center could no longer hold. High and low had been rendered meaningless. The real center of gravity was in corporate sponsorship and the show itself was to generate audience for AT&T, the modern Medici. The recently unbundled AT&T aggressively promoted the show as an extension of its own new brand per-

Culture Incorporated: Ma Bell celebrates fifty years "with the arts."

sonality. MoMA knew it was onto something. For the right choice was not between High and Low but between MCI, Sprint, and AT&T.

To hard-liners, the resulting cultural porridge is the result of watering down the stock. But the crowds out front don't care. Cultural soup is precisely what happens when interchangeable experiences get mixed up. The edutainment stew is strangely more tasty for both the store and the museum. How can you keep them apart? Who wants to? When experiences become similar, storytelling becomes intense, attention getting becomes crucial, and narrative courses overlap. They have become, from a cultural point of view, cross-branded.

When the Art World Went Pop

If one were looking for the moment where the crisscross between the marketplace and the museum took place, one would have to trust the artists themselves. After all, before art historians and students, before architects and shopkeepers, before gallery owners and collectors, the individual artists were the people most sensitive to the shifting currents. It's their livelihood. Since Romanticism, they have become the avant-garde. In marketing lingo, it's what they *own*. The rise of Pop Art in the 1960s was not so much the entrance of the moneychangers into the temple as it was the awareness that if artists were going to tell new tales they were going to have to go where the action is, they were going to have to go shopping. And in the world before Prada, Gucci, and Hermès, the action was quite clearly happening on the shelf down at the appropriately named *super*market.

The genius of Pop Art was, of course, that it never pretended otherwise. It loved the commercial brand. Let the moody Eeyores of Abstract Expressionism such as Franz Kline, Barnett Newman, and Clyfford Still mull things over down at Rothko's chapel; the Pop Artists of the 1960s were on their way to the A&P. Then off to the bank. No lugubrious rigors, no tortured disquisitions on the meaning of paint, no metaphysics of marginality for them. Just get me to the package, Pop said; we'll unwrap it.

But once you say that Pop loved branded packages, what's left? Not much. Pop was a dead end. Like Dada, which also idealized the container (recall Man Ray's *Pechage* or Duchamp's *Boîte en Valise*), it was dull art. It was meant to be. Pop was devoid of complex aspiration by design. It was a mirror always, never a lamp. By the end of the 1960s, Pop had essentially lost its way. Fast-moving consumer goods (FMCGs), canned food, cosmetics, plastics, glitz, oversize packaging, emblems, audiovisual aids, blinking lights left the studio and returned to the store. Slow-moving luxury goods took their place.

How Corporations Branded Art to Brand the Corporation

Although much is made in the Academic-Museum Complex on the prescience of artists, on how they are, in Percy Bysshe Shelley's famous dictum, the "hierophants of unapprehended inspiration . . . unacknowledged legislators of the world," the Pop Artists seemed to know that the *true* panjandrums of the art world were not the curators on museum mile or the academics in some art history department but rather corporate marketers on the twenty-fifth floor of the Philip Morris Building. To the new corporate Medici of the late twentieth century, a work of art was a story that you could lease, just as it was done in the Renaissance. As Lorenzo de' Medici paid to have himself painted into various works of art, as the various mendicant orders such as the Franciscans and Dominicans paid to have their saints painted, corporations found they could put themselves into the artscene by judicious patronage and incessant public relations. Having their brand names involved with brand-name artists could cause the value to spill over to them. Art nirvana: the perpetual-motion machine of meaning—art branding corporation and corporation returning the favor by sponsoring branded art; the sponsored museum sponsoring the sponsor.

This convergence was more than on the surface. Commercialism was exploding at the very center of the high/low split as merchants were becoming patrons, yes, and museums themselves were becoming the necessary intermediaries. Not only was the stuff of adcult becoming the subject matter of artcult, the commercial process itself was becoming the mechanism of display. Not just "Here, paint this" but "Here, let us show this (along with our logo)." It became the mu-

Philip Morris—whoops! Altria—lends a hand to "those in need" by sponsoring art.

seum's job to drive both sides of the market. The museum became the gearbox, the meshing of patron and producer. As with popular music, *selling out* moved from opprobrium to high praise.

By the 1980s, the Bronx Museum of the Arts even started a program to help inform young artists how the art world *really* works and how to master it. Every year almost forty budding artists are selected for a twelve-week course in career management. What's career management for an artist? It's gallery representation, learning the role of the art critic, self-marketing, grant writing, insight into museum prac-

tices, how to pitch your product, what to look like, what to wear, and how to be interviewed. In short, the museum helps you contrive your career. These are serious artists in this program. Two thirds have master's degrees. All you need, the museum seems to be saying, is a little less MFA and a little more MBA. The Pop Artists, their tongues held in cheek, had it right. Taste can be marketed. Art is just another word for branding.

And so Museumworld became just another edutainment, an entertainment corporation struggling to compete for attention. Predictably, it intermingled with its commercial cousins precisely at those points it publicly spurned. The museum travels out into the literal space of the commercial corporation (the Whitney even had a branch in the Philip Morris Building), and the corporation uses the concept of the museum as a way to market its own cultural capital (*Philip Morris Presents the American Masters at the Whitney*). In addition, the Container Corporation of America, for example, commissioned many pieces of art for its Great Ideas campaign that began in the 1950s, and Chase Manhattan Bank collected art up until the 1980s as a way to showcase its cultural commitment. The modern corporation often invokes the claim of art. Carillon Importers, the company that had the Absolut account for years, had this motto: "Marketing after all is an art of its own," and Philip Morris proclaimed, "It takes Art to make a Company Great" without a smirk. Andy Warhol's pithy one-liners, such as "Art? I don't believe I've ever met the man," or "Making money is the highest form of art," became accurate descriptions of what art was coming to mean. Museums were places not just to showcase art but to create it.

As museums became factories of branding, a new mutant, the corporate museum, evolved. Instead of being reviled, it was revisited. So in the 1980s such industry-specific museums as Cleveland's Rock and Roll Hall of Fame and Museum, bankrolled by various record labels; the Museum of Television & Radio in Manhattan, supported by the networks; or the Newseum in the District of Columbia, funded by the Gannett conglomerate of newspapers and television stations, became tourist destinations. At a more specific level of unalloyed intermingling there is the World of Coca-Cola in Atlanta, Kellogg's Cereal City in Battle Creek, or, better yet, almost the entire town of Hershey,

Pennsylvania. Here in these venues, product advertising is showcased as art. Ads are blown up, framed, and heroically lit. The audience gasps with appreciation. The idea that what they know about these heavily advertised fast-moving consumer goods deserves museum space is profoundly affirming and not just a little disconcerting. Often museumification dispenses with the charade and just celebrates its marketing: Frederick's of Hollywood Lingerie Museum in Los Angeles and the Tupperware Visitors' Center and Museum north of Orlando are places to admire and buy stuff.

If you really want to see this corporate/museum juggernaut running at the speed of a thirty-second commercial, look at the incredible growth of children's museums. Why the explosion? Here is the fertile ground to plant the brand seed. Children in the Saint Louis Zoo pet animals at the Emerson Electric Children's Zoo, watch a show at the Bank of America Amphitheater, study bugs at the Monsanto Insectarium, and view the underwater antics of hippopotamuses at the Anheuser-Busch Hippo Harbor. How about the Please Touch Museum Presented by McDonald's in Philadelphia, the General Motors Center for African-American Art in Detroit, and the Mattel Children's Hospital at UCLA?

Most crass, however, is at the prestigious Field Museum in Chicago, where Sue, the most completely preserved fossil of a *Tyrannosaurus rex*, is presented by a corporate consortium that includes McDonald's and Walt Disney World Resorts. Two plastic models of Sue are trucked around the country each displaying the McDonald's name, just as Philip Morris, in palmier days, used to truck around a copy of the Declaration of Independence as part of a freedom-of-speech exhibit. Here, at the extreme, the museum is just another marketing plasma gone pop, the cozy symbiosis of corporate and art worlds acting as one, impossible to divide.

The Museum as Factory: Some Recent Examples

To see the convergence of art and commerce, observe the art museum as it competes for attention. The openings of museum shows have become like Hollywood premieres, events complete with promos and glitz. They are "building the brand." And the brand is not just the museum or the corporate sponsor, but the collection itself. Here's how it works.

In the late 1990s, the Brooklyn Museum of Art contracted with Charles Saatchi to put his collection of British art alongside other certified works as examples of modern sensational art. The exhibit was called *Sensation: Young British Artists from the Saatchi Collection.* Below, the museum admitted that the show was being underwritten by Mr. Saatchi. Mr. Saatchi is nothing if not savvy about how one generates value for interchangeable objects. For a time in the 1980s, he and his brother Maurice were two of the most important advertising men in the world, heading the eponymous Saatchi & Saatchi. The pair did the wondrous British Airways ads as well as the controversial ads that many contend resulted in the election success of Margaret Thatcher. The show was also funded by Christie's, which took many of Saatchi's works to market. The Brooklyn Museum had, in essence, rented out its galleries to lend Saatchi legitimacy and, in so doing, increase the value of his collection. The quid pro quo was certainly worth it. Mayor Rudolph Giuliani graciously threatened to remove city funding if the museum insisted on showing such objects. In so doing, he activated the op-ed regulars and upped the gate.

A short time later the Guggenheim curated a retrospective of the clothing of an Italian designer, Giorgio Armani. Spiraling up the same walkway where masterpieces of modernism (and motorcycles) usually appeared were suits and dresses. The gatekeeper problem here was not just that the exhibit was sponsored by *In Style,* a gossipy magazine from AOL Time Warner, but that Mr. Armani was said to have donated $15 million to the museum. True, the collection of four hundred pieces was stunning, but it was four hundred pieces of what? The magnificent expression of exquisite tailoring (the garments were beautifully presented) and the heroic lighting (the clothes were literally haloed) made fashion and fabric into objects of adoration. Oscar Wilde said that "A really well-made buttonhole is the only link between art and nature," but still this show was a stretch. At least down the block at the Met, when clothes are displayed, it is in the service of historical context, not commercial adoration.

A little back scratch-ing? The Giorgio Armani retrospective at the Guggenheim in 2000 came at the same time as a contribution.

These were not the first examples of back-scratching brands. The land between High Aesthetica and Low Vulgaria has been well traveled. In retrospect, the turning point in the migrations of art and commerce occurred some years ago when objects from the People's Republic of China appeared almost simultaneously in a department store (Bloomingdale's) and in a museum (the Metropolitan). In 1980, Bloomingdale's, then the flagship of luxe lite consumerism, organized two exhibits of China's cultural legacy. On the selling floor, the department store sold knockoffs of the "timeless, aristocratic and rare" Chinese goods. A few months later the Met showed the real things, organized and installed by Diana Vreeland, grande dame of high fashion, longtime editor of *Vogue,* and compatriot of the Bloomingdales. Such synergies were not unnoticed. Museums have wised up: they've learned to put the store *inside* the museum.

Museum Logos

We now accept that what's on the showroom floor of a museum will be accorded the same kind of spin as, say, the introduction of a new model of foreign car or some designer's show during fashion week. Is there a Manhattan museum without a huge logo, the literal brand? The Museum of Modern Art cleverly uses its trademarked MoMA logo on almost every thing it gets its hands on and the Whitney Museum presents its new chunky logo in splashy advertisements. But if you want to see logocentricity, consider this: when the Museum of Contemporary Art in Los Angeles wanted to spotlight itself, it hired TBWA\Chiat\Day, the high-profile advertising agency that created the Energizer Bunny, Taco Bell's smirking Chihuahua, and the quirky sock puppet for Pets.com. What the agency did for the museum was to site it as just another entertainment offering, just like a movie premiere, or new TV show. They took the ubiquitous black-and-white museum labels and made them into billboards, literally. So a billboard near the Crazy Girls strip club in Los Angeles reads:

> *Nudes 2001: Bodies, dimensions variable. A study of First Amendment rights, entertainment and business all acting in concert to provide a debate among lawyers, politicians and the general public. On loan from The Museum of Contemporary Art, Los Angeles.*

Similarly wry wall-text-as-poster was stationed near a well-known church in Hollywood, a public golf course, and at busy intersections. The labels even appeared on coffee cup sleeves, gas pump handles, and coat hangers carrying dry-cleaned clothing. Not to be outdone, across town, the more prestigious Getty Museum used the same kind of send-up of the catalog entry in newspaper ads. "Long before the scooter craze, the gift of choice was an illuminated manuscript," reads the copy in a Getty ad featuring an A.D. 1240 painting.

Museums in the Land of Disney are simply acknowledging the obvious: in a world of interchangeable entertainment choices, the museum is just another venue selling sensation. Not to mark off your territory and instead depend on the myth of redemptive high culture to protect you is a sure way to be passed by. Brand today or be forgotten tomorrow. Manhattan museums are a bit more self-conscious but every bit as competitive.

American Museums Are Not Alone

Lest we think ours is the only country in which the museum currently generates value for commercial products, we might look at those cultures that are often the most censorious. While the English are forever invoking the purgative and redemptive powers of art, if you watch closely they are also out back banging the pots and pans. Observe the Tate Modern. Here hordes of visitors pour into an old power station, funneled first past the café and bookshop before even approaching any of the exhibitions. The Tate logo is everywhere, on everything, logorrhea. The cavernous space is unencumbered by divisions between art and commerce. You don't go into a restaurant; the restaurant is in there with the art. And vice versa.

You can even see this amalgamation in the name change. The Tate has dropped the definite article, and the four museums are now simply Tate Britain (on Millbank), Tate Modern, Tate Liverpool, and Tate St Ives. The Tate brand is clearly commercial; the museums are franchises of it. Although original funding came from lottery money and government subsidies, the Tate conglomerate now has to match these funds through its own initiatives—hence the café, shop, restaurant, and endless promotional campaigns, one of which even includes a tie-in with Coffee Republic. The coffee cups bear the logo *la Tate*, a pun on caffelatte.

The Tate has been one of the few holding-company museums to acknowledge and even celebrate the impact of commercialism on itself. In a refreshingly self-reflexive show in 2002–2003 called *Shopping: A Century of Art and Consumer Culture,* the Liverpool branch coproduced, with the Schirn Kunsthalle of Frankfurt, the first serious retrospective of the impact of shopping on the creation of art. When you walked into the show, you were smack in the middle of a perfect replica of a Tesco supermarket, complete with shelving containing products and checkout aisles. In fact, a real live store manager came in each week to change the prices and refresh the vegetables. The exhibition also included major installations and environments such as

Claes Oldenburg's *Store* (1961) and the Pop ensemble creation *The American Supermarket* (1964) as well as works by artists as varied as Eugène Atget, Berenice Abbott, Walker Evans, Andy Warhol, Roy Lichtenstein, Christo, Duane Hanson, Barbara Kruger, Jeff Koons, and Andreas Gursky. Here was ample proof of the impact of consumption on the fine arts, architecture, film, music, aesthetics, structure, to say nothing of the environment. The only analogy was religious culture of the Renaissance. Like religion then, consumption is now everywhere. *Shopping: A Century of Art and Consumer Culture* wasn't tongue in cheek or even cheeky about this transformation of value systems. It was the Tate's frank acceptance that buying stuff has been an essential part of urban life throughout the twentieth century and that because of it Museumworld itself has been transformed.

It's the Amenities, Stupid

Although Tate Liverpool didn't foreground this, it implied that museums themselves are well on their way to becoming just another self-enclosed shopping venue. Just as Higher Ed, Inc., has used the classroom as the loss leader and just as the megachurch uses the Sunday service as enticement to weeklong activity, the art collection is becoming the come-on promise of the museum. The space increases the value of the objects, but many museums have made a tidy profit from renting their floor space as places to gather, to shop, to party, to be married, just like their religious and academic cousins. Want to party at the Met? You can rent the Temple of Dendur for $50,000 and party down, as long as there is no wine (spills), no balloons (wayward), and no confetti (mess). Chicago's Field Museum grossed as much as $1 million in "event income" in 2002 and expects to increase this by 75 percent in the next few years. If you want to party down at L.A.'s Museum of Contemporary Art, plan ahead now. It's usually booked up. As we will see in the next chapter, the next step is to condominiumize museum space so that ultimately you can live there.

Until that happens, the real day-to-day money is to be made in selling part of the experience, what is called in marketing the *takeaway*. Just as successful churches have exchanged sensations of forgiveness and salvation for attention, just as elite schools have made acceptance and affiliation the product of value, so the successful museum is able to consecrate not just the objects within its borders, but the actual experience. Museums generate a consumption community. Though we see Disney doing this with confected happiness or Harley-Davidson exporting danger into such objects as jackets and pullovers, still it is something of a shock to realize that this is also part of the museum attraction. The artifacts are the concrete symbols of the attraction, yes, the objective correlative of enlightenment. Coming out of a museum, you should feel better, you should feel self-satisfied. You should have felt *awe*. And you are part of a community of consumers. You've got the bag of goodies to prove it.

As might be expected, such realization is not the acknowledged goal of the enterprise. Intellectual enlightenment is the goal. Philippe de Montebello, the director of New York's venerable Metropolitan Museum of Art, made the *public* case, saying, "Our purpose is not to pull the crowds. Museums will lose. They do not do Disney that well." He said this, however, while sponsoring an exhibit of Jackie Kennedy

Jacqueline Kennedy: The White House Years, a show at the Met in 2001, proved no one is exempt from becoming a block-buster, especially one sponsored by L'Oréal and Condé Nast.

fashion memorabilia. To be fair, Mr. de Montebello did cancel a show of Coco Chanel's work at the Met that was to be sponsored by Chanel. But that was only when critics howled after they were informed that Karl Lagerfeld, the current head of the illustrious French fashion house, had demanded a say in the conception of the exhibit. Still the Met thought nothing of having Tiffany & Co. underwrite a show on the heritage of Charles Lewis Tiffany and Louis-François Cartier, arguing that this was okay because Tiffany's work had been created at or before the turn of the century, none of it is still sold by the firm, and the Cartier show ended with objects made in 1930, so Cartier didn't benefit. But that misses the point: these stores were building their brands, and the Met was helping.

As with the church service, the unacknowledged center of the museum experience has become the sense of being *in* the museum. And how can you brand that? Simple. You attach a story to each object, not just in the wall text but in the catalog copy. Then you refabricate the now-branded object and sell it as a memento of the experience—the souvenir. In a sense, the souvenir is a commercial relic, an object fetishized by a narrative, and that narrative surrounds the original object inside a museum. In 1999, according to the American Association of Museums, admissions, shop sales, reproduction royalties, and special events paid for almost 30 percent of the average operating budget. Since you really can't control corporate, governmental, and individual giving, and since you can't drain capital from your endowment or, worse, sell off parts of your collection without risking opprobrium, the question is how to increase the flow of objects leaving your museum. And to maximize your profits from them you have to load them with value, namely, with brand narratives. To make the process still more demanding, you have to do it in such a way that you don't risk losing the tax advantages of being a nonprofit. As with churches and schools, which are also treading the high wire, this is where the real art is effected, the art of applying the brand.

Art Museum, Inc.

American art museums are nonprofit organizations and so are tax-exempt. Almost anything you give to them is tax-free. Inside them, however, are stores. The stores are for-profit (and how!), and they pay the unrelated business income tax on the sale of a portion of their product line. But their overhead is carried as if they were contained inside the protected institution. It's a fine line. If museums start to behave too much like businesses (which is of course precisely what they must if they want to survive) these tax advantages could be threatened. So they are going to behave like schools hyping their logoed paraphernalia or churches selling their burial plots and Starbucks coffee, very carefully. Here are the profit centers of Museumworld.

The store

Oddly enough, the museum store has been around a while. The Victoria and Albert Museum in London had one of the first retail outlets. A century ago, you could buy a plaster cast or photos from the V&A collection. Then, almost by accident, accountants discovered that there was real money to be made. They were astonished to find that about one in five visitors bought something. But where to put the store? You put the store at the end of the exhibits, and you sold souvenirs of what had just been seen.

Americans contributed the next ingredient: the shopping bag that mentions the show you have just seen for which you had the good taste to buy those mementoes. Consumer nirvana. You affiliate with the show and then show your affiliation. Later, luxury stores climbed onto the shopping-bag bandwagon, making the same kind of changes to their bags that the museums had done and for much the same reason.

If you look at museum stores now, you'll see the next step occurring. The store is moving *in front* of the ticket taker, *before* the show. You don't have to go through the gallery to get to the shopping. In fact, better yet, the store has jumped loose of the museum and is off site. In so doing it's lost some of its tax-free protection, but it has also achieved the stand-alone efficiencies of a retail franchise. You can now buy that souvenir/relic/talisman of the show, not just the suitable-for-framing poster and the suitable-for-showing museum bag, but an entire ensemble of whirligigs and trochees often entirely unrelated to the collection. You never have to enter the gallery space.

Go to the museum and see the good stuff. Then buy some of it at the store. Then show your friends. The shopping bag lets you show your good taste to all.

William the Hippo is the Tony the Tiger identification character of the Metropolitan Museum of Art.

So in Manhattan, the Met, which is usually the museum most concerned about the dumbing-down behavior of other museums, has a minichain of three off-premise stores: one in Macy's, another in the Mid-Manhattan Library, and a third in Rockefeller Center. It also has a nifty icon, a faience hippopotamus from the Egyptian gallery nicknamed William. Just like its counterparts in the commercial world, William the logo is on prints, ceramic sculptures, T-shirts, ties, and is also a stuffed toy. The Met does about $90 million a year selling such trinkets, with a gross margin of about 50 percent, which is about 10 percent higher than you'd find at Bloomingdale's.

The venerable British Museum is no slouch in this off-site retail. It has even figured out that the best place for museum retail is in Heathrow Airport, Terminal 4. Forgot to see the museum? Don't fret. Here's your last chance for souvenirs. And you can get them duty-free. In fact, you can even call ahead and never have to go to the store; the booty is delivered to you on the plane.

If you note the current explosion of museum space you will find one constant: the gift shop is running the show. The deal with Mammon is worth it. For instance, the Met estimates that without the stores' contribution to income the real cost per person of admission would be close to $75.00. From 1992 to 1997, gallery space at 185 of the largest museums had increased by 3.3 percent, selling space by a whopping 28 percent. Some of this stuff hardly qualifies as souvenirs. It's straight junque. My personal favorite—aside from museum baseball caps, of course—is the Philadelphia Museum of Art tattoo collection of artworks. You can decorate yourself with van Gogh's sunflowers. The PMA also hawks pasta in the shape of Rodin's *The Thinker.* I've eaten some; it's quite tasty.

If you really want to see the trinketizing of branded stuff, look at the catalog sales. At Christmastime the catalog retailers most omnipresent in my mailbox are the big-city museums. Like the UNICEF catalogs of my childhood, they fairly reek of doing well by doing good. I love reading the catalog copy. How about this from the Museum of Fine Arts, Boston: a necklace "is adapted from Alfabeto di Lettere Iniziali, etchings from 18th-century Italy in our collection of Prints and Drawings"; while porcelain bowls are "similar to an early-15th-century Ming bowl from our Art of Asia Collection." Although they may well lose their Pink shirts in the process, you can certainly understand why all the museum directors piled onto the dot-com Web site debacle. Here was the perfect medium; explode the J. Peterman verbiage. Save the postage. And to the consumer the value was obvious: you never had to budge from your Barcalounger.

Not only has the museum store jumped loose of the exhibition space and migrated into such forms as the off-premise store, the catalog, and the Web site; it has even jumped loose of its own skin. Next time you go to the mall, have a look at the Museum Company. Just as the Nature Company, a fellow retail outlet, has pithy sayings carved on stones, deer-head weather vanes, flocks of ducks on ties, moose pajamas, and reams of notices proclaiming how a percentage of their profits "goes back to nature," the Museum Company does the same using objets d'art. The Museum Company even has a plaque on the entrance proclaiming:

Because Museums play a unique role in preserving mankind's great cultural achievements, we encourage you to visit and support your favorite museum. For our part, the Museum Company is committed to dedicating a share of our profits to museums.

The store makes its profits by selling Michelangelo's *David* in Christmas garb, a *Mona Lisa* stamp pad, *Venus de Milo* on a paperweight, *Queen Nefertiti* as magnetic note pad, Degas handbags, and numerous plastic and plaster reproductions of nameless classical statuary with labels such as Eternal Love or L'Amour. There are even freestanding collections: The Greco-Roman Collection of Jewelry, The Middle Eastern Collection, and the Russian, Celtic, and African collections of knickknacks. About 5 percent of the retail price ends up back at the original museum.

What's the future of the museum store? If it follows high-end retail, it may imitate luxe designers such as Armani, Lauren, Dior, et al., who have been able to colonize floor space in department stores; museums will consider this venue as well. Here's why: The museum store typically offers 8,000 to 10,000 SKUs (stockkeeping units, as they are known in the trade) of which maybe half are books. The Web site sells about 600 to 800 SKUs, while the catalog features 500 to 700 SKUs.

Getting into a department store means a museum can move the high-profit items and vary them in conjunction with changing exhibits. And this is to say nothing of the possibility of extending the brands to places like apparel. Once you start seeing William the hippo displacing the Lacoste alligator and the Lauren polo pony, you'll know that the ultimate transformation has happened. Instead of commercial culture using museums to generate value, museums are reversing the process.

The restaurant

Look again at the omnipresent plans of museum expansion, and you'll see the other profit center that is gobbling up space. Just as the store has crossed the boundary to get *outside* the museum, the restaurant is crossing to get *inside,* to mingle with the collection, to make the eating experience an intimate and uppercrusty event. If you ever ate at the British Museum in the old days, you would think you had been in the dreary catacombs. The restaurant was down in the cellar, and it was dank. Eat in the museum's restaurant today, and you can have a gourmet meal overlooking the recently renovated central core.

Why no one thought of this before is a marketing mystery best explained by whoever was running the place. Curators, like academics, eat from paper bags at their desks. They never saw the attraction of leaving crumbs on the gallery floor. To maximize returns, the modern food court should be placed in such a way that not only do you see the works, but you see the consumers of the works. And they see you. Since the museum experience is all about browsing, about gazing, about being a *flâneur,* what better place to observe than from your comfy chair behind a menu? Tuck in your napkin, and *bon appétit.*

Having a good restaurant on the premises also pumps up a museum's bottom line in unexpected ways, most importantly by increasing the "dwell time" of museum patrons. Plus, a few glasses of wine doesn't hurt when it comes to spending money in the museum store. The chef can even theme the menu so that it excites the very taste buds woken up by the art. When the British Museum recently featured a festival of Japanese art, the menu included a "Mt. Fuji–inspired" creation of chicken-salted jellyfish. When "Cleopatra of Egypt" arrived, so too did Lamb Tajine with couscous.

Even better, the typical museumgoer is so willing, nay eager, to affiliate with the place that usual price sensitivity is dulled. After all, it's the experience that counts. He wants to linger and feel good about himself surrounded by the world of privilege and luxury. And museums are realizing how much this can be worth. Most catering companies give museums a percentage of their turnover, which can range anywhere from 8 percent for a full-service restaurant to 25 percent for a café with a high volume of coffee and light snacks. The British Museum gets between 15 and 20 percent of the restaurant's annual revenue, which was about $4.2 million in 2001. The Europeans too have already learned that where interchangeability and high markup exist, deluxe branding will follow. In Paris you can have a delightful dinner on the sixth floor of the Pompidou Center at Chez Georges, a Costes Brothers restaurant complete with a panoramic view of the Fourth Arrondissement. If you want a meal at the Guggenheim Bilbao, book several days ahead and bring a fat wallet.

If things continue as they have, museums may take a card from the Las Vegas deck and rent their space and clientele to designer chefs as a way to brand themselves. Almost overnight Vegas, a place known for its $10 all-you-can-eat buffets, was overrun with designer eateries: Piero Selvaggio's Valentino, Stephan Pyles's Star Canyon, Joachim Splichal's Pinot Brasserie, Kevin Wu's Royal Star, and Wolfgang Puck's Postrio, to name a few. Casinos used to compete by offering the fill-your-plate-cheap meal. The upscaling of food is succeeding because the casinos are offering the same luxury experience as the museum, the sense of self-satisfaction, of striking it rich, of privilege. Go to the Guggenheim branch in the Venetian hotel, have dinner at Eberhard Muller's Lutèce, and *then* go to the casino to be plucked and boiled.

The architecture

We usually don't think of museum architecture as a competitive amenity, but that is precisely what it has become. Again, if your product is interchangeable with your competitors', then you have to change the story, or in this case the box. Since the end user can't distinguish between this Monet haystack and that Monet haystack, you have to make sure that your container is unique. And that is precisely what architecture does and why it has become so important. As the ever-expanding vaulted cathedral of medieval times separated the mendicant orders each offering a similar mass, so too the flamboyant museum container separates the curatorial orders offering similar art.

New museums with cutting-edge designs (and *memorial opportunities* for the donors) are sprouting like Monet water lilies. Additions or entire complexes are blossoming in San Francisco, Austin, Fort Worth, Las Vegas, Cincinnati, Los Angeles, Denver, Minneapolis, Chicago, St. Louis, Boston, Hartford, Akron, Washington, D.C., Miami, Saratoga Springs, and seemingly all over Manhattan. The now somnolent Guggenheim Wall Street and the temporarily suspended Whitney notwithstanding, major additions are happening to the American Folk Art Museum, MoMA, and the Brooklyn Museum of Art. Whether they get built or not is another question, but one simple reason for the importance of museum architecture (aside from similar insides) is because it is far easier to find the money to build a new container than it is to find the money to fund the more important but dull endowment. You get your name on the door, as the Bigelow carpet ad used to say, when you give the building (or a wing, or at least a room), which may be grander than getting your name stuck on a wall list somewhere.

Looking at the history of museums as container one sees the sweep of modern marketing. In the twentieth century, the museum went from depot to objet d'art to a self-contained edutainment world. Consider Paris. There, museums used to be housed in converted palaces and stately homes (the Louvre Palace); then they moved into industrial edifices: railroad stations, power stations, public schools, and abandoned government structures (the Musée d'Orsay, across from the Louvre, was once a train station). Then museums were perceived as a kind of retail entertainment, a way to brand the experience (the next-door Pompidou). Since the 1990s the museum has become the ultimate object on display; think of the Cité des Sciences et de l'Industrie, a stand-alone, self-contained world unto itself, eerily close in spirit to the dreaded Euro Disney.

The exhibition

Meanwhile, what's in the container has been shaken up, again thanks to competitive branding pressures. Museums don't compete just with one another. Museumworld has to take on all comers in the edutainment industry. No subject has been hotter in recent years than the choice of what edgy thing to display. The role of the curator is to be a brand manager, and the exhibition space is the delivery space of sensation. As we know from the marketplace, if there are many suppliers of the same product you will be rewarded by doing something—anything!—different. Getting *buzz* is, after all, at the heart of branding and often the only way to get talked about is to be cool, even outrageous. To do this you either have to have a more-talked-about inventory than your competitor or you have to open your doors wider and take in new stuff from the outside. In this context, note that *sensationalism* has become so new a genre of painting that the Brooklyn Museum staged an exhibition headlined *Sensation,* and that "sensational" has become a term of approbation. A generation ago it would have been one of derision.

You can see this shift to emotionality in how Museumworld has expanded. As a with-it curator you take fashion seriously and foreground designers such as Dior or Armani; you show cloying pictures of Weimaraner dogs in various human poses; display lots of common things like guitars, motorcycles, or sneakers in terms of design if not aesthetics; have tie-ins with a theme park (Disney) or movie (*Star Wars*); or even collect things that define your state, as in "Made in California." And of course emotional branding may mean showcasing such matters as *Piss Christ,* cow dung, and the Virgin Mary doing horrendous things. In a world of art overload, there is so much background noise that someone, all too often the curator, must yell really loud to be heard. "Over here! Look at this!" After all, when there is a show entitled *Hip-Hop Nation: Roots, Rhymes and Rage* at a major big-city museum, you know the center of gravity has shifted. The ticket taker has indeed replaced the gatekeeper when graffiti, comics, pulp magazine covers, and chocolate become canonical. Essentially, what is really daring about many postmodern shows is not that they make the museum dangerous (What is *that* doing in *here*?) but that they may scare away deep-pocket patrons (How can we support a museum that does *that*?).

By generating sensation in the place of reflection, the modern museum is becoming self-consciously contentious. While the public may think that being called racist, revisionist, hegemonic, elitist, politically correct, mercenary, greedy, sexist, or self-serving are terms of opprobrium, for many in Museumworld it is their only salvation. If you are a marginal supplier in the educational business or the religion business or the soap business, the reward of finding a story that puts you on the edge and makes you dangerous can really be a savvy move. In fact, it may be the safe way. The best-selling shampoo of recent years has been a onetime laggard, Clairol Herbal Essence. Why? The soap company Procter & Gamble has run a campaign in which a woman taking a shower is clearly pleasuring herself and rhapsodizing about this "orgasm in a bottle." Museum culture has become event culture and events have one thing in common. They must be talked about, become part of the buzz, generate emotion.

The Future of Museumworld, Inc.

Occasionally the various parts of the modern museum experience come together in an exhibition, or sometimes in the reformatting of an entire museum, that give a hint of what's to come. Let me give an example of each. The prescient exhibition was one appropriately called *Brand.New* at the Victoria and Albert in 2000–2001, and the prescient new infrastructure of the borderless museum is the New York–based Guggenheim. Both museum show and showy museum hint of the direction of Museumworld as it moves in fits and starts, slouching toward Brandville.

The Victoria and Albert (V&A) Museum isn't usually thought of as a museum on the edge, but it most assuredly is. And not by desire. It's been shoved to the edge by the fierce London competition. Although it receives a government subsidy of about £24 per visitor (!), one of the highest per capita subsidies in the country, it is still dependent on generating flow at the turnstile. The venerable V&A has tried rather unsuccessfully to reposition itself as a museum of design, which historically makes sense, but unfortunately design is not a tourist destination. For a while, back in the 1980s, it even tried advertising itself as "a café with art on the side." The campaign was short-lived, thankfully.

Like its sexy colleagues, the V&A has also turned to architecture to spruce up its image, but this makes little sense as it sits in a wondrous Beaux Arts bunker. Still, in keeping with the modern museum temper to make the package the exhibit, plans for a futuristic "spiral" construction by Daniel Liebeskind have been put forward. Then they were taken back, savaged by critics and local residents on the grounds of both aesthetics and cost. Alas, so far, these marketing and architectural tactics have failed in making the museum anything other than a wondrous *cabinet* of curiosities, albeit one on steroids.

Until it can figure out what to do with its sublime collection of Plunder and Stuff, the V&A is going to have to find an audience to tide it over. In 2001, it did. It foregrounded commercial objects, objects storied not by antiquity but by advertising. This old dowager of a museum dedicated its floors and walls to what is on the floors and walls of its neighbor Harrods. It showcased the worldwide brands of the fast-moving consumer goods (FMCGs).

What made the V&A exhibit on brands provocative was that for the first time that I know of objects of *only* commercial value made their way onto the sacred grounds. The entire collection of the *Brand.New* exhibit was made up of the flotsam of everyday life, the grocery store as reliquary, the department store as cathedral. This might have been acceptable for Tate Liverpool, but it was hardly of V&A caliber. However, what held all the dreck together was the interlinked narrative of commercial life, the fictions of stuff. *That* was the real subject of the show.

Rather like Dante's "Abandon all hope, ye who enter here" over the portal of Hell, we were told on entering the exhibition, "Brand value relies on consumers accepting, believing in and wanting to associate themselves with a created identity—which may be quite unrelated to a product's actual ingredients or effects." Indeed. As if we didn't know. But as we moved into the exhibit, we moved deeper into the land of Peter Pan and the Lost Boys, into a world made up of almost-make-believe characters such as the Queen Mum and Martha Stewart and stories such as "Pulmo Expectorant" and "Hello Kitty." After passing through the stages of what to many critics (and there were more than a handful) was Consumerist Hell, each labeled in Dantesque terms, such as the circles of Authority, Authenticity, Status, Irreverence, Friendliness, and Loyalty, we ended up in what Kurt Vonnegut would have called the Land of And So It Goes. This final circle was called Subversion, in which the hat was tipped to the forces of those who use branding to subvert what they would call the dominant paradigm. Here culture jamming becomes culture. The brand brandished against branding. Lest we forget what is really dominant, however, the last thing you saw on leaving the Land of Brand Subversion was the V&A's own logo, a belated reminder that museums and other cultural establishments invest as much in the branding game as does anyone else. Ah, the truly Divine Comedy.

As with a show of this nature, the requisite hefty catalog is a kind of aide memoire as well as coffee-table souvenir. With this exhibition, however, there were two catalogs: one, a standard reprisal called *Branded?* by Gareth Williams, the other an extended collection of articles making the art-historical case for the exhibit called *Brand.New.* Both books pay a backhanded compliment to the surging power of commercialism and the suppliance of art.

Williams's book is essentially a dictionary review of forty brands, ranging from Apple to Pampers. What the question mark is doing in the title is curious, almost as if Mr. Williams, a curator by trade, is not entirely sure he wants to admit this stuff into the inner sanctum. But *Brand.New,* a collection of essays edited by the other curator, Jane Pavitt, is far more interesting. It takes one of the standard aspects of the museum—the *catalogue raisonné*—and makes it party to commercial branding. The book looks yummy, full of lush images and printed on thick, vellumesque paper. Here critics, historians, sociologists, designers, as well as observers from the business world have a go at explaining why this vulgar stuff really does belong in these hallowed halls.

Of course the obvious reason it's here is that the V&A has always had a bias toward manufactured goods. Originally founded as the Museum of Manufacturers to glorify the artistic and cultural nature of goods, the V&A made the statement early that machine-made things are called *goods* because they do indeed make life easier. But there is a deeper and more cogent reason than Victorian optimism. If museums are the repositories of cultural memory and knowledge, then like it or not this commercial culture is the stuff to preserve. As opposed to art, which we pretend to appreciate, these literally storied goods do indeed get used, used to the point of being used up. In these objects, and in the narratives that explain and generate their value, reside some of the shared knowledge of this generation.

With this in mind, it's bittersweet fun to watch curators shiver as they open the door to the very stuff they have tried so hard to keep out.

> *From cornflakes to cars, our daily lives are increasingly dominated by branded goods and brand names; the brand is the prefix, the qualifier of character. The symbolic associations of the brand name are often used in preference to the pragmatic description of a useful object. We speak of "the old Hoover," "my new Audi," or "my favorite Levi's"—not needing to qualify them with an object description. The brand is at the heart of this process for many of the goods we buy and sell.*

Page for page, this catalog is one of the best introductions to understanding the impact of telling stories about FMCGs ever assembled. That it should come in a non–business school, non–advertising agency, nonacademic setting possibly shows where the future understanding of branding may be coming from. In a sense, perhaps museums are the appropriate place to discuss the nature of branding because the viewer/consumer does indeed play a central part in the adventure/experience. Maybe like the transformation of the visual arts with the rise of the engaged audience of Impressionism, a new realization will appear that consumption itself is not divided into producer/consumer (or artist/viewer) but is an ongoing interaction. Maybe branding will be seen—literally—as an ongoing interchange rather than as a one-way indoctrination.

While museums have been responsible for preserving and glossing the artscapes of the past, perhaps they will do the same with brandscapes. In fact, just as we ask what a brand means we also ask with an exhibition like *Brand.New*, what does a museum mean? Or to restate the famous definition of poetry by Archibald MacLeish that a "poem does not mean but be," so we might ask (as do a number of commentators of the show) that in the modern world a brand does not mean so much as *be*. It just *is*. It starts attached to the object and finally is inseparable from it. But it is always, like a work of art, being negotiated.

If art is the stuff that generates shared experience, then in a sense these brands are the truly modern art. They direct the flow of cultural capital. Maybe the Pop Artists were right; it just took the curators a little longer to figure it out. Admittedly, brands are weightless, ineffable, and in each instance transitory and on the take. Yes, sure, of course. But in the sense that they are the repeated aura of object, the triggers of emotion, they indeed are the proper stuff of display and reflection. Rather like the strong and weak forces in nature, art proper is the strong force of gravity, but the commercial branding is the weak force of consumption. In this sense, branding is the art in things.

Brand.New struggled to make a point that may be too obvious. While we may say that this branded stuff is cultural trash, we must also recognize that trash is a legitimate aesthetic category. Trash, junk, garbage, and refuse represent the result of consumption. It is the antithesis of art. Art is what cannot be used up, what cannot be exhausted. It never gets thrown out. Art cannot live, however, on its own. On the other side of the divide, without the never-ending drumbeat of advertising, PR, packaging, and product design, branded objects would have no significance. Hence the nifty conundrum: does stuff get to be trash by being consumed and does it get to be art by not being consumed? Which is the arbiter of meaningful value? The hermetically sealed and untouched object in the galleries or the ripped-open and devoured object in the Dumpster?

Go-Go Guggenheim . . . Gone?

If there is something important about the stuff we don't privilege, stuff that by its very sugar-coated nature holds our attention and gives us pause not to experience arm's-length awe but I-want-it-now desire, then we might consider the agent provocateur of the museum world Thomas Krens and his groundbreaking museum, the New & Improved Guggenheim. For Krens may be doing to art what the megachurch is doing to religion and what mass-provider schools are doing to education—he is making it not just unmysterious but accessible. As we have seen, this process is fraught with danger because brands themselves are aspects of magical thinking. Before observing the rebranding of the Guggenheim and the firestorm it has caused, a bit of institutional history, for when you examine the Gugg from a marketing point of view, you see that what looks to be risky behavior may indeed be sensible.

On museum row the Guggenheim has always been the perennial struggler. Its collection of "nonobjective painting," aka abstract art, was important, to be sure, but it was hardly the crowd pleaser that was down the street at the somber Met or several blocks away at the serious Whitney or over at the exciting MoMA. In a word, the core collection is dour. What really separated the museum was not the contents but the wrapping, the Frank Lloyd Wright package. In fact, this wondrous building has always depended, to some extent, on the dreariness of the rest of the surrounding Museumworld. The Guggenheim has the building as art, and it has art in a building.

But deep inside the Gugg there has always been a time bomb slowly ticking. It's not just the art; the endowment is puny. There is no mound of cash in the cellar. Museums set their clocks in terms of operating expenses. The Guggenheim's endowment equals just about one year of its operating expenses—compared with almost eleven years at the Metropolitan Museum. So this museum has to continually refashion its brand. It has to keep moving, going new places, letting new stuff in. One thing is certain: audience attention is not coming from the permanent collection and protection from vagaries of the marketplace is not coming from the endowment. Hilla Rebay, the adviser to Solomon Guggenheim when he was bitten by the art bug (and other bugs as well—spiritual and erotic), knew the problem. Under Rebay's spell, Guggenheim started his buying spree, which both made and debilitated the museum. He bought 150 Kandinskys in 1929 and swiftly piled up works by Moholy-Nagy, Leger, Delaunay, Gleizes, Chagall, and Modigliani. These are not just difficult paintings, they are unremitting melancholy. People will pay to cry but not to be depressed. There's not a real "destination piece" in the bunch.

Rebay and Guggenheim found this out in 1939, when they opened the Museum of Non-Objective Painting in a converted car salesroom on East Fifty-fourth Street. The place was like a scene out of the Addams family, with gray velour walls, drab seats upholstered in plush velvet, recorded music by Chopin and Bach, and continually burning incense. Aargh. The paintings were hung touching the ground, sup-

posedly to mediate between heaven and earth. The few visitors who were willing to have a look didn't bother either curator or patron. They came. They left.

Now you understand why Rebay fought so hard for Frank Lloyd Wright to design a new building in Manhattan. Wright had been an *enfant terrible,* to be sure. He was a bully and a showoff and a philanderer and a pariah. But he was a master of pay-attention-to-me architecture. That's why Rebay defended his cost overruns, his unwillingness to adapt to zoning, and his attacks of spite. This museum needs the combative spirit, or, as Rebay famously wrote to Wright in 1943, "I need a fighter, a lover of space, an agitator, a tester and a wise man." Essentially this collection needs a director who can mimic the architect, not the mumpsy painters.

To the founders, the Wright building was to emphasize the religious nature of the collection. Hence the famous spiral based on ancient Mesopotamian ziggurats, sites of prayer. In most museums, space is organized like a book with chapter heads, subheads, paragraphs, sentences, and words. You start at the beginning and read until the end. You know you are at the end because you are in the gift shop. But the Guggenheim asks you to go up and down in a chambered nautilus as well as move back and forth. There is no mandate for progress. You never finish. You are both inchworm and crab—back and forth, up and down. There's no gridlike structure of parallel galleries and cross-connection rooms that imply itinerary. The Gugg doesn't act like a funnel moving you closer and closer to the exit buyhole. You don't need to drop popcorn on the way in to find your way out. It's a museum built for browsers, wanderers, *flâneurs,* people who expect the unexpected.

Of all the museum directors who came to their posts in the heady 1990s, Thomas Krens was the best match of director and institution. Krens is a marketer, a brandmeister, a mover, if not by choice then by necessity. If he can't generate enough flowthrough, the museum will wither. Remember, he has that problem down at the bank. So he's been very aggressive not only in what he puts on the walls and floors but where he finds exhibition space. To do this, Krens has taken extraordinary chances not just with the brand but with his endowment.

He has gobbled up principal. In fact, he's spent almost $23 million just to cover operating expenses and debt. In Museumworld that's unheard of—in fact, scandalous.

As I write, Krens has just been bailed out by Peter Lewis, the philanthropist whose previous claim to art fame in Museumworld was his candid admission that he had become chairman of the Guggenheim's board by more than doubling Ronald O. Perelman's $20 million contribution. With refreshing candor, he told Deborah Solomon in a *New York Times Magazine* piece on the mess at the Gugg, "I bought myself the job." Lewis also bought himself the responsibility of putting the books back in order and, with a gift of $12 million and some "tough love," he has done just that, at least for a month or two. There is no doubt, however, that in the incredibly competitive world of fund raising for high-cult venues, Krens is the Vulgarian to art historians and the Profligate to contributors. To other museum directors, however, he may well be the Harbinger.

So What Did Krens Do Wrong?

In a nutshell, here is the problem. Is Krens spending too much money letting in the wrong kind of art as well or the wrong kind of customer? While much has been made of his willingness to gamble with what he exhibits, the really edgy shows are few and far between. Of the more than 150 exhibitions in the 1990s, only two really shocked: the motorcycle show and the Armani exhibit. If the Guggenheim brand is that it colonizes the extremes, then such shows make sense. For all the PC-and-diversity talk of opening up the museum, of making it democratic, of being inclusive, Krens has been the notable exception among museum directors. He's really walked the walk. Worse, he made no pretenses. To him the museum was a sponsor, yes, but it was also sponsored. It had a brand but could also carry the brands of others. In a provocative play on the adage that it is easier to ask for forgiveness than permission, Krens actively solicited what are euphemistically called *subventions*. He even set up a Web site expressly to garner corporate monies, an act hardly calculated to garner support from his colleagues in Museumworld.

Exhibition
Sponsorship

Exhibition sponsorship at the Guggenheim Museum provides
corporations with a unique opportunity to partner with one of
the world's leading international museums. Through this
program, corporate sponsors help enable the development and
presentation of the finest in cultural programming. The
Guggenheim's exhibition sponsorship program offers sponsors a
flexible, multilevel engagement.

The Guggenheim works with
its corporate sponsors to
maximize benefits,
including:

• prominent corporate
acknowledgment
• special events
• acknowledgment on
museum Web site
• acknowledgment in press
and media campaigns
• licensing of museum
image and artworks
• complimentary corporate
membership with full
member benefits.

For more information, contact:
Corporate Sponsorship
Solomon R. Guggenheim Museum
1071 Fifth Avenue
New York, NY 10128
(212) 355-6394
E-mail: sponsorship@guggenheim.org

Bottom: Pierre Auguste Renoir, *Woman with Parrot (La Femme à la perruche)*, 1871.
Oil on canvas, 92.1 x 65.1 cm. Thannhauser Collection, Gift, Justin K. Thannhauser
78.2514 T68.

*The Guggenheim knows
what to foreground when
it trolls for sponsors on
its Web site.*

Worse, Krens mucked around with the canon, not just letting in new stuff but letting in stuff with filthy lucre attached. First was the infamous motorcycle show. In Upper Aesthetica anything with an internal combustion motor attached to it is suspect. So it was bad enough that iron and rubber in the service of making noise should be foregrounded on the elegant walkways; Krens inserted too many of his favorite German machines (BMWs) and then placed those initials on the cover of the catalog along with a full-color photo. If you saw the show, you also saw the problem. He let in an entirely outré group of museum visitors from Lower Vulgaria. Seeing gearheads with long hair and bellies the size of beer kegs who truly appreciated the aesthetics of sculpted iron and plastic ogling and ahhing the objects as if they were Bernard Berensons was simply too much. But they knew what to do when the visit was over. The best-selling souvenir from the gift shop? The Guggenheim motorcycle jacket at $345.

So too with his Armani show Krens let into the clubhouse all the neighborhood riffraff, this time not greasy men with bandanas as hats so much as fashionistas with bandanas as scarfs. Again he raised eyebrows and hackles, not just because of the content—*schmatte*—but because of the whispers. Usually, in the same breath, critics like to mention his cross-branding deals with the German clothing company Hugo Boss. But the really disconcerting whispers were for the crowds. And I mean *crowds*. The place was packed. People were pausing in front of draped mannequins and torsos with hushed reverence. Such sacrilege. We have been taught to reserve those reverential moments for standing in front of altars or in front of Old Masters.

As if his choice of objets d'art weren't scary enough, Krens also dared to reconfigure both the place and container of art. In addition to the original museum on Fifth Avenue and the dried-up one in New York's SoHo, there is a robust Guggenheim in Bilbao, a pocket museum in Berlin (a joint venture with and, alas, *inside* Deutsche Bank), the Peggy Guggenheim palazzo in Venice (which Krens inherited with the job but expanded), and the Guggenheim.com fiasco, now off-line. Who knows what will happen to extending the brand in Rio de Janeiro other than that Krens keeps demanding more concessions to jack up his wobbling brand. He and the mayor of Rio have signed an agreement to build a $130 million museum designed by the French architect Jean Nouvel and expected to open in 2007. As with the hugely successful Guggenheim Bilbao, the Guggenheim Rio de Janeiro will be financed by Rio as part of a larger project to revive its waterfront. Such a delicious irony that the shipbuilding port, one of the most common symbols of national glory in the nineteenth century, should become one of the harbors of modern culture in the twenty-first.

Museumworld, like its counterparts the church and school world, is ripe with tender egos. Often there is fierce competition just below the after-you-Alphonse exterior. The truism that the battles are most intense when the stakes are smallest is never truer than with high-cult nonprofits. Under the facade of "We're just here to help you" is "My way or the highway." And when there is excess inventory, as there is in these three suppliers of culture, the volume goes up to, as they say in *This Is Spinal Tap*, eleven. What makes matters still more strained is the concept of pretended decorum. In these often cloyingly polite worlds it's bad taste if you ever comment on the taste of your competitors, whoops, colleagues. Just as raucous Fox News made it possible (unavoidable) to criticize television journalism, so the Guggenheim made it possible to criticize museums. If you listen to the criticism of Krens's Guggenheim, you can hear the refrain of "It's just fashion" forever being reiterated. "This museum is acting as if it were on Seventh Avenue." It "relies on sexy sensationalism to sell." It "is changing the hemlines too quickly." The Guggenheim is, in a word that is not used but implied, "pornographic." But at least museums are being talked about.

What is often missed is Krens's understanding of the marketing mess he's in and how expanding the brand by extending the franchise is really a sensible way out. True, it's not the only way and it's a dangerous way. What he is driving for is, in his terms, borderless exhibition space with "discontiguous galleries"—what in marketing would be called brand inclusion and extension at the same time. Get more excluded stuff included, and then get it into new venues. This is the new "international museum," a global showroom that respects no geographical limits and essentially extends the franchise to where the market demands. You judge success by the length of the line out front as well as the number of lines at your other sites. To old-style gatekeepers this is the dreaded "McGuggenheim," Chicken McNuggets in Prague.

And the word you hear next is that Krens is "selling out," not just giving up on his inventory but devaluing everyone else's. He's literally selling pieces and in so doing deflating the values of others. When a superstar museum sells a piece by Rothko, the Rothko oeuvre loses value. When Warren Buffett sells General Electric, the market price goes down. At least for a while. *Deaccessioning,* as it's called euphemistically, is taboo in Museumworld. It's abhorred not because there is any intrinsic problem but because it shows that (1) art is not endless and timeless but part of slow-moving fashion, (2) it unsettles the donors, who realize they may not have gotten the perpetual acknowledgment they bargained for, and (3) it lessens the market value of other museums' collections whenever a museum starts selling off parts of its inventory. Thus the gentleman's agreement among directors of art museums that they buy and sell preferably only to each other, if ever. To Krens, getting rid of excess stock is a cost of doing business. And it's healthy to occasionally churn inventory. Not only did he sell some paintings—a Modigliani, a Kandinsky, and a Chagall—but he sold them through Sotheby's, thereby circumventing the usual behind-the-back gentleman's sale to other museums. The Gugg pocketed some $47 million for works that usually lived in storage.

Critics rarely mention that the major museums show only a tiny portion of the collection. Hundreds, nay, thousands of images live below the floorboards or out in New Jersey warehouses gathering dust and dubious value. If art is so important to see, then why not let the market circulate them? Why does no one mention the obvious connection between confining supply and increasing market values? Essentially, museums have forced us to go to them. If museums are so concerned about introducing the unwashed to the cleansing powers of art, why don't they give up the obsession with ownership and share works? It's a feckless question. One might as well ask, if the Ivy League is genuinely concerned about education, why doesn't it shunt some of its billions over to K–12, or if churches really care about the poor and downtrodden, why don't they spend a little less on building massive temples and a bit more on soup kitchens?

Krens's real sin was not that he was developing a franchise that he himself proclaimed as a new kind of museum: the never-ending gallery. His real sin was where he was willing to put these galleries and who he was willing to let in. While it's fine to share inventory with the Russians (his deal with the Hermitage), the Spanish (Bilbao), the Germans (Deutsche Guggenheim Berlin), the Italians (a second Venice Guggenheim), the Austrians (a tie-up with the Kunsthistorisches Museum in Vienna), and now a new outpost in Brazil, he grabbed the third rail of high cult when he put art near the hands of the worst kind of heathen: the thrill seeker: he opened a branch in (oh, my God!) Las Vegas.

The Store to Settle the Score: The Other Venetian Guggenheim

In going to Vegas, Krens subverted the entire history of museums. The idea of museum was always to keep the mob at bay. The very word *mob*, a Victorian coinage, carried the threat within its etymology. *Mob* was a slang version of *mobile vulgus,* the rabble on the move. Cultures must be kept separate, and the aspiring middle class had the most at stake if the proles got out of hand. Museums are kept locked not just to keep art in but to keep Visigoths out. Nowhere is this conflict more easily observed than on the untrammeled grounds of American cultural soil. Here the *vulgi* could really be mobile. And the word you heard after Las Vegas was mob—not art, but the literal mob, as in The Mob.

The impresario of the "new," reformed Vegas, Steve Wynn, is not the first to exploit the connection between low and high culture but the most accomplished. He understood that as long as the casinos were interchangeable, the only way to separate one product from another was by changing the brand narrative. And he was the first to change the narrative by flooding his casinos with *Kultur,* building kitsch into the architecture, and confecting a world of outrageous fantasy drawn from the Land of High Cult.

Back in the 1980s, Wynn opened the first megacasino, the Mirage, a literal dreamworld. However, his masterwork at the end of the twentieth century was an industrial-strength casino deluxe called Bellagio. In the center of a cement block of a hotel that looks eerily like Sing Sing was the Bellagio Gallery of Fine Art. Out in front was an old-time sign in marquee plastic letters set against a white background surrounded by baroque decoration. It said: "Now Appearing: van Gogh. Monet. Cézanne. Picasso." The sign looked just like other "Now Appearing" signs announcing Paul Anka and Elvis look-alikes. It was a joke, yes. But his art collection was no joke. It was the real McCoy.

The Bellagio collection is superb, the "best money could buy," and his visitors were duly impressed. It's a collection of the greatest hits, one piece from every canonical big shot. These include Cézanne's *Portrait of a Woman* (1900), Miró's *Dialogue of Insects* (1924–25), Picasso's *Portrait of Dora Maar* (1942), and van Gogh's *Peasant Woman Against a Background of Wheat* (1890). As you leave the gallery, you are funneled into the museum store. Don't all real museums shunt you into the store before letting you back onto the streets? After all, you need to buy some souvenir of your experience, and, rather amazingly, the Bellagio Gallery has almost exactly duplicated the museum experience except that the store is about the same size as a double-wide trailer. Here are the wall posters in tubes for mailing, post cards of paintings, trinkets, shot glasses, and paraphernalia all duly embossed with the images you have just viewed. Plus there are books on art including the *catalogue raisonné* of the Bellagio collection, all done up exactly as you would find at the Met or the National Gallery: glossy photos, learned text.

Krens saw Wynn and upped him a chip or two. Not only does Krens have two museums inside a casino (Sheldon Adelson's Venetian, the Bellagio's slightly more luxurious next-door neighbor); he had them designed by Rem Koolhaas, fresh from Prada. As opposed to Wynn's rather dreary suite of dark rooms, these Guggenheim galleries are appropriately called "treasure boxes." They sparkle. The larger gallery (called the "big box") is filled with objects from New York and the other smaller one (the "jewel box") is affiliated with the Hermitage, the Russian national gallery in Saint Petersburg. At the husk level, both galleries are untreated orange-colored Cor-ten steel sheds, almost industrial warehouses. The larger gallery features a seventy-foot-by-seventy-foot pivoting door, as well as a functioning industrial bridge crane hovering close to the ceiling and suspended from tracks at either side of the space—with a lifting capacity of thirty-five tons. It feels suspiciously as if you are in Costco or Sam's Club. The artworks are even held in place by magnets, as if to make light of the usual museum protocol of wall hanging. It's as though Krens is saying, Here it is, come and get it while it's hot.

Critics claimed that Krens was out to make a buck. Of all things! Bad enough that the Venetian Resort Hotel Casino chipped in to the tune of $30 million for the two Guggenheim rooms, worse was that the surrounding space was almost a parody of high cult. The Venetian is an almost perfect mimicry of Italian scenes done up by Disney Imagineering. And what was going to appear in the big box but the very same shows that had caused such a ruckus in Manhattan: the motorcycle show and the Armani collection.

In the last few years I've spoken to several museum directors and a number of professors of art history. I've been amazed at how many of them are keeping their fingers crossed that Krens will fail in Vegas, proving once and for all that art may be for the people, yes, but not for those kind of people, not for *them*. In fact, the iconoclastic Dave Hickey, who teaches art theory and criticism at the University of Nevada in Las Vegas, says as much. "Very few people care about art here," he says. "And that's okay with me. Art is not a required course in this culture. It's an elective." The bottom line may well prove high cultists right. The Venetian has fallen way behind its projections of how much revenue it would find in the treasure boxes. In fact, as I write this, it keeps shuttering the gallery space until blockbusters can pass through.

Show Business Means Having Something to Show

Say what you want, Thomas Krens is doing very much what Bill Hybels does at Willow Creek or what the admissions directors at Ivy League schools or brand managers at Unilever are doing. He is, in the tradition of the carnie, forgetting what is inside the tent and concentrating on how long the line is out front. He is working the crowd. And until recently, that's been fine. Art museums depend on audience mobility, on tourism, on people moving around looking for "something to do." The various Guggenheims are whirling the turnstiles, no doubt about it. The New York, Berlin, Bilbao, and Venice venues together had almost 3 million visitors in 2000. And once the Guggs-under-construction are finished, their total visitor numbers could reach 6 million, as much as the Louvre and more than the mighty Met. But they may not be whirling fast enough. Things are slowing down. Like the Prada store in SoHo, the joint may occasionally be jammed, but it's hard to tell how much product it is moving. The cash registers are suspiciously silent.

What I find refreshing about Krens is his candor. He's doing what all great directors have done. He's opening, not closing, doors. Recall the blockbuster shows of J. Carter Brown of the National Gallery of Art or the razzmatazz of Thomas Hoving at the Met. They knew what Barnum knew: before the show you gather a crowd. And you gather a crowd by telling a story; you generate what Barnum called *hokum*. Remember the Helga nudes of Andrew Wyeth or the *Harlem on My Mind* exhibitions put on by Thomas Hoving? They mimicked the famous Armory show by getting new people to come into this forbidding site. They promised something you had never seen before. They promised danger. We forget that the Met, once an elitist, stiff, gray, and slightly moribund entity, came alive with these shows. We also forget Hoving was roundly criticized. The chattering class response to this kind of museum behavior is as uniform as it is predictable: they are craven, without critical rigor, apparatus-free, no intellectual foundation. So too Krens is hectored as a programmer, a huckster, a Barnum, or worse, a Babbitt, willing to sacrifice a good long-term name for short-term economic gain.

If you listen to what competitors say about Bill Hybels at Willow Creek: that he is overlooking Scripture, that he is dumbing down salvation, that his back door is letting out almost as many penitents as are coming in the front door, you can appreciate the old guard's take on Krens. If Willow is excoriated as McChurch, then the Guggenheim is McMuseum. If Willow is debasing the integrity of sanctified truth, the Gugg is doing the same with sanctified art. If Willow is branding the unique with the customer-based desires, so too is this museum. It's the Phoenix University of Museumworld.

In fact, what Hybel and Krens are doing is replacing the narrative of the unique with the concept of a brand. What you can find here, they seem to say, can be found elsewhere. We know that. So we are just showing it in a new way. And that, more than any other claim, may mark their great attraction. And their downfall. They may be opening their doors too wide. They have attached their brand to the category, to the commodity, not to the particular, the unique—too many people are being saved, not enough condemned; too much art is being let in, not enough kept out. Can art, like luxury, exist without sacrifice and exclusion? Is the very phrase "art for all" like "affordable luxury"—a contradiction? Should they learn from the Ivy League that you build brand value by rigorously patrolling the front door?

The Future of Museumworld

What we see from looking at the branding of privileged space is that, although the specific innovations continually push the edges, each of these institutions is gathering strength as it merges with the other. If the university is the sacred grove, the museum the sacred reliquary, and the church the sacred temple, the successful ones are essentially moving the same story. In a way we may be returning to Renaissance unity: church/school/museum, all in one. Each of them deliverers a specific experience, namely, the sensation of uplift, the marketing of sublimity, the transfer of transcendence, the democratization of epiphany.

In addition, if one extrapolates from the current convergence of museum as secular cathedral and luxury shopping experience as a branch of Museumworld, it's possible to envision what the next generation of branded euphoria will be like. The experience will be simultaneously commercialized and sacralized—the postmodern mall. After all, that is precisely the nature of brand behavior, the slip-streaming of product behind story. More specifically, that is precisely the narrative claim of luxury.

That the public-sphere, meaning-making institutions—churches, schools, museums—should be in cahoots with the high-end market-place is distressing to critics, who, after all, have a vested interest in *not* sharing the Word with hoi polloi irrespective of price. In each case, *selectivity* is the product. And they have another point: salvation, education, and art should not be in competition with theme parks, movie theaters, and television. Congregants, students, and art patrons should not be considered clients, customers, or tourists. Pastors, professors, and curators should not be carnival barkers. But, like it or not, they increasingly are. The battle for attention, for market share, is transforming not just these institutions, it is transforming the very nature of how we live our day-to-day lives. It is transforming the very nature of community. How distraught should we be that these three primary generators of cultural capital are not just converging with one another but are marketing themselves in a way not seen since the Renaissance?

5.

When All Business Is Show Business, What's Next?

Love it or hate it, consumerism is us. From mall to museum the same impulses and gratifications govern commerce and culture; it all depends on what you're shopping for. But even more important is the process itself—the commercial or cultural experience as entertainment, as social ritual, the sense they provide of being part of a scene. Consumerism is the last shared public activity.

—Ada Louise Huxtable, *The Wall Street Journal*

Twenty-first-century organizations have to compete on brands because they have nothing left. They can't get product differentiation; they can't get superior pricing, distribution or promotion, so branding strategy is it.

—Don Schultz, *Measuring Brand Communication*

There is no disputing the transformative power of commercial branding in rearranging the world of manufactured things. In these pages I've argued that innovations in commercial branding have also rearranged the world of beliefs. I've tried to show how certain suppliers of religion, art, and education are layering commercial templates over their often antiquated delivery systems. As much as these high-culture institutions have held the vulgar marketplace in disdain, individual innovators have adapted self-fictionalizing techniques with varying degrees of success. In so doing, the successful belief and learning suppliers have moved from gatekeepers to ticket takers. Marketing culture may not be so bad. In fact, it has been a source of rejuvenation. And from a consumer's point of view, it means a much less patronizing and much more responsive relationship with what used to be an arm's-length culture. Word that once came from on high now comes from the *felt needs* of the consumption community.

In fact, the branding of cultural capital may be the next step in the evolution of modern community. In *Bowling Alone: The Collapse and Revival of American Community,* Harvard professor Robert Putnam bemoans the social gaps generated by such private pastimes as solitary driving, couch-potato TV viewing, and electronic keyboarding. Three machines—the automobile, television, and computer—have increased the distances between ourselves and others. According to Putnam, they generate communication with a responsive instrument at the expense of human connectedness. The interaction draws us away from one another and increases loneliness and anxiety. Fewer and fewer of us find time for the League of Women Voters, the United Way, the Shriners, the monthly bridge club, or even a Sunday picnic with friends. Modern misguided me-ism threatens safe neighborhoods, equitable tax collection, democratic responsiveness, everyday honesty, and even individual health and happiness.

The decline of public socializing over the past two generations— club attendance has fallen by more than half, church attendance is off, home entertaining is off, even fewer card games are played—is undeniable. But why is this important? According to Putnam, because a society that is wound in social fibers is healthier, both for the group and for the individual. The states that have the highest club membership and voter turnouts also have the most income equality and the best schools (and those that have the lowest have the worst).

Putnam has many detractors, most importantly political scientist Everett Ladd, the executive director of the Roper Center for Public Opinion Research. Ladd made the compelling argument that just because one set of institutions is declining (say, the Elks Club and Boy Scouts) is not to say that others aren't taking its place (Sierra Club and youth soccer, for example). And this is to overlook an obvious refrain since World War II, namely, that there was more community when we were growing up than what our kids experience. Yet, although we claim to want community, we often try hard to escape it. Raymond Williams's observation in *Keywords: A Vocabulary of Culture and Society* that "unlike all other terms of social organization, *community* seems never to be used unfavorably, and never to be given any positive opposing or distinguishing term" seems worth considering.

So what does bowling alone have to do with the kind of cultural branding we have been observing? Cultural anthropologist Grant McCracken sees the underlying phenomenon of modern life as surplus, what he calls *plenitude,* and it is the center of modern life: lots of interchangeable objects and services, lots of stories, lots of media in which to tell them. Plenitude would seem to discourage community because it entails a shallow and ahistorical affiliation. But the opposite is also true: what branding does is to give the consumer something to hold on to, some knowledge or story to cluster around. In this sense, if community groups are the necessary matrix of culture then perhaps branding is changing how they are held together.

Community Defined by Consumption of Brands

The goal of much human storifying is how to spread common knowledge and belief. This knowledge is crucial if we are to know who/where we are and how to treat each other. Cultural literacy is the basis of community. Branding is one way to generate this literacy because the brand story depends not just on communal adoption (consumption) but shared individual understanding (recognition). Hard to believe, but knowing what's in a Big Mac (two all-beef patties, a special sauce . . .) has much of the same kind of unifying force as knowing who played third base for the Yankees, which, in a way, has the same force as knowing what's in Deuteronomy 2:18.

In 1987, an English professor at the University of Virginia, E. D. Hirsch, published a book called *Cultural Literacy* that had the daunting subtitle *What Every American Needs to Know.* The thesis was compelling. If we want community, we first need to share a culture. While Putnam bemoans the loss of shared socializing, Hirsch says we need shared knowledge. With this in mind, some years ago I took a

much-shortened list of what "every American needs to know" to my
class of juniors and seniors. I made up the list by choosing the lower-
right-hand entry from each page in Hirsch's Appendix, cleverly entitled "What Literate Americans Know," so it is an almost random
sample of "the really important stuff" of community. I asked my students to "briefly define or explain the following":

Ampersand	Auschwitz	Biochemical pathways
Bundestag	Neville Chamberlain	Complex sentence
Cyclotron	Dog in the manger	Elysian Fields
Federalism	Indira Gandhi	D. W. Griffith
Hoover Dam	Installment buying	Joseph and his brothers
Leibnitz	Ferdinand Magellan	Herman Melville
National Guard	Nucleotide	Paradox
Planets	Prosecution	Reign of Terror
Sacred cow	Shawnee Indians	Battle of Stalingrad
Taproot	Topsoil	Vector
Winnie the Pooh	Richard Wright	Zurich

Of course, they were soon bored. Who cares about this school stuff?
they seemed to say. I asked them to continue the process, only with
these entries:

Just do it	Uh-huh	Colonel Sanders
Morris	Feel really clean	Heartbeat of America
Mummm, Good	Kills bugs dead	Mrs. Olsen
Fahrvergnügen	Quality is Job One	Why ask why?
Two scoops!	Because I'm worth it	Tony the Tiger
Have it your way	99⁴⁴/100% pure	Master the moment
57 Varieties	Speedy	Never had it, never will
White knight	Jolly Green Giant	Mountain grown
Mr. Whipple	Do you know me?	Be all you can be
Betty Crocker	Still going	Snap, Crackle, Pop
Aunt Jemima	We try harder	That's Italian

They were so excited that they started shouting out entries for me to
consider. Clearly they liked this version of what Americans *really*

know, partly because it was thrilling to think that what they knew had any value, but it was also because they realized that they shared something they understood. Blacks and whites, males and females, front row and back row, do have a common culture. Professors Hirsch and Putnam are correct. There is a cohesive power in sharing. Some of my students are embarrassed, of course, that cultural junk food is what they share. Perhaps they realize there is nothing behind this knowledge, no historical or cultural event, no reason to know it. Yet it is precisely the recognizance of jingles and brand names, precisely what high culturists abhor, that links us as members of various communities. More than anything else, this paper-thin familiarity is what gives commercial branding its incredible reach and equally incredible shallowness. Ironically, concepts in advertising explain the phenomenon: the farther the reach (cost per thousand) the shallower the effect (recall of individual product).

Clearly, much cultural literacy is achieved in the noncommercial world by the same application of brand meanings. And the reason I have mentioned the conjunction of cultural literacy and community is because I think this is the direction in which the megachurch, Higher Ed, Inc., and Museumworld are headed. In a bizarre sense, Las Vegas is the template. A Canadian sociologist, John Hannigan, has coined the phrase *fantasy city* to describe this new mutation—a place to go to consume fictions. Cities used to be based on manufacturing, or hog butchering, or the shouted trading of stocks, or the exchange of goods, or loading things on ships. Now a new kind of urban economy, rooted in tourism, sports, gambling, entertainment, and spending, is reworking the landscape.

Vegas is a fantasy city made up of self-contained city-states atop interchangeable casinos. These city-states have their own narrative embedded in their name and architecture: you choose. Do you want the worlds of faraway (Luxor, Caesars Palace, Bellagio, Venetian); the standard tourist destinations (New York-New York, Paris, MGM Grand Hotel, Mandalay Bay Resort); or an out-and-out fantasy world (Mirage, Treasure Island, Excalibur)? Vegas is just like Disney World. You have your choice of Main Street USA, Fantasyland, Frontier Land, Tomorrowland, Adventureland. As well, the same theme-parking occurs in places such as Seaside (the self-contained experiment in generating nostalgia in the Florida panhandle) and Celebration (the Disney experiment in linking fantasy with town life outside Orlando). They are experiments in branding community for commercial gain.

The Future of Branded Living Space: Megachurch as Minitown

The allure of linking cultural aspiration with living space has always informed community. When you look at most utopian experiments you see they are usually informed by some metaphysical plan, some religious program. After all, this country was founded by Puritans who were trying to link otherworld belief with this-world reality. The City on the Hill was going to be built around Christian apocalyptic vision. So when one of the lower denominations of Protestantism decides to brand living space as with Jim and Tammy Bakker's Heritage USA (at one time the third most visited U.S. tourist attraction, behind Disneyland and Disney World) or Jerry Falwell's Liberty University (to "challenge Harvard in academics and Notre Dame in athletics"), they are squarely in the tradition of our forefathers, although we may be loath to admit it.

The megachurch is at this intersection between sacred and profane. It inspires reverence, awe, and commitment and at the same time it attempts to generate a mimic of village life. It attempts to link Sunday with the rest of the week. Just as the congregation enjoys fellowship in shared faith, the megachurch also provides the interactions of club, family, and business. One of the primary redevelopers of derelict malls around the country has been the megachurch. Old shopping meccas are becoming new religious meccas.

As Patricia Leigh Brown reports in "Megachurches as Minitowns," this is a predictable evolution of reconstituted community. The full-service, 24/7 sprawling megachurch, which offers many of the conveniences and trappings of secular life wrapped around a spiritual core, is essentially subsuming many of the activities previously outsourced by the only-on-Sunday church. It is possible to eat, shop, go to school, bank, work out, scale a rock-climbing wall, and pray, all without leaving the grounds. It's like the New England village on steroids, the church as gated community.

Often these churches seem to fetishize the very objects of community. So at Southeast Christian in Louisville, Kentucky, churchgoers speak of a 22,000-person family, and visitors are regaled with often loopy statistics such as the automated coffeepot that serves five thousand cups an hour. Southeast's size has spawned the invention of the Greenlee Communion Dispensing Machine, which can fill forty communion cups in two seconds. Fellowship Church in Grapevine, Texas, by attracting young congregants and keeping them, has grown from a handful of families to 20,000 members in a dozen years. Fellowship offers a 40,000-square-foot youth center with a climbing wall and video arcade and is creating a lake to encourage father-son bass fishing. Prestonwood Baptist Church in Plano, Texas, has a youth center so elaborate that some have called it "Preston World": fifteen ball fields, a 1950s-style diner, and a fitness center, as well as classrooms and a seven-thousand-seat sanctuary. It is adding a $19 million school, a coffee shop, a food court, a student ministry center, a youth building, an outdoor prayer walk, a chapel, and an indoor commons, modeled on the idea of Main Street. As Ms. Brown concludes, "These churches are becoming civic in a way unimaginable since the 13th century and its cathedral towns. No longer simply places to worship, they have become part resort, part mall, part extended family and part town square."

As I saw at Willow Creek, these seemingly unthreatening churches are becoming a parallel universe, a self-conscious branded community, social magnets drawing in all manner of outside services (the Brentwood Baptist Church in Houston has even incorporated a McDonald's complete with a drive-in window and small golden arches) with all manner of cradle-to-grave services (including in some cases an on-site crematorium). Essentially, the megachurch has the necessary market clout to buy back what we have spent the last hundred years selling off. A study by the Hartford Institute for Religion Research at the Hartford Seminary finds the average annual income for a megachurch is $4.6 million a year, which means it can support all kinds of nonpastoral interactions. In fact, it means the megachurch may be becoming dependent on competitive amenities just as Higher Ed, Inc., has.

Yet in stark contrast to the issues roiling the big traditional churches, these place-based churches offer relief from stresses on American family life, including suburban sprawl, with its vast commutes, and real and perceived dangers. These bastions offer simple things such as multiple entry points, nonintimidating iconography, ATMs, big-time gyms, computer classes, dating services, after-school programs, places that sell real spiritwear, internal clubs to help smokers learn how to quit and bowlers learn how not to do it alone—things usually associated with the marketplace community. If people are shopping for faith, the megachurch fills up the shelves. And since you can't generate brand loyalty on the basis of faith, you essentially do it on the basis of add-ons, on the basis of value added to affiliation, on the basis of providing convenient community.

To hard-pew critics, such belief-as-lifestyle is closer to lifestyle-as-belief. But such marketing is the inevitable development of interchangeable surplus goods. Yes, everything is prepackaged, including extended family. In a historical sense, the church as safe harbor is revived and reformatted to conform to the shoppers' climate-controlled mentality—room-temperature religion. Yes, the megachurch is the religious version of the gated community, and yes, it is religious Disneyland, but it is also the ineluctable result of combining powerful narrative with human yearning and plenty of free parking.

The Future of Branded Living Space: Alma Mater Township

While we usually associate the colonization of living space with religious institutions, the instillation of cultural capital into museums and universities means that they may be the next to extend their brands into generating community. It is already happening with universities; perhaps museums will follow. Nonprofits will be able to bank on the brand equity by extending their stories to living space just as commercial and religious entities have done.

In Higher Ed, Inc., the brand extension happened innocently enough. A generation ago, a number of universities decided to develop so-called research parks. Stanford Research Park, opened by

Stanford University in 1951 as an incubator of university research, catapulted to success on the decision by William Hewlett and David Packard to locate their growing computer company there. In a sense, Silicon Valley, an extension of the Stanford park, followed. A decade later, a consortium of universities in the Piedmont area of North Carolina joined with local government officials to found the Research Triangle Park. With more than fifty companies employing almost 35,000 people, the Park now has only a tenuous academic connection to Duke, UNC, and NC State but a profound perceptual link.

Such success in extending the academic brand did not go unnoticed. The real burst came in 1980, when passage of the Bayh-Dole Act gave schools the right to patent federally financed inventions. The initial beneficiaries were the large research universities. The park concept was made still more attractive because the legislatures realized that State U. didn't have to be a continual financial drain; it could be a source of income. There are now about 130 of these cleverly named parks that are supported by, and in turn contribute to, host universities. Or, at least, that's the hope.

If the results of university-supported research have been mixed, the next development is probably going to succeed. Since selling affiliations of various sorts is now the biggest money maker for universities (and not tuition), why not extend the brand to include older students? In fact, why not forget the students for a moment and create a living environment for alums? University-Linked Retirement Communities (ULRCs) are the watchword for future brand growth. While the golf course may be attractive and living next to a hospital may seem comforting, why not also live next to your alma mater? In fact, why not live *on* campus?

In the last decade these affiliated communities have been growing like collegial ivy. In most cases, the community itself isn't owned by the college or university. The ULRCs are outsourced just as are the teaching and food service. The symbiosis succeeds because universities have such a problem with fixed costs. Although they operate year-round, the academic term lasts only nine months. Summer school has never been a money maker, and no school has ever been able to succeed with a full-year calendar, although some schools attempt to mandate attending a certain number of summer sessions. In the past, universities often rented campus space in the summer to private conventions or private summer schools and struck various lease arrangements that allowed schools to off-load their dormitory services to private developers. The ULRC solves many problems of maximizing the use of facilities. Often the community does have some kind of access to the school that allows residents to take courses free or at deeply discounted prices. The expansion starts simply enough. First, offer spaces to alumni/ae and retired professors; then provide housing for parents of the students/faculty/staff; then extend to relatives of alumni; then take anyone with the money. Is there a better brandstory than lifelong learning? Needless to say, when you look at the brochures, the second paragraph details the proximity to university medical care.

The largest operator of ULRCs is Kendal Corporation in Kennett Square, Pennsylvania, which already has communities at Dartmouth, Cornell, and Oberlin. Classic Residence by Hyatt, the senior living affiliate of Hyatt Corporation, has signed a long-term ground lease with Stanford University to build and operate a 494-unit retirement community near the university medical center. Retirement communities have been built or are planned for the University of Pennsylvania, Penn State University, the University of Michigan, the University of Alabama, Louisiana State University, the University of Notre Dame, Indiana University, the University of Virginia, and Duke University. You don't have to major in Retirement Communities 101 to see the possibilities. All you have to know is that in 2003 the United States had 35 million people over age 65. By 2035 that number will double.

In Gainesville, Florida, where I teach, Oak Hammock is being built at the University of Florida. This appropriately named continuing care retirement community will have 269 living units, comprising 212 apartments and 57 "villas" and "club homes." There will also be 69 rooms for those who need assistance or nursing care. As you might imagine, I get lots of junk mail from it, so I filled out one of its forms. My phone hasn't stopped ringing. I've gotten a ream of brochures assuring me that I don't have to have any connection with the university to join, that I'll be able to go to the hospital or to the football games whenever the spirit and body move, and that I'll "finally have time to work on personal growth" by enrolling in the Institute of Learning in Retirement (ILR), which is in partnership with the Institute on Aging.

Higher Ed, Inc., loves institutes. In fact, in one of the endless brochures there is a picture of an elderly man with books piled up to his chin over which is his freshman first-day-of-classes smile from ear to ear. The brochure concludes with this: "Registrations are now being accepted for upcoming classes." All he needs is a beanie. And, although I haven't corresponded, let alone communicated, with President Charles Young of my university since he arrived there a number of years ago, as you can see, he thanks me for my interest and hopes

UNIVERSITY OF
FLORIDA

Oak Hammock
— at the University of Florida —

From the desk of the President . . .

Thank you for inquiring about Oak Hammock. We, at the University of Florida, are excited about this truly exceptional, world class community.

Thank you for your interest. We hope that you will make the decision to join the Oak Hammock family.

Sincerely,

Charles E. Young

The future of Higher Ed, Inc.: I am invited to spend my twilight days in Oak Hammock at the University of Florida, along with thousands of others.

that I'll join the university family. A week later, I also received a huge postcard from someone else concerned about my well-being asking me, this time in handwritten form, to please let her know how I was coming along with my decision to join "a unique university-affiliated retirement community with all the best that college and life have to offer!"

Not all is lost. If your school doesn't get you for your retirement perhaps they'll get you for your postretirement. *The Wall Street Journal* reported that the hottest brand extender on campus is to sell space in columbariums, which is essentially a crypt built into the campus. This seems particularly appealing in the mid-south where students take their heritage seriously. So for $3,000 a slot, you can rest easy in the University of Richmond, or for $1,800, you can become part of Thomas Jefferson's University of Virginia, literally. Other schools that offer such homecomings are predictably military academies and religious schools. With about half of deaths now resulting in cremation and with other affiliation groups such as family and denominational church receding in importance, the selling of monogrammed strongboxes for your ashes, like rah-rah sweatshirts and logoed mugs, seems alluring. And, since about fifty schools, from the University of Alabama to the University of Virginia, already sell caskets emblazoned with school insignias for about what a crypt would cost, the comparative price advantage seems obvious. Now we're *really* talking spiritwear. According to the *Journal,* the cooperating schools earn about 7.5 to 10 percent on the sales, about what they earn on the sweatshirts and coffee mugs.

Guggenheim Heights? Not Yet, But Kinkadeville Is Up and Going

Museums have been slow to extend their brands into theme parks for the obvious reason: levels of affiliation do not run so deep nor the recognition so high. As we have seen, museums clearly have cross-pollinated with high-end luxury shopping (the Prada home store and its museum-based counterpart) and with themed escape (the art galleries in Las Vegas at the Bellagio and the Venetian). And certainly museums have proved a housing boon to whatever community they appear in, as witness the increase in housing costs near the Queens MoMA or the gentrification of places such as Beacon, New York, when the Art Foundation appeared or Bilbao, Spain, after the Guggenheim.

But the active collaboration between housing development and museum hasn't appeared, yet. That's because museums are almost always built on expensive downtown real estate, where they often stimulate urban renewal but are not, in themselves, places to live. Although the MoMA towers rise above the Museum of Modern Art and although museums have all kinds of travel and entertainment events that crisscross, they really haven't gotten into the themed community. And certainly they have not aggressively entered the columbarium business other than the obvious "memorial opportunity" of paying for a chunk of space on which to emblazon your name—the exception being Salvador Dalí, who made a rather eloquent statement by being buried beneath the toilets of his own museum in Figueras, Spain.

Doubtless, some museum director is, even as I write this, trying to think of a way to leverage his brand by getting some of the enormous amount of unused product out of storage and into productive circulation. Museums have tried leasing paintings for commercial locales as well as to individuals for decorating personal living space. The sticking point is that the art donor usually demands that the gift stay inside the museum, and insurance companies charge prohibitive premiums if the work is moved off premise. So the innovations in renting art have come from the private sector. Landlords of office buildings often contract with a supplier such as Art Assets LLC or Wilson Meany Sullivan LLC to lease art as a way of separating their products. As Barbara Paley, founder and CEO of Art Assets, says, "Landlords are finding it important to distinguish their buildings one from another to attract and keep tenants." Using branded art in the service of branding office space is something that corporations have been doing for decades. Think only of the art collections of Seagram's, Enron, or Citibank, all of which have been unloaded. What is unique is that now building companies are commissioning art, which they essentially lease to other companies as a way of separating the very product—office space—that they have made interchangeable.

True, certain works have made their way from museums into malls and public spaces, and, yes, there are elaborate lending systems that move art from large, overendowed museums into smaller regional ones. But no one has yet figured a way to cross-brand holdings of a specific museum with, say, a hotel chain or a resort. Why not a Guggenheim affiliation with some chain of four-star hotels or a cruise ship? The museum brand may not be sufficiently compelling. More commonly, museums are used as named parts of urban development schemes. But that may change if someone can figure out a way to transport the brand value without moving the product. Contributing to the trend are public policies that mandate that a certain percent of building costs for public works (usually about 1 percent of the budget) be dedicated to art. Since museums play such a crucial role in certifying art, perhaps here they will figure out a way to distribute it as well.

Certainly there are locales in Europe such as Florence, Italy, in which Renaissance art achieves an almost Disneyesque treatment, and quasi shrines such as Givenchy, France, where Monet's house, studio, and garden have become almost a theme park for pilgrims. As might have been predicted, the most innovative transposition of brand from art culture to living space has been achieved by an American, Thomas Kinkade, the self-anointed Painter of Light™. Mr. Kinkade, whose usual niche in American visual culture is at the mall or on the trailer wall, has taken his fluorescent schmaltz to a new level. After having illustrated everything from potholders to Bible covers to screen savers, he is closing in on domestic space. In so doing he has become the richest art brand ever, far surpassing the irrepressible Dalí of the endless lithographs or Mr. and Mrs. Keane of the wide-eyed children fame. Some 20 million of his prints currently hang on the same walls that only recently held the poker-playing dogs and surf-pounding horses. Mr. Kinkade's genius is not with painted images but with extensions of those images. He is, as he himself says, "an art-based lifestyle brand," so he is ripe to become a gated community. Why sell wall hangings when you can sell the entire house?

In the 1990s, Kinkade joined forces with a construction company to build a housing development in . . . where else? California. Part of Hiddenbrooke, a massive housing development centered on an Arnold Palmer–designed golf course, is The Village, a Thomas Kinkade Community by Taylor Woodrow Homes. While the development is hardly in a cozy glen or a bosky dell (it's right next to Interstate 80), the brochure claims that the developer "has translated Kinkade's light-infused artistry into a neighborhood of extraordinary design and detail." In fact, the development looks like any other scruffy area scraped out of California's scraggly central valley, former ranchland a half-hour drive northeast of San Francisco.

Kinkade's métier is the trailer park as gated community. When you think of it, that's what he paints—all those cozy little sugarplum houses bathed in all that amber and lemony light. The vision itself, the brand identity, is to be isolated, insulated, and bomb-shelter safe. Not by happenstance do most of his fairy tale houses have a protective fence out front. It's the New Urbanism made High Victorian, then Shrinky-Dinked. The actual project, The Village, with its narrow streets and

Why own a painting of a bungalow in a bosky dell when you can get a real one in the gated community at The Village, a Thomas Kinkade Community?

mock cobblestone driveways, takes its down-home inspiration from Kinkade's paintings and never lets up. That is as long as you keep your head down so you don't notice all the scrub brush and scraggy hills and Interstate 80. While Kinkade is positioned in the mall as "starter art," in northern California his four home designs (named for his four daughters: Winsor, Merritt, Chandler, and Everett) are hardly starter homes. They are priced from $365,000 to $464,000.

Now admittedly it's easy to take potshots at Mr. Kinkade. He is just such a Happy Meal. But as he commented to Susan Orlean, who did a devastating *New Yorker* portrait of him, "I created a system of marketing compatible with American art. I believe in *aspire to* art. I want my work to be available but not common. It's good to dream about things. It's like dreaming of owning a Rolex—instead, you dream about owning a seventy-five-thousand-dollar print."

The Branding of Larger Community: Cities, States, and Nations

Although it may seem self-evident, whatever it was that drew humans into cathedral/university towns and now compresses traveling/shopping/gambling into Vegas city-state casinos, it is the same yearnings that underlie the newest branded environment, be it New Urbanism, Mallcondo culture, or Kinkadeville. Humans congregate to share stories. The fantasy town is more than economic community and physical safety, it's narrative community, Brandopia. The story is told through a willingness to share a common fiction. Aspirational stories—about religion, knowledge, and art—promise deep and lasting affiliation, and they may finally trump simple commercial stories. The Sacred Grove as Home, Sweet Home.

When humans affiliate with larger entities such as cities, states, and nations, the constructed forms often wobble under the weight of too many conflicting brands. As the built environment gives way to the natural one, the brand is harder to control. To wit: in the recession that followed the 9/11 bombings, New York mayor Michael Bloomberg suggested that New York City make up for its $4 billion shortfall by granting corporate naming rights to portions of the park system. So just as corporate interests have branding rights to sports arenas, the mayor suggested that places such as Randall's Island be leased out for corporate sponsorship. This mayor understands the value of naming rights. Every time his name is mentioned, his news service is plugged. And certainly the city has a history of such exchanges. In 2000, the Selwyn Theatre on Forty-second Street signed an $8.5 million, ten-year deal to change its marquee to the American Airlines Theatre. Or consider the complete commercialization of Times Square, in which entire buildings have been transformed into billboards.

Such exchanges of public space are fraught with misreading, as detractors were quick to suggest. Even the usually dour *New York Times* was giggling in the Style section that the famous New Yorkers' verbal abuse might be branded as well as its equally famous traffic jams. Imagine how much law firms would pay to have their messages embedded in the sirens of police cars or ambulances. Ditto car alarms, the nighttime sound track of many New York streets. Franz Lidz, a writer at *Sports Illustrated,* had more sport on the *Times's* op-ed page by suggesting that Nathan's Famous hot dogs should donate millions to the United Nations and change the name to United Nathan's. And the Calgon bath oil bead company might do well to prop up the Algonquin, thus creating the Calgonquin. Museums could cobrand. The Lefrak City complex in Queens could bequeath part of its profits to the Frick Collection, thereby forming the LeFrick & Frak Collection. Similarly, if U-Haul hitched itself to the Museum of Modern Art, would arts patrons think twice about spending a day at U-MoMA? Thankfully Crazy Eddie is no more; otherwise it might underwrite the Guggenheim Museum. One Crazy Guggenheim, according to Mr. Lidz, was quite enough.

In truth, however, most Western cities have already rented out their public spaces. Once city spaces became interchangeable, with few intrinsic differences, selling the naming rights to such places as stadiums and parks was inevitable. Why not externalize the public costs? Given a choice between higher taxes and name changing, many city dwellers prefer giving up language to giving up money. And what's the difference between a wealthy benefactor exchanging naming rights for a putative gift and a corporation cutting the same deal for cash? When telephone exchanges such as 212 or zip codes such as

90210 become distinctions, you know something profound has happened to our ability to generate neighborhood status. Universities, churches, and museums may be next to enter the fray.

States pose a slightly different problem. In the United States, few of the fifty entities have distinct brands. Maine and Oregon are known for their coasts, the expanse of Texas and Alaska defines them, northern and southern California center around San Francisco and L.A., Hawaii is lush, and Florida's narrative is easily understood in terms of oranges, hanging chads, and retirement communities. The rest of the states have to depend on such often ludicrous slogans, called *wordmarks*, as "Virginia Is for Lovers," "You've Got a Friend in Pennsylvania," "Arkansas: The Natural State," "Oklahoma Is OK," "Illinois: Right Here Right Now," and "New Hampshire: Live Free or Die" (from which some wag suggested that New Jersey should be "Breathe Deep and Die").

So it's interesting that two states in the middle of the continent have self-consciously attempted to reposition themselves not on the map but in the minds of possible consumers. Since 1947, there's been a movement in North Dakota to shorten the title to Dakota because "North" adds nothing but a needlessly chilly direction. This renaming was quite a joke to the columnist Dave Barry, who suggested dropping Dakota and going with North. The North droppers, however, have been gathering steam as the diversifying population is becoming more savvy in telling its story.

While the North Dakota brouhaha has all the elements of sending up the branding craze, to the south the state of Nevada is taking it seriously. Realizing that what it literally owns is often barren, desolate, and intimidating, Nevada recently launched a campaign called "Bring It On." The *It* seems to refer to some mysterious cosmic force. Ads, usually placed in outdoor adventure magazines and billboards, feature tattooed men with surfboards suspiciously looking at sand dunes, bearded men peering out into bogs, and exhausted bicyclists halfway up rock faces under such headlines as "You Are a Predator of Life," "You Stalk Adventure," and "Can You Handle the Truth?"

Admittedly, the idea of branding geographic entities with such wordmarks approaches the stuff of parody—remember Jonathan Swift's *Gulliver's Travels* and the inhabitants of Laputa, who had to

Is this how to brand a state? "What kind of animal are you?" asks Nevada.

have their ears slapped with bladders to force them to concentrate on reality. It is also, however, the stuff of modern tourism. The turning point came in the 1950s when David Ogilvy, the heavily self-branded adman, transformed Puerto Rico from a rogue outpost into a vacation and business paradise. Ogilvy would boast, "I gave the facts, no hot air, no adjectives," but of course the secret was in knowing what information to foreground as fact and what to neglect. What's true with tonic water (Schweppes tonic water), shirts (Hathaway), cars (Rolls-Royce), and gasoline (Shell) is also true with nation-states. Thus in "Falling in love with Old San Juan," "Honeymoon in Puerto Rico," and "On a Picnic in Puerto Rico, I discovered a new kind of rum," Ogilvy completely overlooked the political and environmental squalor to focus on this being the ideal place for romance, relaxation, and mild licentiousness. Here, in his own words, was the brand statement:

We started a kind of endorsement campaign for Puerto Rican rum by bringing married couples to the island to make a pitch for the drink. Up until that point, women had never appeared in liquor ads—never! The ads we shot did feature women: in each of them, the man would have a drink in his hand, but the woman would not even have a drink in front of her—we had to make believe she wasn't drinking at all!

No one doubts that this rebranding didn't just transform Puerto Rico but opened up the entire Caribbean to a radically new image.

The Brand State

What makes this kind of nation branding modern is not just the sophisticated use of commercial marketing techniques like focus groups, test runs, and market segmentation, but also the realization that narrative influences perception. The old ad campaign for *Rolling Stone* magazine was right: perception *is* reality. Recently there has been such a spate of serious articles and op-ed pieces on "Brand America" that nation branding has become an important aspect of foreign policy. Modern political branding is different from historical propaganda if only because it is being taken seriously by all concerned. As opposed to the megachurch, Higher Ed, Inc., and Museumworld, the diplomatic world is acutely aware that it is in the marketing business. No one pretends otherwise. After all, diplomats are politicians, which, as former Clinton adviser and current TV pundit Paul Begala famously observed, is just showbiz for ugly guys.

Charles Skuba, erstwhile adman, comments on this development in image making in "Branding America," published in *The Georgetown Journal of International Affairs*. At almost the same time Peter van Ham, a senior research fellow at the Netherlands Institute of International Relations, does the same in "The Rise of the Brand State" in *Foreign Affairs*. Both observers make the case that in the next generation of diplomacy the ability to brand your nation before your competition does it to you is going to become crucial. Essentially, both men argue that those states that successfully fictionalize themselves to others, rather than those states that fictionalize themselves to themselves, will prevail. Old-style nationalism, in which the focus was on telling stories internally (*our* history, *our* bloodlines, *our* manifest destiny), will take a backseat to branding, telling your story to others (What we can do for you? Where do you want to go today?).

In "The Rise of the Brand State," van Ham points out what seems obvious. We now know each other not by how we talk among ourselves but how we are spoken to. As he says,

> Look at the covers of the brochures in any travel agency and you will see the various ways in which countries present themselves on the world's mental map. Singapore has a smiling, beautiful face offering us tasty appetizers on an airplane, whereas Ireland is a windy, green island full of freckled, red-haired children. But do these images depict real places, existing geographical sites one can visit? Or do the advertisements simply use cultural stereotypes to sell a product?
>
> Over the last two decades, straightforward advertising has given way to branding—giving products and services an emotional dimension with which people can identify. In this way, Singapore and Ireland are no longer merely countries one finds in an atlas. They have become brand states, with geographical and political settings that seem trivial compared to their emotional resonance among an increasingly global audience of consumers. A brand is best described as a customer's idea about a product; the brand state comprises the outside world's ideas about a particular country.

As we have learned, branding occurs wherever a surplus of fungible objects appears. It is demonstrably true that, like soap powders, meat patties, or credit cards, the nations of the world are becoming indistinguishable. Geographical boundaries are relatively unimportant. Iron curtains and Berlin Walls rust and crumble. As in earlier times, when similar machinery effaced product differences so that commercial brands became necessary, modern globalization is doing the same thing. Consumption habits of both commercial and cultural brands are threatening to make nation-states equally indistinguishable. As companies face the challenge of marketing in an environment where their products and services often are perceived as just generic commodities, as universities, churches, and museums struggle to break away from the generic, so too nation-states have to differentiate or die.

What we increasingly share as individuals is not ancestry, religion, literature, language, or ideology but an ephemeral knowledge of the difference between Coke and Pepsi, which Prada purse is hot, or what's in a Big Mac. What we increasingly share as nations is not a unique past but the same flyby culture of what we are consuming right now. To rise above the cluttered landscape, the successful nation-state must be able to define and promote its unique narrative, albeit a transitory one. The unbranded state will have a difficult time attracting economic and political attention. It has no voice through which to tell stories. No one will listen. Think Canada and perhaps even Russia. But it can work the other way too. A state can be too well branded and have too much voice. Think Israel and perhaps the United States of America.

Image and reputation are thus becoming essential parts of the state's strategic equity, its export capital, what it offers to those it wishes to influence. Like a branded product, the branded state depends on expectation and satisfaction. Do you believe the story? Better yet, do you buy it? Are you satisfied? What is being transferred is not old-style us-versus-them politics but us-versus-them feelings. As van Ham says, we now talk about a state's personality in the same way we discuss the products and services we consume, describing it as "friendly" (i.e., Western-oriented) and "credible" (ally) or as "aggressive" (expansionist) and "unreliable" (rogue). The battle is for audience share—the new market of diplomacy.

Although unsettling to conservatives and old-style nationalists, this outward expansion of narrative may actually become a positive development, gradually supplanting nationalistic me-first-ism. The brand state's use of its history, geography, and ethnic motifs to construct its own distinct image may become less combative as it exchanges depth for breadth, specific affiliation for wider consumption, and increased concentration on audience desires. To make the sale, you have to talk the consumer's language, not just your own. By penalizing chauvinism and provincialism, the brand state may prove pacifying.

So at one level, nation-states are branding themselves for tourist and trade reasons. Tony Blair's "Cool Britannia" is square in the David Ogilvy tradition of exporting emotion. Canada has an active branding campaign under way that involves not just separating from its southern neighbor but controlling its position by emphasizing exactly this separation. As of yet there is no distinct Canadian voice. More suc-

cessful is Belgium, where Prime Minister Guy Verhofstadt has hired a team of image makers to introduce a new logo and hip colors. Estonia is launching itself aggressively as "Scandinavian," while Poland's leaders have tried to reverse the perception of their nation as backward and conservatively Catholic. In the globalized future, brand states will compete not only among themselves but also with superbrands such as the EU, CNN, Microsoft, and perhaps even the Roman Catholic Church (the oldest and most recognized brand state in the world). And it is here in the land of supranational brands that we may see the future of the megachurch, Higher Ed, Inc., and Museumworld as cultural capital starts to flow across the weakened national brands.

Brand U.S.A.

In this context, what will the United States of America come to mean? On one hand, of course, *we* know that "America" and "Made in the U.S.A." stand for individual freedom and prosperity. But we are also aware that to much of the world the country is seen as a selfish and rapacious despoiler of precisely the same values. Brands often merge as opposites in the minds of the global consumer. For example, in many ways, Nike, Microsoft, Marlboro, Coke, Levi's, and McDonald's are as much vehicles of contradictions as they are actual products.

George Bush's appointment in 2001 of the often-nicknamed "most powerful woman in advertising," Charlotte Beers, as undersecretary for public diplomacy and public affairs in the State Department acknowledged this conundrum. As expected, such an appointment of an image juggler from Madison Avenue rather than a career diplomat from Foggy Bottom met with arched eyebrows. The common refrain: Statecraft is *not* selling soap. But to some degree, of course, that is exactly what diplomacy has become. Hearts and minds are the goal, not territory and natural resources. Who knows? Perhaps von Clausewitz's famous observation that "War is the natural extension of diplomacy" will be changed by future conflicts so that branding plays the ultimate role of war.

Although Ms. Beers has since retired, her appointment is worth considering not just in the context of nation branding but also in the general sense of how meaning is manufactured and transmitted in the modern world. To what degree is a nation like just another cultural fiction, a *habitus,* like a church, a university, a museum, or a tourist destination? The most trenchant criticism of the Beers appointment came from Naomi Klein, author of *No Logo: Taking Aim at the Brand Bullies.* In a piece for the *Los Angeles Times,* Ms. Klein gives her take on commercial branding when applied to geopolitical matters:

> *In the corporate world, once a "brand identity" is settled upon by the head office, it is enforced with military precision throughout a company's operations. The brand identity may be tailored to accommodate local language and cultural preferences (like McDonald's serving pasta in Italy), but its core features—aesthetic, message, logo—remain unchanged. This consistency is what brand managers like to call "the promise" of a brand: it's a pledge that wherever you go in the world, your experience at Wal-Mart, Holiday Inn or a Disney theme park will be comfortable and familiar. Anything that threatens this homogeneity dilutes a company's overall strength. That's why the flip side of enthusiastically flogging a brand is aggressively prosecuting anyone who tries to mess with it, whether by pirating its trademarks or by spreading unwanted information about the brand on the Internet. At its core, branding is about rigorously controlled one-way messages, sent out in their glossiest form, then hermetically sealed off from those who would turn that corporate monologue into a social dialogue. The most important tools in launching a strong brand may be research, creativity and design, but after that, libel and copyright laws are a brand's best friends. When brand managers transfer their skills from the corporate to the political world, they invariably bring this fanaticism for homogeneity with them. . . . From a branding perspective, it would certainly be tiresome if we found ourselves simultaneously admiring and abusing our laundry detergent. But when it comes to our relationship with governments, particularly the government of the most powerful and richest nation in the world, surely some complexity is in order.*

Klein's concerns are logical if you perceive branding as a one-way, univocal, "yelling down the pipe" kind of communication. If branding is how you stamp the ownership message on the bleating steer, then she is correct. Much as we may comfort ourselves in seeing branding this way (if only because it exonerates us of any responsibility as consumers), such is rarely the case. Commercial narrative, like any kind of storytelling, depends as much on the listener as on the storyteller. The audience is always negotiating meaning, affirming and subverting. It would be as easy and as naive to think that Osama bin Laden, carefully dressed in fatigues and sitting calmly before a rocky outcrop, cradling his Kalashnikov rifle and flashing his Ironman Triathlon Timex watch, was understood the same way by all viewers. "You have to choose your side," he told the world's one billion Muslims, and leaned back contentedly for a sip of water. Not so simple. Islam is as multifaceted as Christianity. The Arab states are as complex as Western liberal democracies.

Admittedly, part of any audience will be confused by almost any statement, especially if the statement is complex. But powerful brands can harness this ambiguity by not denying it. As Allen Rosenshine, chairman and CEO of Omnicom Group's BBDO Worldwide, put it:

> *It is wrong to dismiss branding as inappropriate [in diplomacy] just because it is mainly associated with commercial enterprises. On the contrary, branding precepts can be quite effective in persuading antagonists that our social, political, and economic systems are worthy of respect rather than contempt. Branding is based on the notion that promoting a specific relationship between a product and its user creates psychological value for the product in addition to the benefit of its actual performance. This means creating a relevant linkage, both rational and emotional, between the product and the lives of the people you hope will use it. Branding America thus requires presenting a nation that offers something people can value and aspire to with their minds and hearts. It goes beyond statistics that measure life in material terms. More important, it must capture the sense of decency, fairness and opportunity that characterizes our country. In commerce, branding teaches us that we cannot simply dismiss or ignore what the competition promotes. Branding insists we accept what the customer thinks, even*

wrongly, as the state of the market. This means we cannot counter people's hatred just by telling them how much we love America. . . . Successful branding requires credibility. If we say the soap smells like fresh flowers when in fact people don't think so, we may sell someone one bar but not another. At the end of the day, the usual critics notwithstanding, what makes us good at selling soap can help us sell America.

Of course, it's one thing to plan the meal, quite another to cook it. Determining exactly how to brand the American stew, a narrative seasoned by ambiguity and contradiction, will not be easy. "Getting the word out" is complex when the single descriptor of this brand is not *overnight* or *cool* or *the real thing*. In fact, if there is a single word that the U.S.A. brand boils down to, it is *complexity*. The one thing you don't want it to boil down to is *arrogant rogue*.

Perhaps this kind of storytelling won't work in a world already overwhelmed with so many competing fictions. Perhaps television and the Internet have jaded the audience to any story that requires deep reading and concentration. But not to attempt it, not to use language, images, and sounds to make a narrative, is to abrogate the very process that has made a better life for so many people across most of the globe. We have created plenitude, the heart of branding; now the question is do we know how to distribute it. This much seems clear. The extrapolation of branding from fast-moving consumer goods to slow-moving cultural services to even slower moving nation-states is happening with or without government sponsorship.

We have come to live in a world of continual and often frantic storytelling, be it on the shelves of the supermarket or inside our own heads. It's a highly unstable world, partly because the flashdance stories that draw a crowd are up for grabs and in part because the media that carry them are so cheap. Paper is expensive, radio and television are cheaper, but the Internet is essentially free. If anything, we know too much. Mark Twain's "A lie can travel halfway around the world while truth is putting on its shoes" has never been more appropriate.

Brand clutter of all kinds—commercial, cultural, and political—is overwhelming. Many brands have the shelf life of a hothouse tomato. But who can tell how powerful the branding of culture, social place, and nationhood will ultimately be? Will it erect or destroy the Berlin Walls of separation? Who knows? We may cluster around political and cultural capital in the twenty-first century the way we clustered around physical territory or designer jeans in the twentieth. While it would be nice to think that this eternally encouraging market for the narratives of social meaning will result in the cosmopolitanism envisioned by the Enlightenment *philosophes,* that a Universalism of Nonmaterial Branding will end in a crescendo of hosannas, that globalization will mean worldwide community, such may not be the case.

We have been in this New Brand World a short time, and it is often a scary and melancholy place. This is a world not driven by the caprices of the rich, as was the first industrial age. Nor is it being whipsawed by marketers eager to sell crapular products. They contribute, to be sure. Our world is being driven primarily by the desire of the massclass of consumers, most of them young, for deep meaning *inside* the material world. Plenitude is no longer the goal of the developed world; finding and sharing the wealth of meaning is.

As we have seen, these fictions have become the dominant meaning-making system of modern life because of our deep confusion about consumption, not only about *what* to consume but *how* to consume. The idea that they create artificial desires rests on a wistful ignorance of history and human nature, on the hazy feeling that there existed some halcyon era of noble savages with purely natural needs. Once fed and sheltered, our needs have always been cultural, not inborn. Feed us food, then feed us stories.

We may well find that the increasing Nikefication of such social constructions as faith, history, art, place, politics, justice, and culture and making them in any way analogous to blue jeans and sneakers is demeaning to the human spirit. We may find that community based on consumption of brand fictions instead of concepts like bloodline or received beliefs of a promised hereafter is constricting instead of liberating. Transforming the end user from penitent to believer to customer to client to companion strikes many observers as not just inappropriate but deeply offensive.

The audience for megachurches, mass-provider universities, blockbuster museums, and other social constructions may have little of substance in common with the special bonhomie of Apple computer users, the hand waving of Saab and Vespa drivers, the shared glee of TiVo users, or the raucous fraternity of Harley-Davidson gearheads. That contrived community of any kind should be created by sharing brands and/or the confected stories they retell is dreary and depressing to some, as doubtless it should be. That the putative civilizing rituals should behave like so much soap powder is insulting to many. What these modern markets in belief, knowledge, and art tell us is that no hierarchy is currently exempt from internal competition and the very concept of disembodied authority is if not questionable then at least discussable. What branding tells us is that often the hierarchy and authority reside not in intrinsic qualities but in the ability to generate compelling narrative.

Let me close with a personal note. I grew up in a little town in northern Vermont. It was ripe with community—perhaps overripe. After World War II, the state emptied, not just because jobs were elsewhere but because there were too much community, too much social knowledge, too much intimacy. Men and women who had been off to war were not ready to return to confinement. My grandfather had a small community store. Often he sold on credit. My mother told me that if he did not know the customer, he extended credit on the basis of smell. If the customer smelled of sheep, no credit; of cows, perhaps; of horses, credit. He practiced a kind of smell profiling. Much of my family went to California, the land of milk and honey.

I return to this world every summer. In the last generation people are moving back to my little town. This state has gone from Ethan Allen to Calvin Coolidge to Howard Dean. For a while it even had a new wordmark, clearly designed for flatlanders: *the beckoning country.* In this process of rebranding, social and cultural capital is being redistributed. Social place and cultural value are up for grabs. This may be refreshing if also traumatic. Elms and white churches are no more. The community store is a 7-Eleven. Downtown is a pedestrian mall with Crate and Barrel and Abercrombie & Fitch. After years of contention, an ugly Wal-Mart has arrived out by the interstate next to a cluster of big-box stores. It seems so wasteful and unhistorical. My mother used to complain that it was rootless. The Episcopal Church no longer runs the show. The families who can trace their heritage to the *Mayflower* no longer decide who's in and who's out. Few of them live here anymore. Pictures of Ben and Jerry's cows appear on mailboxes where real cows used to graze in the fields. Not too far from where I live is a statue of a man taking a photograph of a moose and a farm that raises wildflowers for profit. The local museum no longer just shows quilts collected a generation ago but sponsors a circus and last week a Willie Nelson concert. Anyone with a fistful of cash can join the country club. There are some budding megachurches a few towns over, which are causing the shivers. The local university is floating a new bond issue not for classrooms or labs but for a student union. It claims it has to "stay competitive."

Who knows? Maybe marketing meaning, status, and belief like so much soap and toothpaste to be moved off the shelf will be more equitable and, ironically, more stabilizing than previous systems. The risk, of course, is that you can't get this toothpaste back in the tube. Once the merchants have entered these temples, things are never going to be the same. I often think of Wilde's observation that "the brotherhood of man is not a mere poet's dream: it is a most depressing and humiliating reality." That may be so, but I prefer this new branded world and the free-for-all community it provides. It seems more fair and democratic—in a strange way more honest and liberating—to let these time-bound institutions go pop. In the end, however, the rest of the world will decide if it's really worth the price.

Notes

Chapter 1:
Branding 101: Marketing Stories in a Culture of Consumption

2   A marketing professor: Both studies referenced in Sarah Schmidt, "Advertisers Sear Brands into Eager Preschoolers," *The Gazette* (Montreal), May 6, 2003, p. A1.

2   As Richard Sherwin has shown: *When Law Goes Pop: The Vanishing Line Between Law and Popular Culture* (Chicago: University of Chicago Press, 2002).

10   To some sociologists: Of all the French sociologists, Pierre Bourdieu has been most influential in appreciating how competition has moved from economic capital (financial assets, a bank account) to social capital (networks, a Rolodex) and cultural capital (skills and knowledge, an Ivy League diploma, and a seat on a museum board). His *Distinction: A Social Critique of the Judgement of Taste* (Cambridge, Mass.: Harvard University Press, 1984) has had a profound effect on the study of the consecrating institutions of education, religion, and the arts.

14   "I've never seen": www.storytellinginorganizations.com/ext-pub-news-12-2003.asp 2000 INC. 500 Conference.

14   Or, as another master of this: www.drdifferentiate.com/.

24   "Whether one adopts": Susan Fournier, "Consumers and Their Brands: Developing Relationship Theory in Consumer Research," *Journal of Consumer Research* 24 (March 1998): 361.

25   the *Diderot effect:* This concept was first discussed by Grant McCracken in *Culture and Consumption* (Bloomington: Indiana University Press, 1988), Chapter 8.

28   As Margaret Mark and Carol Pearson: *The Hero and the Outlaw: Building Extraordinary Brands Through the Power of Archetypes* (New York: McGraw-Hill, 2002).

35   Colin Campbell, an English sociologist: *The Romantic Ethic and the Spirit of Modern Consumerism* (London: Blackwell, 1987).

37   As Herbert Muschamp, design critic: "Seductive Objects with a Sly Sting," *The New York Times,* July 2, 1999, p. B35.

37   "Modern exchange is *not* materialistic": Neil Cummings and Marysia Lewandowska, *The Value of Things* (London: Birkhauser, 2000), 76–77.

38   The case has been consolidated: Barry Hoffman, *The Fine Art of Advertising* (New

York: Harry Abrams, 2003); Charles A. Goodrum and Helen Dalrymple, *Advertising in America: The First Two Hundred Years* (New York: Harry Abrams, 1990), and the Taschen series (Cologne, Germany) edited by Jim Heimann, *All-American Ads of the 60s* (2002), *All-American Ads of the 50s* (2002), *All-American Ads of the 40s* (2002), *All-American Ads of the 30s* (2003), *All-American Ads of the 70s* (2004).

38   "A brand is a name": As quoted in Philip Kotler, *Marketing Management: The Millennium Edition* (Upper Saddle River, N.J.: Prentice Hall, 2000), 404.

Chapter 2:

One Market Under God: The Churching of Brands

48   Each day about two more: David B. Barrett, George T. Kurian, and Todd M. Johnson, eds., *World Christian Encyclopedia: A Comparative Survey of Churches and Religions in the Modern World* (London: Oxford University Press, 2001).

49   as Toby Lester reported: "Oh, Gods," *The Atlantic,* February 2002, pp. 37–45.

56   And if religion were a company: Thomas A. Stewart, "Turning Around the Lord's Business," *Fortune,* September 25, 1989, p. 116.

57   As Lawrence Moore, the historian: *Selling God: American Religion in the Marketplace of Culture* (New York: Oxford University Press, 1994).

57   When the Pew Research Center: *What the World Thinks in 2002* (www.people=press.org/reports/display.php3?ReportID-165).

57   "I follow religion": Ibid., p. 3.

58   What's extraordinary: Chris Shea, "Supply and Demand Among the Faithful," *The New York Times,* March 24, 2001, p. B9.

59   In 1950, *Fortune* magazine: As quoted in Kit and Frederica Konolige, *The Power of Their Glory: America's Ruling Class* (New York: Wyden Books, 1978), 321.

61   As Nicholas Lehmann argues: *The Big Test: The Secret History of the American Meritocracy* (New York: Farrar, Straus and Giroux, 1999).

61   Stay home and be a star: And where did the SAT come from? Harvard. It was the brainchild of Harvard's James Bryant Conant and Henry Chauncey. Launching a revolution against their own class of privileged white Anglo-Saxon Protestants, Conant and Chauncey wanted to put into place a system that would skim the best and brightest from all social classes, educate them, and place them in positions of power and responsibility. They succeeded—and in so doing helped take down an entire Protestant brand.

61   Since 1991, the mother Church: Gustav Niebuhr, "Protestantism Shifts Toward a New Model of How 'Church' Is Done," *The New York Times,* April 29, 1995, p. 12.

62   In every church I attended: As one wag recently said of his church's meltdown, "I am just thankful that the church's founder, Henry VIII, and his wife Catherine of Aragon, his wife Anne Boleyn, his wife Jane Seymour, his wife Anne of Cleves, his wife Katherine Howard, and his wife Catherine Parr are no longer here to suffer through this assault on our traditional Christian marriage."

64   In other ads: The Church Ad Project also publishes marketing books such as *From Disciple to Apostle: A User-Friendly Manual for Church Membership* and *Advertising the Local Church: A Handbook for Promotion,* as well as T-shirts, radio spots,

a pastoral card care system, and information on how to negotiate the rates for and placement of ads in your local newspaper. It also sells books by other publishers, such as *The Proverbial Marquee: Words to Drive By,* which gives helpful suggestions on what to put on your sign with movable letters; *Stealing Sheep: The Hidden Problems of Transfer Growth,* which "is not a polemic against the church growth movement" (but really is); and *Facing Reality: A Tool for Congregational Mission Assessment,* complete with CD-ROM, for "assessing the growth potential and opportunities facing the local church." Clearly, rebranding is the order of the day.

65   If you wonder how: Richard Tomkins, "Brands Are New Religion, Says Advertising Agency," *Financial Times* (London), March 3, 2001, p. 13.

66   Among the most important ministers: The best and just about only history of advertising is Stephen Fox, *The Mirror Makers: A History of American Advertising and Its Creators* (New York: Morrow, 1984).

67   "I am not a doctor": Bruce Barton, *The Man Nobody Knows: A Discovery of Jesus* (Indianapolis, Ind.: Bobbs-Merrill, 1925), 125, 126, 136, 138, 139, 140.

69   In the world imagined by advertising: Richard Simon, "Advertising as Literature: The Utopian Fiction of the American Marketplace," *Texas Studies in Language and Literature* 22, no. 2 (1980):154–174.

71   Recent surveys show: Robert Marquand, "Influence of New Age, Megachurches Grow Among US Worshipers," *The Christian Science Monitor,* August 19, 1996, p. 1.

71   The Pentecostals have clearly: Katrina Burger, "JesusChrist.com," *Forbes,* May 5, 1997, p. 76. For demographic information on American Protestant churches, see Laurie Goodstein, "Conservative Churches Grew Fastest in 1990s, Report Says," *The New York Times,* September 11, 2002, p. A16.

71   They are the bourgeois: David Brooks, *Bobos in Paradise: The New Upper Class and How They Got There* (New York: Simon & Schuster, 2000).

75   In *Acts of Faith:* Rodney Stark and Roger Finke, *Acts of Faith: Explaining the Human Side of Religion* (Berkeley: University of California Press, 2000).

77   "Zip codes are another": ReVision Starter Kit 12. If you want to see the ReVision questionnaire, go to www.percept1.com/pacific/PDF/Context/StarterKit.pdf.

79   Paul Ormerod points out: *Butterfly Economics: A New General Theory of Social and Economic Behavior* (New York: Basic Books, 2001).

80   As Malcolm Gladwell: *The Tipping Point: How Little Things Can Make a Big Difference* (Boston: Little, Brown, 2000).

80   These churches even have: Charles Trueheart, "Welcome to the Next Church," *The Atlantic,* August 1996, pp. 37–58, and Gustav Niebuhr's series on megachurches in *The New York Times:* "Missionaries to Suburbia: Megachurch," April 16, 1995, p. A1; "The Minister as Marketer: Learning from Business," April 18, 1995, p. A1; and "Protestantism Shifts Toward a New Model of How 'Church' Is Done," April 29, 1995, p. A12.

81   To look at it another way: Trueheart, "Welcome to the Next Church," p. 38.

82   Piling on is even legitimated: Marc Spiegler, "Scouting for Souls," *American Demographics,* March 1996, pp. 42–54.

87   Now it brings: Ibid., p. 50.

89 In the twentieth century: Robert Marquand, "Upstart Churches Chart New Directions in Protestantism," *The Christian Science Monitor,* April 10, 1997, p. 1.

90 Art historian Leo Steinberg: *The Sexuality of Christ in the Renaissance and in Modern Oblivion* (New York: Pantheon Books, 1983). See also Jaroslav Pelikan, *The Illustrated Jesus Through the Centuries* (New Haven, Conn.: Yale University Press, 1997), and David Morgan, ed., *Icons of American Protestantism: The Art of Warner Sallman* (New Haven, Conn.: Yale University Press, 1996).

91 It's the Next Thing: Laura M. Kaczorowski, "Willow Creek: Conversion Without Commitment," Distinguished Majors Honors Thesis, University of Virginia, May 11, 1997, is one of the best introductions to the church: available at www.religiousmovements. lib.virginia.edu/nrms/superch.html. Another megachurch worthy of mention is Saddleback (120 acres, 19,000 attendees) in Orange County, California, if only because its pastor, Rich Warren, has written the megabestseller *The Purpose-Driven Life: What on Earth Am I Here For?* (Grand Rapids, Mich.: Zondervan, 2002), full of daily exercises for success in coping.

92 Bill Hybels: Gregory Pritchard, *Willow Creek Seeker Services: Evaluating a New Way to Do Church* (Grand Rapids, Mich.: Baker Book House, 1996), p. 81.

92 Getting parishioners off the Interstate: William Langley, "God's Shopping Mall," *The Sunday Telegraph* (London), June 4, 1995, p. 14.

93 "When I was in London": As quoted in ibid., p. 15.

95 Gregory Pritchard: Ibid., pp. 119, 147.

98 The MBAs reveled: James Mellado, *Willow Creek Community Church: Harvard Business School Case Study 9-691-102* (Cambridge, Mass.: Harvard Business School, 1991).

99 All in all: Ibid., p. 1.

99 In an analogy: Lee Strobel, *Inside the Mind of Unchurched Harry and Mary* (Grand Rapids, Mich.: Zondervan, 1993).

100 He is absolutely sincere: Mary Beth Sammons, "Full-Service Church: For Willow Creek Faithful, Singular Success Is God's Work," *Chicago Tribune,* April 3, 1994, p. 1.

102 When men want to talk: In the bookstore there was a special section of books for men. The titles were revelatory: *Minute Meditations for Men; With God on the Golf Course; Reel Time with God; With God on a Deer Hunt; Faith in the Fast Lane; 15 Minutes Alone with God for Men; A Look at Life from a Deer Stand; What a Hunter Brings Home; Where the Grass Is Always Greener; Every Man's Battle: Meditation for Men; A Man After God's Own Heart; The Ultimate Fishing Challenge; The Ultimate Hunt; As Iron Sharpens Iron: Building Character in a Mentoring Relationship; Wild at Heart: Discovering the Secret of a Man's Soul; With God on the Open Road; Fight on Your Knees: Calling Men to Action Through Transforming Prayer; A Man's Role in the Home; 4th and Goal: Coaching for Life's Tough Calls;* and *The Power of a Praying Husband* (Audiobook, Prayer Pak, and Study Guide).

103 Plus, men would spend almost: For an introduction to how men spent their time in the company of other men, see Mark C. Carnes, *Secret Ritual and Manhood in Victorian America* (New Haven, Conn.: Yale University Press, 1989). For instance, almost half the male population in the beginning of the twentieth century belonged to a single-sex fraternal lodge. The megachurch is currently one of the few places men can now congregate guilt-free with other men.

Chapter 3:

School Daze: Higher Ed, Inc., in an Age of Branding

110 Counting in everything but: Kenneth N. Gilpin, "Turning a Profit with Higher Education," *The New York Times,* October 20, 2002, sect. 3, p. 7.

110 "After a few months": Janet MacFadyen and Dick Teresi, "Hard Knocks," *Forbes FYI,* September 16, 2002, p. 100.

110 The remaining 20 percent: Louis Menand, "The Thin Envelope: Why College Admissions Has Become Unpredictable," *The New Yorker,* April 7, 2003, p. 88.

111 In 1970, when I entered: Walter P. Metzger, "The Academic Profession in the United States," in *The Academic Profession,* ed. Burton Clark (Berkeley: University of California Press, 1987), 243.

112 This is an industry: Nick Bromell, "*Summa cum Avaritia:* Plucking a Profit from the Groves of Academe," *Harper's,* February 1, 2002, p. 71.

112 College enrollment hit a record: The best place to see this kind of statistic is the National Center for Education Statistics, published by the U.S. Department of Education; see, e.g., www.nces.ed.gov/pubs2002/2002162.pdf.

113 Enrollment in degree-granting: Ibid.

113 Meanwhile, 10 percent: *Digest of Educational Statistics,* 1999: www.nces.ed.gov/pubs99/digest98/chapter3.asp.

115 Whenever someone: When the chief financial officer of the foundation embezzled more than $700,000 in 2003, the university president said, "The university, of course, was very chagrined and surprised at what happened," and we went on about our business.

115 Americans donate more money: Solomon Moore, "A Look Ahead . . . ," *Los Angeles Times,* April 3, 2000, p. H1.

115 Private dollars now account: For the corresponding decline in state aid, see June Kronholz, "Schools Trim State Ties," *The Wall Street Journal,* April 18, 2003, p. B1.

116 Since the 1980s: *Digest of Education Statistics,* 1996: www.nces.ed.gov/pubs/96/d960006.html.

117 Having poor sporting teams: For instance, William Bowen and Sarah Levin, in *Reclaiming the Game: College Sports and Educational Values* (Princeton, N.J.: Princeton University Press, 2003), make the case that sports revenues and reputation are progressively driving the Ivy League and other elite universities.

123 "The system at Duke": Daniel Golden, "Study Break: At Many Colleges, the Rich Kids Get Affirmative Action," *The Wall Street Journal,* February 3, 2003, p. A1. This groundbreaking article won the 2003 Pulitzer Prize for education reporting.

124 So the 977 doctorates: Karen W. Arenson, "Job Listings Decline 20% at Colleges," *The New York Times,* December 14, 2002, p. A17.

127 They have to protect: One of the few studies, in fact, the only study, I've seen detailing how successfully specific schools send their graduates on is Elizabeth Bernstein, "Want to Go to Harvard Law?" *The Wall Street Journal,* September 26, 2003, p. W1, in which the reporter had to hand-count the various applications to Harvard Law from individual schools to figure out who was accepted where. The schools could easily do this but won't.

128 Students are taught: Florence Olsen, "Phoenix Rises: The University's Online Pro-

gram Attracts Students, Profits, and Praise," *The Chronicle of Higher Education,* November 1, 2002, p. 29.

130 As Derek Bok: Concern about the academic-industrial complex is already becoming something of an industry in itself. See some recent examples: David Kirp, *Shakespeare, Einstein and the Bottom Line: The Marketing of Higher Education* (Cambridge, Mass.: Harvard University Press, 2003); Eric Gould, *The University in a Corporate Culture* (New Haven, Conn.: Yale University Press, 2003); and Christopher Newfield, *Ivy and Industry: Business and the Making of the American University 1880–1980* (Durham, N.C.: Duke University Press, 2004).

135 At least 27: Yilu Zhao, "More Small Colleges Dropping Out," *The New York Times,* May 7, 2002, p. A28.

139 When its English Department: Jeffrey Toobin, "Letter from Cambridge: Free Expression and Civility Clash at Harvard," *The New Yorker,* January 27, 2003, p. 32.

140 "Harvard's brand licensing program": Interbrands, an ad agency, *Brands: An International Review* (London: Mercury Books, 1990), p. 69.

142 "When Harvard takes a step": As quoted in Christina Hoff Sommers, "The Fonda Effect," *The Wall Street Journal,* March 9, 2001, p. W15.

142 Harvard, in Harvard fashion: Sara Rimer, "Harvard Is Returning Donation from Jane Fonda for New Center," *The New York Times,* February 4, 2003, p. A14.

144 "What this idealized picture": Nicolaus Mills, "The Endless Autumn," *The Nation,* April 16, 1990, p. 529.

150 Even *The Atlantic:* Don Peck, "The Selectivity Illusion, *The Atlantic,* November 2003, pp. 128–130.

150 "When the *U.S. News & World Report*": "Learning Beyond Measure," *The New York Times,* September 17, 2002, p. A29.

152 So Elisabeth Muhlenfield: Jay Matthews, "The New College Game," *Newsweek,* September 1, 2003, p. 42.

154 "Yes, we're targeting": As quoted by Daniel Golden in "Religious Preference: Colleges Court Jewish Students in Effort to Raise Rankings," *The Wall Street Journal,* April 29, 2002, p. A1.

155 For years, the Pew Foundation: For more on this subject, see Nicholas Confessore, "What Makes a College Good?" *The Atlantic,* November 2003, pp. 118–126.

155 "When *Consumer Reports* rates": Robert L. Woodbury, "How to Make Your College No. 1 in *U.S. News & World Report*," *Connection: The Journal of the New England Board of Higher Education,* Spring 2003, p. 20.

157 "Competition among schools": Gordon C. Winston, *The Positional Arms Race in Higher Education,* Discussion Paper 54, Williams Project on the Economics of Higher Education, Williams College, April 2000, p. 4.

160 "I think branding": "Ivy Envy," *The New York Times Magazine,* June 8, 2003, p. 76.

160 The 743 students: Karen W. Arenson, "CUNY Pays for Top Students and Throws in a Laptop," *The New York Times,* May 11, 2002, p. B2.

161 In a report: John Pulley, "Tuition Discounting Hurts Low-Income Students and Some Colleges, Study Suggests," *The Chronicle of Higher Education,* May 14, 2003; electronic edition: www.chronicle.com/prm/daily/2003/05/2003051402n.htm.

163 As a *Fortune* magazine: Jeremy Kahn, "Is Harvard Worth It?" *Fortune,* May 1, 2000, p. 200.

163 As Alan B. Krueger: The study from the National Bureau of Economic Research is available at www.nber.org/papers/w7322.

165 So the University of Houston: Greg Winter, "Jacuzzi U.? A Battle of Perks," *The New York Times*, October 5, 2001, p. A1. See also Michael J. Lewis, "Forget classrooms. How Big Is the Atrium in the New Student Center?" *Chronicle of Higher Education*, July 11, 2003, p. B7.

165 *The Wall Street Journal:* Pooja Bhatie, "Phi Beta Cafeteria," *The Wall Street Journal*, November 8, 2002, p. W1.

169 And if you come across: Freshman English at my university became so eccentric that in 2003 the provost removed it from the English Department and set up a controlled course complete with lecture and discussion groups. He claimed that we were not doing our job and he was being besieged with complaints. In fact, the man who then took it over, an erstwhile classics chairman, called what the English Department had been doing "a fraud against the state." Thirty years ago, when I started teaching, I remember my chairman saying that as long as we were responsible for Freshman English we could go about teaching upper-division literature courses. Talking about literature was the reward for teaching composition. Full professors had to teach one lower-division course a year. But during the 1990s this was seen as an unproductive way to spend our resources, and writing courses were offloaded onto grad students. When we were finally relieved of almost all our writing courses, many in the department breathed a collective sigh of relief. Most of my younger colleagues considered teaching writing to be time-consuming and not very helpful in building careers as critics or the reputation of the department as an academic powerhouse in what is commonly misnomered theory.

169 When the National Alumni: See www.goacta.org/publications/Reports/shakespeare.pdf. This group is now called the American Council of Trustees and Alumni.

170 The full descriptions: See www.english.ufl.edu/courses_archive.html#grad.

173 "English R1A: The Politics and Poetics": As quoted in Roger Kimball, "The Intifada Curriculum," *The Wall Street Journal*, May 9, 2002, p. A14.

174 "Universities should not": "Letter to Editor," *The Wall Street Journal*, May 17, 2002, p. A11.

175 As Rachel Toor: *Admissions Confidential: An Insider's Account of the Elite College Selection Process* (New York: St. Martin's Press, 2001), p. 4.

175 This same phenomenon: Jacques Steinberg, *The Gatekeepers: Inside the Admissions Process at a Premier College* (New York: Viking Press, 2002).

177 These "unpaid professionals": Andrew Zimbalist, *Unpaid Professionals: Commercialism and Conflict in Big-Time College Sports* (Princeton, N.J.: Princeton University Press, 1999).

177 Many don't graduate: For this information I'm indebted to a four-part exposition of the Florida athletic program by Carrie Miller and Bob Arndorfer that ran January 12–15, 2003, in *The Gainesville Sun*.

177 At Florida he had founded: For more on this ranking system, see www.thecenter.ufl.edu/.

178 According to the U.S. Department of Education's: The report can be seen at www.acenet.edu/bookstore/pdf/2002_new_professoriate.pdf.

180 Barry Munitz: As quoted in David L. Kirp, "Higher Ed Inc.: Avoiding the Perils of Outsourcing," *The Chronicle Review,* March 15, 2002, p. 13.

181 In a recent report: See www.amacad.org/publications/monographs/Evaluation_and_the_Academy.pdf.

182 In typical complexity: See www.hno.harvard.edu/gazette/2002/05.23/03-grades.html.

182 "When you send in your resume": As quoted in Davidson Gold, "In a Change of Policy, and Heart, Colleges Join Fight Against Inflated Grades," *The New York Times,* July 4, 1995, p. A8.

182 "I'm sure you can understand": Letter from Sheila Dickinson, director of UF Honors Program, to instructional staff, January 2, 2003.

183 A report by Valen Johnson: *Grade Inflation: A Crisis in College Education* (New York: Copernicus Books, 2003).

185 Here's how it works: Carrie Miller, "The Future of Bright Futures," *The Gainesville Sun,* April 7, 2002, p. A1.

186 About half the states: June Kronholz, "More Students Win Scholarships Based on Merit, Not Need," *The Wall Street Journal,* September 23, 2002, p. B1.

188 "While the public": David Kirp, "The New U," *The Nation,* April 17, 2000, p. 25.

189 "Attend a conference": Michele Tolela Myers, "A Student Is Not an Input," *The New York Times,* March 26, 2001, p. A19.

190 "Confidently, with generosity": Judith Shapiro, "Keeping Parents off Campus," *The New York Times,* August 22, 2002, p. A23.

Chapter 4:

Museumworld: The Art of Branding Art

194 Four percent of American museums: Ann Hofstra Grogg, *Museums Count: A Report* (Washington, D.C.: American Association of Museums, 1994), p. 33. Two excellent sources of information about modern museums are a special edition of *Daedalus* (Journal of American Academy of Arts and Sciences), Summer 1999, and Mark W. Rectanus, *Culture Incorporated: Museums, Artists, and Corporate Sponsorships* (Minneapolis: University of Minnesota Press, 2002).

194 In 2000, more than a billion: Cathleen McGuigan and Peter Plagens, "State of the Art," *Newsweek,* March 26, 2001, p. 52.

194 They even have a consortium: Carol Vogel, "Dear Museumgoer: What Do You Think?" *The New York Times,* December 20, 1992, sect. 2, p. 1.

195 According to *The Official: A Higher Standard: The Museum Accreditation Handbook* (Washington, D.C.: American Association of Museums, 1997), pp. 19–20.

197 If cities cut museums loose: *Museum Financial Information* (Washington, D.C.: American Association of Museums, 1999), exhibit 54.

197 The Europeans are facing: "When Merchants Enter the Temple," *The Economist,* April 21, 2001, p. 64.

200 "There is something": Joseph Epstein, "Think You Have a Book in You?" *The New York Times,* September 28, 2002, p. A17.

200 "Thank goodness": All letters are from *The New York Times,* October 1, 2002, p. A30.

203 In a McLuhanesque observation: Douglas D. Paige, "Should Copy Writers Be Cultured?" *Printer's Ink,* October 1, 1954, p. 25.

211 In "The Work of Art": Walter Benjamin, "The Work of Art in the Age of Mechanical Reproduction," www.bid.berkeley.edu/bidclassreadings/benjamin.html.

211 Relic transportation: Patrick J. Geary, Furta Sacra: *Thefts of Relics in the Central Middle Ages* (Princeton, N.J.: Princeton University Press, 1978).

213 As the English critic/novelist: See especially Chapter 3 of John Berger, *Ways of Seeing* (New York: Penguin Books, 1972).

217 "My profits": P(hineas) T. Barnum, *Struggles and Triumphs, or Forty Years' Recollections of P. T. Barnum* (New York: Knopf, 1927), rpt., p. 18.

219 In *Struggles and Triumphs:* Ibid., p. 102.

221 Although no one has: *The Economist,* May 1, 1993, p. 97, as quoted in Bruno S. Frey, *Arts & Economics: Analysis and Cultural Policy* (New York: Springer, 2000), p. 36. Only about 3 percent of the Guggenheim's collection has ever been on display at one time: see Geraldine Norman, "Art Without Gallery Hangups," *The Independent* (London), April 14, 1991, p. 12. The same is probably true at the Met, but it won't give out such information. Instead, Mr. de Montebello says he shows about "90 percent of what you would like to see." See Judith H. Dobrzynski, "Hip vs. Stately: The Tao of Two Museums," *The New York Times,* February 2, 2002, sect. 2, p. 1.

223 They took the legendary: Janet Tassel, "Reverence for the Object: Art Museums in a Changed World," *Harvard Magazine,* September–October 2002, pp. 48–51.

224 The Williams mafia in particular: Krens was not alone. The mafia includes luminaries such as Earl A. Powell III, director of the National Gallery of Art; Glenn Lowry, director of the Museum of Modern Art; James N. Wood, director of the Art Institute of Chicago; Michael Govan, director of the Dia Art Foundation; Roger Mandle, president of the Rhode Island School of Design; and the late Kirk Varnedoe, former curator of painting and sculpture at the Museum of Modern Art and professor of art history at Princeton University's Institute for Advanced Study.

224 Here is verbatim: Dobrzynski, "Hip vs. Stately: The Tao of Two Museums."

229 Jesse McKinley, "Art Is Long? So Are the Lines," *The New York Times,* March 28, 2003, p. B37.

231 As David Brooks: Ibid.

233 If you want to find out: Rem Koolhaas, et al. *Harvard Design School Guide to Shopping* (Cambridge, Mass.: Harvard Design School, 2001).

235 The 1990–91 MoMA show: *High & Low: Popular Culture and Modern Art* (New York: Museum of Modern Art, 1990).

238 By the 1980s: Ken Johnson, "Newcomers Ready for Marketing, Accounting . . . and, Oh Yes, Creating," *The New York Times,* August 10, 2001, p. B36.

243 "Long before the scooter craze": Greg Johnson, "Museums See Advertising in a New Light," *Los Angeles Times,* February 1, 2001, p. C1.

244 In a refreshingly self-reflexive: Christoph Grunenberg and Max Hollein, eds., *Shopping: A Century of Art and Consumer Culture* (Stuttgart: Hatje Cantz, 2002).

245 It's usually booked up: Brooks Barnes, "Museums' New Mantra: Party On!," *The Wall Street Journal,* July 19, 2002, p. W4.

246 Philippe de Montebello: "When Merchants Enter the Temple," *The Economist,* April 21, 2001, p. 64.

247 In 1999: Jason Edward Kaufman, "In a Downturn, Museums Remain Big Spenders," *The Wall Street Journal,* August 21, 2001, p. A17.

250 The Met does about $90 million: Judith H. Dobrzynski, "Art (?) to Go: Museum Shops Broaden Wares, at a Profit," *The New York Times,* December 10, 1997, p. A1.

250 For instance, the Met estimates: Ibid.

253 The British Museum: Jennifer Conlin, "The Art of Dining," *Time,* August 13, 2001, p. 52.

256 Although it receives: Julian Spalding, "Keep Our Museums Free for All," *The Scotsman,* October 21, 1997, p. 17.

258 With this exhibition: Both books published by the V&A, London, 2000.

259 "From cornflakes to cars": *Brand.New* (London: Victoria & Albert, 2000), p. 16.

261 The Guggenheim's endowment: Deborah Solomon, "Is the Go-Go Guggenheim Going, Going . . . ," *The New York Times Magazine,* June 30, 2002, p. 36.

261 There's not a real "destination piece": Too bad that the infamous Albert C. Barnes Collection in Philadelphia, gathered at almost the same time and now the center of a never-ending scandal, had not been exchanged with the Guggenheim. Imagine how different the Guggenheim would be with the 353 Renoirs, Cézannes, Matisses, and Picassos of the Barnes collection.

263 In Museumworld: For more on this, see Lee Rosenbaum, "The Guggenheim Regroups: The Story Behind the Cutbacks," *Art in America,* February 1, 2003, p. 91.

263 With refreshing candor: As quoted in Solomon, "Is the Go-Go Guggenheim," p. 39.

269 Plus there are books on art: Wynn has since sold his hotel but not the art collection. It is now called Le Rêve Collection and will appear in his new casino of the same name.

270 "Very few people": See www.lasvegasweekly.com/2001_2/10_04/news_upfront4.html/.

Chapter 5:
When All Business Is Show Business, What's Next?

274 In *Bowling Alone:* Robert Putnam, *Bowling Alone: The Collapse and Revival of American Community* (New York: Simon & Schuster, 2001).

274 Putnam has many detractors: Everett L. Ladd, *The Ladd Report* (New York: Basic Books, 1999).

275 Raymond Williams's observation: Raymond Williams, *Keywords: A Vocabulary of Culture and Society* (New York: Oxford University Press, 1985), p. 76.

275 Cultural anthropologist Grant McCracken: *Plenitude,* an online book, can be read at www.cultureby.com/books/plenit/cxc_trilogy_plenitude.html.

275 In 1987, an English professor: E. D. Hirsch, *What Every American Should Know* (Boston: Houghton Mifflin, 1987).

277 A Canadian sociologist: John Hannigan, *Environmental Sociology: A Social Constructionist Perspective* (New York: Routledge, 1995).

279 As Ms. Brown concludes: Patricia Leigh Brown, "Megachurches as Minitowns," *The New York Times,* May 9, 2002, p. D1.

279 A study by the Hartford Institute: As quoted in ibid.

282 The largest operator: Andrea Stone, "College Towns Attracting New Class: Retirees," *USA Today,* April 2, 1996, p. A1.

284 *The Wall Street Journal:* Anne Marie Chaker, "The New School Spirit, Burial Plots for Alums—Cash-Hungry Universities Sell Space in Campus Vaults," *The Wall Street Journal,* July 10, 2002, p. D1.

285 As Barbara Paley: Sheila Muto, "Office Owners Turn to Art to Lure Tenants," *The Wall Street Journal,* May 21, 2003, p. B4.

288 But as he commented to Susan Orlean: "Art for Everybody," *The New Yorker,* October 15, 2001, p. 124.

288 So just as corporate interests: Michael Cooper, "Mayor Warns About Deficit While Promising to Rebuild," *The New York Times,* January 31, 2002, p. A1.

289 Even the usually dour: John Leland, "And Now, Unveiling RCA Battery Park," *The New York Times,* February 10, 2002, sect. 9, p. 10.

289 Franz Lidz, "John Q. Public Library," *The New York Times,* February 10, 2002, sect. 14, p. 13.

291 "We started a kind": For more, see www.intuart.com/dotcommune/advertising/puerto.html.

293 "Look at the covers": "The Rise of the Brand State: The Postmodern Politics of Image and Reputation," *Foreign Affairs,* October 2001, p. 2.

296 "In the corporate world": Naomi Klein, "Brand USA," *Los Angeles Times,* March 10, 2002, p. M1.

297 "It is wrong to dismiss": "Now a Word from America," *Advertising Age,* February 18, 2002, p. 15.

Index

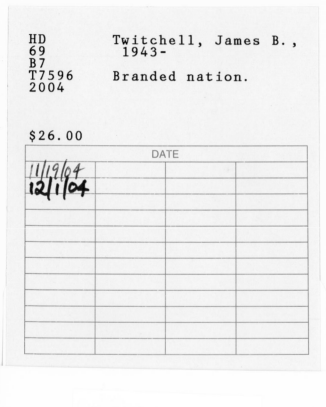

HD
69
B7
T7596
2004

Twitchell, James B.,
    1943-

Branded nation.

$26.00

DATE			
11/19/04			
12/1/04			